"If you want to ....plained, elusive characteristics of successful leadership, this explains it in detail like I've never seen before. If then you want an action plan to reach the highest levels of leadership, it's all here. A masterpiece – and written in simple language too."

"The
have
profe
most
recol
make
even
it to
busir
trade
parer
defin

"Thi
powe
insta
richn
of L
genu
their
you a
choo

"The
I hav
leade
enha
mast
new

and inspirational leader and I am adding this book to my list of 'essential reading' for leaders I coach and mentor."

Deborah A. Armstrong, Vice-President Human Resources, Rockwell Automation

"James Scouller offers a thoughtful, well-researched, practical explanation of how we can integrate 150 years of leadership theory to help people become better leaders. He identifies the missing link in many leadership development programs, books and models, arguing that leaders can learn to express their 'authentic presence.' After three decades of teaching leadership, I have now found a book that **MBA** students and future leaders can use as a tool to develop themselves. If they want to grow their emotional intelligence and learn how to become level 5 leaders, they need look no further than The Three Levels of Leadership."

Larry Bienati, Ph.D, Senior Principal, CTM Inc. & Leadership Lecturer,
California State University System

"James Scouller playfully asks whether the world needs another book on leadership before proving over 300 concise, easy to read pages that the answer is an emphatic yes. 'Three Levels' is not a book for the faint hearted however. James tackles the hardest area for the modern leader, that of the psyche and asks leaders to take a long, hard look at themselves in the mirror. Those that can take it will be rewarded with a manual packed full of practical wisdom and exercises to tackle the psychological blocks we all face but sometimes draw back from. By the end, I was arm in arm with James, agreeing that it's hard to imagine anything that could help a leader's growth and effectiveness more than self-mastery."

Tony Langham, Chief Executive, Lansons Communications

"If all leaders, or even a few of them, could take to heart and begin to implement just 10% of what James Scouller proposes in The Three Levels of Leadership, organisations (and one day our world) would become a place that truly does reflect the magnificence of the human being."

Nancy Kline, author of Time to Think: Listening to Ignite the Human Mind

"This book is extraordinarily valuable. In showing the psychological keys to being a leader instead of focusing on just behaviours and skills, James Scouller offers you the opportunity to achieve true self-mastery. This is what sets it apart from other management books. It's a must read for both experienced leaders and those new to leadership."

Kim Morgan, Managing Director, Barefoot Coaching Ltd.

"This is a bold and ambitious book that brings clarity and coherence to the much-theorised field of leadership. Connecting the outer tasks of leadership with the underpinning psychology of presence, Scouller provides an accessible, insightful and pragmatic map for helping leaders to be more effective. Beginning with a refreshingly clear redefinition of leadership, we are taken on an engaging journey from the external aspects of leadership, through leadership as relationship, to a far-reaching model of the psyche and practical techniques that will foster a leader's self-mastery. Leaders at all levels of experience and responsibility will find valuable approaches and tools for cultivating their presence, clarity and impact."

Graham Lee, author of Leadership Coaching: From Personal Insight to Organisational Performance

"I love this book; it is a concise and pragmatic guide to the art of leadership. A must-read for anyone wanting to identify and overcome any perceived personal limitations on their way to becoming a better leader."

Olaf Althaus, Managing Director, CellMed AG

"The Three Levels of Leadership is an exciting new contribution to the world of leadership. It combines the practical with the visionary and the psychological with the strategic, making an important and welcome contribution to our understanding of what it means and what it takes to be a leader. Scouller's ability to organise, distil, pull together eclectic sources and translate them into a powerful model of the psyche is reminiscent of Ken Wilber's prowess. But Scouller wants his book to be practical. Over and again, he pre-empts the reader in asking the killer question: So what? How does this help me as a leader? And he answers clearly in straightforward language that engages the reader in a conversation, making this book a pleasure to read."

Hetty Einzig, Executive Coach

"There are many books that help leaders brush up their skills or get up-to-date on the latest management thinking. And there are plenty that tell us what we "should" do as leaders and how we "should" behave. Very few also challenge us to ask ourselves why we act as we do and offer a psychological model to explain why the deeply held beliefs and insecurities that we all carry, derail us and stop us reaching our full potential. This is where The Three Levels of Leadership is different. It offers practical, succinct leadership definitions and principles, but its real value is that it offers a way of tackling our limiting beliefs and an insight into how, by mastering them, our leadership presence can flow – letting us become the leaders we want to be... and that our people deserve."

Andrew Sedgwick, President, CooperVision Europe

"The Three Levels of Leadership combines extensive hands-on executive experience with rigorous academic research to provide a readable, practical and actionable guide to achieving leadership excellence. A quick read, it condenses modern leadership theory and practice while introducing original new thinking on personal leadership and how to achieve self-mastery. Any leader committed to personal growth and looking for fresh ideas and models to raise team performance will find this book a useful tool."

Bob Coleman, Divisional President, OMNOVA Solutions Inc.

"At last, a book which links the 'outer' facing elements of leadership with the 'inner' development that all true leaders must engage with, if they are to succeed in the long term. The great strength of James Scouller's model is that it allows any leader, whatever their current level of accomplishment, to place themselves on a practical path to leadership development in the fullest sense."

Steve O'Shaughnessy, Chartered Psychologist & Managing Partner, The Quo Group

"The Three Levels of Leadership is a candid, fascinating journey into the keys to effective leadership. It is an essential read for CEOs and Human Resource professionals. Scouller drives the point home that self-mastery is the keystone to a leader's growth and effectiveness. Through his examples, we understand the challenge and means of freeing ourselves from the 'false self,' which helps us create a unique and enduring leadership presence. And he offers a significant piece of wisdom for leaders: that the past is gone, that we only have the now. Scouller reminds us to keenly live in this current state – a message to heed well."

Gregory T. Troy, VP & Chief Human Resources Officer,
Modine Manufacturing Company

"James Scouller distils the work of researchers and academics down to just three levels. The most original and demanding of these is Personal Leadership – how we remove our hidden limits to personal growth. This book will appeal to aspiring and current leaders in any organisation, public or private, who know they could do better, but don't know how. Here at last is the guidance they have been looking for."

Roger Shaw, ex-Vice-President, Schering-Plough Europe

"It happened in the past that I had the chance to read books like this and was disappointed. So reading The Three Levels of Leadership was a surprising experience for me. In fact, there were five surprises. The first was how easy it was to read, even for someone like me (I'm French) who does not speak English as their first language. The second was learning that a leader does not always need a magnificent vision or have to be a Napoleon to be effective. The leader could be me. Yes, me! Or you. Because most of what we need is already inside us, we just need to practise. The third was how realistic the book is, for we learn that we will probably not be strong on every leadership behaviour and that most leaders have weaknesses, so we are not alone. The fourth surprise was learning about the psychology of leaders – this goes well beyond what you will read in other books. And the last surprise was how practical it is in helping you develop as a leader, especially the detailed exercises in self-mastery. This is a book you will want to read again and again."

Jacques-Charles Souleau-Joffre, International Director, OMNOVA Coated Fabrics

"Nothing truly prepares you for your first leadership role. And often there's little to support you as you try to grow as a leader. This book helps you with both in a way that's readable and understandable. It's the first book I've read to unite our thinking around leadership and human psychology in one model and will be a valuable source of reference to leaders as they face and address their limiting beliefs. More important, it offers a framework for developing yourself that's well explained and points the way to straightforward implementation. In short, it's a 'must' for leaders in any walk of life. However experienced we think we are as leaders, we should all strive to improve ourselves. We owe this to the teams we lead and those who pay us; indeed we owe it to ourselves. Invest time in this book and it will be time well spent."

Chris Williams, Managing Director, Northern Europe, Videojet

"This book provides an excellent understanding of what leadership is and how to achieve it. Apart from the ideas presented, it is easy to read and the ideas outlined can be put into place quickly. It will prove an invaluable tool for both leaders and coaches who work with leaders. The author's expertise lies in how he has put together what it takes to be a great leader and managed to do this in an accessible manner. Occam's Razor is the term in science that says the simplest solution is usually the most effective. I think readers will see this in action in this book."

Gladeana McMahon, Chair, Association for Coaching UK; Co-Director, Centre for Coaching

"If you're an aspiring leader, a **CEO**, a middle manager, outdoor leader, teacher or anyone who leads on a daily basis and want to be the best you can be – The Three Levels of Leadership is for you. Based on extensive personal experience and research, but easy to read, it neatly brings together existing theories and models on leadership. It enabled me to identify why certain leaders I've worked with have been successful and why others haven't – and allowed me to start applying these same lessons to my own leadership. I'm certain I'll refer to this book again and again."

Francesco Bove, Outdoor Education Lecturer & Instructor

"James Scouller has used his long and varied business leadership experience and time as a coach to leaders to present a unique, practical approach to leadership. The Three Levels of Leadership is a very valuable tool."

Tariq Rashid, Finance Director, Muraspec Ltd

"How do you become a better leader? The Three Levels of Leadership answers this comprehensively. I don't normally read books like this, so I was surprised when James Scouller went beyond practical advice on how to improve your skills to address leaders' issues of self-doubt. Surprised too to find it easy to read – it feels as though you are having a conversation with him, not listening to a lecture. However, the second part of the book is challenging as it forces you to reflect on stuff you may not have considered before. The genius of this fascinating book is that it's equally helpful for experienced and inexperienced leaders, whether in business or elsewhere."

Tim Garnham, Group Development Director, Minerva plc

"There are many books on leadership. They offer interesting leadership theories and philosophies that are worth reading. But this one is different – it is a book to read, digest and act on. Although it is written in simple language, the ideas it presents are complex. Yet if leaders fully digest its message, they will have a means to challenge and grow beyond their own patterns of leadership. Gandhi directed us to Be The Change. James Scouller's book shows us How To."

Anne Welsh, Director, Synthesis-in-the-City and Senior Trainer & Supervisor, London Institute of Psychosynthesis

The Three Levels of Leadership

How to Develop Your Leadership Presence,
Knowhow and Skill

James Scouller

First published in 2011 by Management Books 2000 Ltd
Forge House, Limes Road
Kemble, Cirencester
Gloucestershire, GL7 6AD, UK
Tel: 0044 (0) 1285 771441
Fax: 0044 (0) 1285 771055
Email: info@mb2000.com
Web: www.mb2000.com

British Library Cataloguing in Publication Data is available

ISBN 9781852526818

Contents

Preface

Who This Book Is For

There are two kinds of leaders, both of whom influence others to make things happen: thought leaders and executive leaders. Thought leaders include philosophers, scientific thinkers and spiritual teachers. Executive leaders direct small groups, organisations and nations. They include owners of small-medium sized businesses, department heads, prime ministers, chief executives, head teachers and army commanders.

This is a book for executive leaders. Executive leaders who want to grow in their role.

What It's For

This book is a manual for your development as a leader. It will help you understand what leadership is; your unique purpose as leader; the key leadership behaviours; and above all, how to develop your leadership presence, knowhow and skill.

It unites previous leadership thinking and modern psychology in one simple model and explains the practical steps you can take to become the best leader you can be. It explains "presence," that hard-to-define characteristic of many great leaders. It introduces a new model of the human psyche and exposes the hidden psychological blocks to growing as a leader. Finally, it explains how to achieve self-mastery. Self-mastery is the key to addressing these inner blocks, letting your leadership presence unfold and quickening your growth as a leader.

Why We Need It

You may be thinking, "There must be hundreds of books on leadership, why do we need another?"

Well, if you manage to read them and pull the many ideas on leadership together, you'll find the list of styles, character traits and behaviours they demand of leaders is so long it's bewildering. This leaves many leaders confused about their role, the personal qualities it demands and how to behave to best effect. Now some leadership books do give clear advice on what to do, but they don't address a leader's psychology. In overlooking this, they ignore the reality that many leaders cannot and will not follow their advice because of subtle, unnoticed psychological blocks.

This leaves leaders trying to do the best they can while wrestling with their greatest, but unseen fears. Like the fear of failure, criticism and humiliation. Or the fear of feeling powerless, inadequate or disliked if they make decisions others disagree with. You see, there is nothing like a leadership role for exposing you to your greatest (but often unrealised) fears.

Yet leaders have a huge effect on our world, for good or ill. So it's surprising no one has integrated previous leadership research and modern psychology into one complete, authoritative model to teach people how to develop as leaders. And it's also surprising that no one has offered leaders the chance to understand and master their own psyches. We need good leaders, especially now during a time of global economic crisis, but in my view, the path to becoming a better leader remains poorly lit.

Jim Collins highlighted this problem in his best-selling book, Good to Great, when he wrote about Level 5 Leadership. For those not familiar with his book, he and his research team studied 28 companies over five years to find out why some made the leap from good to great – and stayed there – and others didn't. He discovered seven success factors. The first and perhaps most important was what he called Level 5 Leadership. Every one of the companies that went from good to great had level 5 leaders during their transition phase whereas the comparison firms did not.

Level 5 leaders display what Collins called "a paradoxical blend of personal humility and professional will." They aren't charismatic, but under their leadership the right things happen. *The trouble is, he wasn't able to say what you need to do to become a level 5 leader.* He concluded that, "Our research exposed Level 5 as a key component inside the black box of what it takes to shift a company from good to great. Yet inside that black box is yet another black box – namely, the inner development of a person to level 5. We could speculate on what might be inside that inner black box, but it would mostly be just that – speculation."

This book opens that inner black box. The inner development that Collins speaks of is what I call personal leadership and this book shows you how to work on it.

This Book's Style

I'm guessing that like most leaders you don't have much spare time. So in writing this book I've followed two principles:

- *Plain English.* I've kept the language as simple as possible. I see no reason to add unnecessary complexity. Nor do I want this book to be hard to read.

- *No padding.* My aim has been to keep this book compact. This means every page matters. I know how frustrating it is to read a book while feeling it could be 80% shorter. So you won't have to hunt for the useful stuff on the assumption that it's scattered here and there. You will find that I repeat certain themes, but only because repetition is sometimes necessary for key messages to get through. However, I've made sure this book is no longer than it needs to be.

This Book's Structure

The book is organised into two parts.

Part One comprises chapters 1 to 4 and presents the foundational ideas. Its first aim is to demystify leadership and clarify the purpose of a leader. It promotes the idea of shared leadership, but affirms there is one responsibility that belongs uniquely to the leader. This is why, in a group, the leader remains first among equals. Its second aim is to introduce the *Three Levels of Leadership* model. This is what it offers by chapter:

- Chapter 1 defines leadership and reveals the simple, but perhaps surprising purpose of a leader.

- Chapter 2 introduces the more complete model of leadership that I feel we've been lacking. This is where I unveil the Three Levels of Leadership – the three levels being Public, Private and Personal Leadership.

- Chapter 3 goes into the Three Levels model in more detail. It offers two self-assessment exercises, lists the key public and private leadership behaviours – in other words, what leaders have to do – and introduces what personal leadership involves. Personal leadership is the key to developing your presence, knowhow and skill.

- Chapter 4 summarises the key points from the first three chapters to give you a quick source of reference as you move on to part two.

Part Two covers chapters 5 to 10. It builds on part one by going into the detail of personal leadership. Its focus is on how you can grow your leadership presence, knowhow and skill. Thus, it looks closely at how to work on the three elements of personal leadership: Technical Knowledge & Skills, Attitude Towards Others and Self-Mastery. Most of the book is devoted to part two and this is what each chapter covers:

- Chapter 5 explains what presence is, how it shows itself and how it's different to charisma. It lists the seven qualities of presence and argues that everyone can express their unique presence by practising self-mastery.

- Chapter 6 outlines the technical knowhow every leader needs and how to gain it. It discusses the skills that support the public and private leadership behaviours and what you can do to learn them. And it contains a self-assessment exercise to help you decide on your learning priorities.

- Chapter 7 clarifies why the right attitude to other people is so important. It explains what it involves with the help of a five-level model and real-life examples. It reveals why some leaders don't display the right attitude and outlines what you can do to avoid the same happening to you. Finally, it highlights the importance of self-mastery in developing the right attitude and behaviour towards others.

- Chapters 8 and 9 are both on self-mastery. Chapter 8 explains what Self is and the fears and psychological blocks it has to master by offering a new, practical model of the human psyche, drawing on the latest thinking from psychology and neuroscience.

- Chapter 9 builds on the model by outlining the principles of personal change, the obstacles you are likely to meet and how to overcome them. It then offers six practical techniques to help you work on self-mastery. Where necessary, I've included scientific data to support them.

- Chapter 10 summarises the key themes to tie it all together.

Throughout the book, my aim has been for you to see the big picture while giving you enough detail to take action on your growth as a leader. Thus, at times I have referred you to the notes at the end of the book to avoid a chapter wandering too far off its main purpose. You don't have to read these notes, but if you want to go deeper into the model of the psyche and some of the science behind it, you'll probably wish to do so.

Like many authors, I faced the question of gender. In other words, do I write "he," "she," "he or she," "his," "her" or "his or her"? I chose to use the masculine gender. It's just a way of keeping things simple and avoiding clumsy writing.

Sometimes you will find I recommend or mention coaching. Now being a professional coach, I'm open to the charge, "You would, wouldn't you?" And of course, I would, because I believe in the power of a coaching relationship. So I feel caught in a dilemma. I could avoid mentioning coaching, but I'd be stifling my view that it's one of the most effective ways of enabling personal change. Or instead, I could be honest and suggest it when it makes sense to do so, but risk being accused of selling coaching. So damned if I do and damned if I don't. Thus, when writing, I applied this test: am I sure coaching can offer significant help and do I feel I'd be withholding valuable advice if I didn't mention it? Only if the answers were yes and yes did I choose to mention coaching.

Website Tools

This book offers you practical tools. You can download copies of some of them from the book's website, which may make them easier to use. The downloadable tools are:

- The two self-assessment exercises in chapter 3. They will help you decide which leadership behaviours to work on first.

- The self-assessment exercise in chapter 6. Designed to help you see your technical knowledge and skills learning priorities.

- Five of the six self-mastery techniques in chapter 9.

You can find the website at www.three-levels-of-leadership.com.

Acknowledgements

My eyes used to glaze over when I read authors' acknowledgements, but that's before I'd written a book. Now I understand why authors say what they do. They know they couldn't have completed their work without help. And it's the same for me. So I'll keep this short, but there are people I want to thank.

First, I couldn't have written this book if I hadn't had the experience of being a leader. So I thank those in my career who saw potential in me and helped me become a chief executive. Their feedback and belief in me (which often exceeded my own) was crucial. Then there were the colleagues who had to work alongside me and put up with my strengths and weaknesses. I learnt more from them than perhaps they know. The experiences I shared with them – especially the most difficult ones – have helped me and this book enormously.

Second, while knowing first-hand what it's like to lead was essential, it wasn't enough. Only through working on my own psychology (which is a continuing project) under the guidance of various teachers over the years and having the privilege to act as coach to many leaders did this book become a real possibility. Thus, I have to thank both my teachers and my clients.

Third, thank you to my many test readers – friends, ex-colleagues, clients and ex-clients – who read certain chapters and gave me their reactions, advice and comments. They are all busy people and generously gave their time. Their feedback has made this a better book.

Finally, there's my family. They're the ones who had to tolerate hearing about the writing of this book for the past two years. My elder children, Mark and Charlotte, managed to avoid having to spend too much time on the text because they live elsewhere – although both gave me wise advice at certain points – but my youngest son, Sam, wasn't so lucky. He was good enough to give me a 22-year-old's perspective on four of the chapters and that kept my feet on the ground. And last, there is Trish, my wife. I now know that writing a book is probably hardest for the person closest to you. Trish has had to put up with me using every spare moment on this book and now she's hoping to get her husband back. Trish, your patience and understanding gave me the all-important space and time to write this book. To you, my love and thanks.

James Scouller
Flitwick, Bedfordshire

Part 1

The Foundational Ideas

Part 1 – The Foundational Ideas

Part 1 has two aims.

First, to demystify "leadership" and clarify the purpose of a leader to help a difficult role become more doable and enjoyable. It promotes the idea of shared leadership, but affirms there is one responsibility that belongs uniquely to the leader. This is why, in a group, the leader remains first among equals.

The second is to introduce the *Three Levels of Leadership* model. It integrates the findings of previous leadership research and offers a new, practical framework to help leaders understand what to do in their role and how to realise their potential.

◇◇◇◇◇◇◇◇◇

1

◇◇◇◇◇◇◇◇◇

Leadership & The Leader

Three Inner Issues

In working with leaders, I've found they typically face three inner, psychological challenges in their roles:

- First, unhelpful or vague beliefs about leadership and the role of the leader, which make it harder for them to do their job.

- Second, subconscious fears about themselves. They may, for example, have doubts around their ability to do their job, or concerns about their likeability. These fears can cause rigid, defensive behaviours, reducing their skill, flexibility and effectiveness.[1]

- Third, gaps in their knowledge and behavioural skills.

This chapter focuses on the first issue, as does chapter two. Later chapters will look at the second and third issues.

What Is Leadership?

When I ask clients, "What does the word "leadership" evoke for you – what images, words, symbols, feelings or people spring to mind?" I get responses like "vision," "inspiring," "greatness," "Winston Churchill," "Superman" and "awesome." The underlying idea is clear: leadership is a major, even heroic challenge, needing exceptional qualities.

But do most of us believe we have these qualities? I suspect not. Thus, it shouldn't surprise us if, deep down, many leaders see the leadership challenge as intimidating. Now if – like many leaders – they also privately fear they may not be up to the task, the pressure and unease they feel increases. In my work with clients, we'll often look at their unconscious fears and the negative beliefs behind them. But that won't be enough to achieve the change they want if the way they see leadership only heightens their sense of inadequacy. So we also work on their ideas around leadership and the leader.

If you ask business leaders to define "leadership," most – in my experience – find it difficult. And this is part of the problem. You see, if leaders hold an intimidating – but fuzzy – idea of leadership, it can make it harder for them to lead effectively. Why? Well, partly because it may create towering, unrealistic expectations about the impact they should have. And partly because the idea's vagueness makes it impossible to know if they are doing a good enough job – for how can you measure yourself against something that's undefined?

So can we define leadership in a practical way to help leaders perform better in their role? I believe we can. Here's my definition:

> Leadership is a process that involves setting a **purpose and direction** which inspires people to combine and work towards willingly; paying attention to the **means, pace and quality of progress** towards the aim; and upholding **group unity** and **individual effectiveness** throughout.

Having offered this definition, there are two points I want to stress. The first is that leadership has four dimensions, as the words in bold italics above and the diagram (figure 1) highlight.

Leadership starts with setting a purpose, vision and goals we care about – that motivate or even inspire us. It's also about results, progress and the practical management of the task – planning, finding resources, solving problems and following up. And it includes people handling – that is, paying attention to individual effectiveness and building and upholding group unity.

Some authors define leadership more narrowly, putting the emphasis on vision and the art of inspiring others to greater heights.[2] Why this more limited view? Perhaps because in the last twenty years there has been much debate on the contrast between leadership and management. This led some authors to stress the points of distinction – with vision and inspiration being key ones. But I feel some imbalance has crept in.

Figure I
Leadership's Four Dimensions

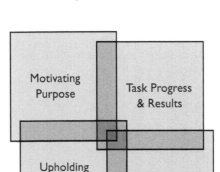

There *is* a distinction between leadership and management. Leadership is more about change, inspiration, setting the purpose and direction, and building the enthusiasm, unity and staying power for the journey ahead. Management, on the other hand, is less about change, more about stability and making the best use of resources to get things done – good administration, essentially.

But here's the key point: leadership and management are not separate. And they are not necessarily done by different people. It's not a case of, "You are either a manager or a leader." Leadership and management overlap. Frankly, I find it hard to imagine a good leader who's not also a capable administrator. Admittedly, I also find it hard to imagine a good leader who wanted to be only an administrator because of their natural drive for change – but that's a matter of emphasis, not of outright separation.

My point is that in striving to highlight differences between leadership and management, some authors have unwittingly separated the two and there lies the mistake. They have a different emphasis, but they complement each other. We need both.

So yes, the inspirational side of leadership must be present. You do need a purpose, a vision, that excites – or at least motivates – everyone. But it won't be effective if no one translates the vision into reality or responds to the surprises and failures along the way. And it won't be enough if no one is attending to team atmosphere and maintaining individuals' confidence and enthusiasm. So, for me, effective leadership has to have the management and two people dimensions alongside the inspirational aspect. Otherwise, it won't be practical leadership.

The second point is that I've described leadership as a "process." What I mean is that it's a series of choices and actions around defining and achieving a goal. This is significant because it means *leadership is a practical challenge that's bigger than the leader.* You see, we often confuse "leadership" with the role of "leader," assuming they are one and the same. But leadership doesn't have to rely on one person – anyone in a group could potentially exert leadership. That is, anyone could play the leading role in one of the four leadership dimensions.

In fact, I'd go further. I'd say that not only can others exert leadership; they must exert it at times if a group is to be successful. Why do I say this? Three reasons:

- First, as you will read in chapter 3, there are so many public leadership behaviours (34), one person is unlikely to be good at all of them, so it makes sense to draw on others' strengths.

> *Note: when I say "public" leadership behaviours, I'm using a model I introduce in the next chapter. Public leadership covers the actions leaders take in a group setting, for example, a meeting, or when trying to influence the organisation as a whole. It excludes individual handling of group members as, for example, in appraisal discussions. Those are what I call "private" leadership behaviours.*

- Second, making one person responsible for all 34 behaviours can overload them and frustrate their colleagues, many of whom may be qualified and keen to lead on certain issues.

- Third, shared leadership means more people take part in the big decisions, which promotes joint accountability – a key feature of a high performance team.

What Is a Leader For?

Now if leadership is a process where more than one person can exert leadership – why do you need a leader? What is he or she there to do? Does a team or an organisation really need a leader?

In my view the answer is yes, a leader is needed, *because someone has to make sure there is leadership.* In other words, someone has to make sure all four dimensions of leadership are in force. And this of course is the leader's primary purpose and main way of serving the organisation. When we see the job like this, we realise the leader's role is to serve those they lead, as Robert Greenleaf argued in his book, Servant Leadership.[3] This is a point I'll come back to in Part 2.

Realising that the leader's main role is to make sure there is leadership takes us to another big point: *the official leader does not have to provide all the leadership personally.* And, therefore, he needn't have all the qualities of the "ideal" leader. He just has to make sure all four leadership dimensions are being addressed. If they're not, it's the leader's job to step in and take the lead role – or ensure someone else does so.

Let me give you an example. Imagine a leader and his team are flying in an aeroplane over the Pacific Ocean, hundreds of miles from civilisation. And imagine the plane crashes on a desert island, leaving only the leader and team members as survivors. The leader calls the team together and says, "Now look, none of us have any idea how long we'll be here and I don't have any experience of emergencies like this. Have any of you learnt survival skills to keep us alive while we figure out how to attract attention for a rescue?" Let's say Jack, one of the team members, steps forward and replies, "Yes, I was in the Army Reserve and trained in survival techniques." "Okay Jack," says the leader, "You take charge for the moment. What do we have to do first?"

This is leadership.

The leader doesn't assume he has to have all the answers and lead from the front every time. The leader's role, above all, *is to make sure there is leadership* and, on the island, someone else was better qualified to lead. So he delegated leadership of the situation to that person and played the role of follower, but take note, *he did not delegate his responsibility to make sure there is leadership.*

Do you see the difference?

At some point, of course, the team's challenge will change, so the leader will have to judge when to make another leadership intervention.

So although you can read surveys listing the ideal qualities people want in their leaders, don't assume you can't lead well if you don't have all the right traits.[4] Who does, for heaven's sake? The idea that leaders must be heroes or supermen stops many people from leading because they feel so deficient. And those who are in leadership positions often feel anxious for the same reason.

What traits or qualities do leaders believe they lack the most? From my experience with clients, two qualities – or rather, the absence of two qualities – worry them more than any other. They are, first, the "need" to be a visionary, to be forward-looking, and second, the "requirement" to be inspirational, to be a natural cheerleader.[5]

Now it's true that if a group, team, organisation or even a nation is to achieve exceptional performance, it will need a motivating, perhaps inspirational, vision or direction. And the leader's job is to make sure the group has this exciting sense of destination. But here's the point: it's a bonus if he or she happens to be a visionary who can imagine and express an inspirational future in an exciting, colourful way and move among their people boosting morale. That is one way of leading – and a powerful one too – but it is only one way.

You see, the leader doesn't have to be an inspirational visionary. If he knows what questions to ask in crafting a galvanising vision (we'll look them at in chapter 7), he can create one with his team. And if he gathers around him people who are better at cheerleading, they can help him cover that aspect. But he can never evade his responsibility to ensure the group has a sense of direction and that the atmosphere stays positive enough to reach the destination.

Why Do These Insights Matter?

There are two reasons.

- First, it will be hard for you to grow as a leader if you have a vague, distorted or exaggerated view of your challenge. So understanding "leadership" and the uniqueness of the role is fundamental to a leader's development. It sets the foundation for everything else we'll discuss in this book. Without it, your growth can go awry from the start as there's more risk of you feeling inadequate and anxious about not measuring up. It's that important.

- Second, I have found that when clients reframe their view of leadership and their role as leader in the way I've described, they understand their position better and feel relieved. It's as though weight has slipped off their shoulders and they feel freer to perform as a leader.

This is because they are seeing the idea of leadership clearly for the first time. They don't see it as being so heroic, so extraordinary. And they no longer see the leader as a super-human being with all the brilliance, all the charisma, all the vision and all the answers. Their anxiety level drops, they can start to relax into their role, do it their way and begin to share leadership. And yet they realise they can't give up their responsibility to make sure there *is* leadership – for they now understand what's truly special about their role.

It helps group performance if a leader's colleagues share this view of leadership – because they too have a responsibility to contribute leadership when they are in the best position to do so. Yes, of course, the leader has to make sure he enables them to do so. But it's important they understand that leadership isn't the province of one person. If they do understand this and act on it – and the leader encourages shared leadership without forgetting the one responsibility he can't abandon – the group's performance can soar.

I started this chapter by remarking that leaders often have "unhelpful or vague beliefs about leadership and the role of the leader" that make it harder for them to do their job. We have addressed two of these – the idea of leadership itself and the purpose of the leader – but there are two more problem areas to look at. We'll deal with them in chapter 2.

The Key Points...

- Many leaders' beliefs about leadership and what it means to be a leader are both intimidating and fuzzy. Yet these beliefs usually live on unnoticed. They often cause a leader to feel inadequate and make it harder for him to grow and enjoy his role.

- Leadership doesn't have to be a vague, unpractical, intimidating idea. It's a process that involves:
  - setting a purpose that inspires people to combine and work towards willingly;
  - attention to the means, pace and quality of progress towards the aim;
  - building and upholding group unity throughout;
  - sustaining individual effectiveness.

- Leadership is all four dimensions, not just the first, which is the one many people focus on.

- Leadership and management differ in emphasis, but they are not separate. Leadership has a management dimension. Thus, a leader is also a manager.

- The purpose of the leader is to make sure there is leadership – whether he or she personally provides it or draws on others' strengths, or allows others to lead for a time.

- As a leader, it makes practical sense to share leadership with your colleagues for three reasons. First, you are unlikely to be good at all 34 of the public leadership behaviours and may overburden yourself if you take all of the load. Second, you might frustrate any colleagues who are ready and better able to lead on certain issues. Third, allowing others to take part in the big decisions promotes joint accountability.

- A leader does not have to be an inspirational visionary. It helps if he is, but it's not a deal-breaker if he's not. But if he's not, he'll need to know how to craft a new vision (or bring in an outside expert to facilitate the process) and make sure he has people around him to help with the job of cheerleading.

- The leader's responsibility to make sure there is leadership is the one thing he can't delegate.

- Being clear on leadership and your purpose as a leader sets the foundation for everything to come in the next nine chapters.

◇◇◇◇◇◇◇◇◇

2

◇◇◇◇◇◇◇◇◇

The Three Levels of Leadership Model

The Difficulty of Becoming a Leader

It isn't easy being a leader. Unlike previous less senior roles, you can't hide. Everything you do is visible.

But how many leaders feel they were ready for the role when they first stepped into it? Very few, judging by the conversations I've had with CEOs. Every one I've spoken to said none of their previous roles prepared them for the increase in pressure and exposure they felt when they became leader. But ready or not, others will expect you to make a difference. However, if you don't meet their expectations, criticism will rain down and if the organisation's performance continues to disappoint, you will become the scapegoat. Perhaps the biggest challenge you face is that your ego will be exposed as never before to the fear of failure or of feeling inadequate. But don't expect sympathy. Your critics will say, "You wanted the job, you get the financial rewards – you have to take the pressure that goes with it."

But leaders sometimes make it tougher for themselves. They don't always work as hard as they could on preparing themselves for leadership, nor on continued learning once they're in position. To make it worse, some who take on the number one role come to believe the idea that, "Now I'm the leader, I am the finished article – or at least I must pretend to be." Which is why many leaders don't ask for help after they start. This means the only way they learn is via the school of hard knocks – which can be a slow way to make progress.

The trouble is, leaders have a disproportionate effect – for good or ill – on the organisations they lead. So the question is: given their importance to society, why do we stand by and let would-be leaders so often arrive in the CEO role under-prepared, lacking guidance on how to develop from there on?

I believe one of the chief but rarely talked about reasons is that we continue to hold vague, unhelpful ideas around leadership – most notably around:

1 The idea of "leadership" itself.
2 The fundamental purpose of a leader.
3 What leaders have to do.
4 What they need to work on to become more effective.

After all, if we can't agree what "leadership" means; if we're not clear why the leader's role exists; if we don't know the key leadership behaviours and if we lack a framework for developing leaders... how can we expect anything other than hit and miss results?

Chapter one dealt with points 1 and 2 and offered a clear, practical definition of "leadership" and revealed the surprising simplicity of a leader's purpose. This chapter offers a model to teach leaders not only what they have to do in their role, but also what they have to work on to grow in their role.

Research Into Leadership

We now have a definition of "leadership," but if we're to develop leaders, we must also understand the keys to *effective* leadership.

What are they? Well, researchers have been trying to find the answer for at least 150 years. We can summarise their findings and ideas under five headings, as you'll see in table 1.

Table 1: Lines of Thinking On Leadership

Approach	Summary	Problems
1 **Traits or Qualities**	The idea that great leaders have certain common traits. Led some to assume leadership ability is innate; that leaders are born, not made.	• Findings on the key traits either differ or produce lists so long they are useless.[6] • Even if researchers agree on a trait, they may give it different meanings.
2 **Situational Suitability**	The belief that the person most qualified to meet the demands of the situation should take the lead. Their "qualifications" stem from their expertise or behavioural style.[7]	• Not every qualified person wants to lead. • Who decides who is most qualified? • May lead to frequent changes of leader, which can disturb a group's performance.
3 **Behavioural Style**	Studied leaders' behavioural patterns. Led to Blake & Mouton's view of the ideal style, called "team management," which balances concern for task with concern for people.[8]	• One style may not suit every leadership challenge. • Not every leader can adopt the ideal style, even after training, because of inner blocks.
4 **Flexing Behaviour**	The idea that leaders should flex their one-to-one behavioural style, popularised by Hersey & Blanchard's "Situational Leadership" model, where the leader flexes behaviour to match the competence and commitment of each follower.[9]	• Many leaders display behavioural rigidity, acting the same way repeatedly, even if it's ineffective, as they feel they can't change. • Applies better to "one-to-one" leadership than the "one-to-many" reality of leading a group or an organisation.
5 **Leadership Functions**	Focuses on what the leader has to do in their role. The two leading versions are: (1) The "three needs" model, where the leader has to concentrate on three functions: (a) the task (b) the needs of individuals (c) maintaining the group as a united force. Has become well known through the writings of John Adair.[10] (2) Kouzes & Posner's Leadership Practices model, which describes the ten broad behaviours they believe, from their research, reflects the actions of leaders at their best.[11]	• The three needs model: —Has led some theorists to believe you don't need a leader – that provided the group takes care of the three leadership functions, all will be well. —Omits the "motivating purpose" dimension of leadership. • The leadership practices model: —Shows leaders what they have to do, but not every leader can or will do it because of subtle, inner blocks. —Largely overlooks the "task/ management" side of leadership and ignores other ways of leading in portraying the leader as a visionary hero.

You may have noticed that the first two approaches (Traits/Qualities and Situational Suitability) are better for selecting leaders than developing them.

However, the third, fourth and fifth approaches (Behavioural Style, Flexing Behaviour and Leadership Functions) can help leaders develop their leadership ability. The third proposes that all leaders balance concern for the task with equal concern for people's needs. The fourth suggests leaders match their behaviour to the person before them. One version of the fifth idea argues that leaders should focus on and balance the pressures of task, individual team member needs and group unity. The other version suggests all leaders must perform ten specific behaviours to be effective.

These last three lines of thinking have merit. But each has weaknesses – as you see in the table's right-hand column. The key point is that there are two notable weaknesses common to all three ideas:

- First, they tell the leader what to do, but they don't help the leader perform the key behaviours if they don't come naturally. What about skills training, you ask? This will help some, but for many – and possibly the majority – it won't be enough. That's because, as I'll explain in chapter 3, inner psychological blocks in the form of habits and limiting beliefs can and do stop us from learning new skills and trying new behaviours.

- Second, they don't address the question of leadership qualities. And that leaves a void, because the best leaders I have known had something about them beyond their behaviour – call it their presence – that enabled them to lead successfully. But that "something" varied from person to person.

The Three Levels of Leadership Model

The table confirms the confusing picture facing leaders wanting to do their job well and get better at it. It's not clear how they should behave or what they should do to develop themselves, especially if certain behaviours are awkward for them. And it's unclear whether certain character traits are crucial to successful leadership and whether they can or should do anything to acquire any qualities they're missing.

What *is* clear from this is that existing and up-and-coming leaders and their sponsoring organisations lack a concise, useful framework to guide their development.

So can we integrate the five lines of research and address the missing link – the leader's psychology – in one compact, practical model? Can we create a model to help leaders (1) understand what they have to do to lead effectively (2) express their personality flexibly, but authentically and (3) remove any hidden limits to their growth? The answer is yes, if we come in from a different angle.

That angle is a model I call the *Three Levels of Leadership*, shown in figure 2. It recognises the practical benefits of seeing the leadership challenge through the three lenses of task, individual and group. It accepts that it's important for the leader to develop and express his presence and natural personality traits in a leadership role. And it can help a leader flex his behaviour while remaining authentic and, where necessary, allowing others to lead if they are better qualified.

Figure 2
The Three Levels of Leadership Model

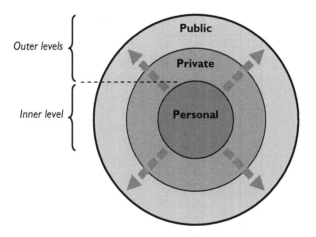

Thus, a leader may take up Blake & Mouton's ideal style *and* adopt other styles if needed – for example, in an emergency, a turnaround, or when the group is new – while staying true to character. The *Three Levels*

of Leadership model therefore enables "authentic flexibility". It does so by encouraging leaders to give up the limiting beliefs that drive their hidden anxieties and burden them with rigid, ineffective attitudes and behaviours.

Underlying the model is the earlier idea that the leader must ensure there is leadership in all four dimensions: (1) motivating purpose (2) task and results (3) upholding group spirit and (4) attention to individuals. To achieve this, a leader has to work at three levels. Two are outer or behavioural levels: public and private leadership. The third – personal leadership – takes place at inner mental and emotional levels. Here's how I define them:

- *Public leadership* covers *the actions leaders take in a group setting* – for example, a meeting – *or when trying to influence an organisation as a whole*. It includes the behaviours dealing with group purpose, group task work and group togetherness building. "Togetherness building" means encouraging group-wide trust and respect and developing an atmosphere in which it's natural to perform to your highest standard, share information and help colleagues.

- *Private leadership* refers to *individual handling of group members*. It includes getting to know your people as individuals; agreeing individual goals to support the group task; reviewing their individual task performance; helping them maintain and improve their performance; helping them grow beyond their current roles; selection; disciplining and removing underperforming members of the group.

- *Personal leadership* is the inner counterpart to the outer levels of private and public leadership. It concerns the leader's *psychological, moral and technical development and its effect on his presence and behaviour* – and therefore on the people around him. At its heart is the leader's self-awareness, his progress toward self-mastery and technical competence, and his sense of connection with those around him. It's the inner core, the source, of a leader's outer leadership effectiveness.

Of the three levels, personal leadership is the most powerful. Imagine dropping a pebble into a pond and seeing the ripples spreading out from the centre. The pebble represents inner, personal leadership and the ripples the two outer levels. Helpful inner change and growth will affect outer leadership positively. Negative inner change will cause the opposite.

In the next chapter, we will look more closely at the three levels and see the specific behaviours underneath the public and private leadership headings.

The Limitation of a Model

Before we move on, let's be clear that a model, however good, is just a simplified representation of a more complex reality. And leadership – and a leader's growth – is an especially complex, fluid, creative and therefore unpredictable reality.

So this model doesn't list every leadership behaviour you can think of, only the key ones. Nor does it classify every leadership behaviour neatly. Consider the example of "management by wandering about" (MBWA), first described by Peters & Waterman in their book, In Search of Excellence. [12] MBWA is, well, walking about your place of work seeing how your colleagues are; finding out what's going on; following up on projects; being visible; saying what you want to say one-to-one; and helping the atmosphere as you go. You couldn't describe it as a public behaviour or a private one because it's both.

What this means is that the Three Levels of Leadership model isn't perfect. But it doesn't have to be. It only has to be good enough to steer you through the many theories around effective leadership and offer a blueprint to guide your growth as a leader.

The Key Points...

- There are differing views on the keys to leadership success. Together, they present a confusing picture. This is why until now we've lacked a simple, complete model to help leaders understand (a) what they have to do to lead effectively and (b) grow in their role.

- The new Three Levels of Leadership model ends the confusion. It combines the previous ideas into one practical model while addressing their key flaw – inattention to the leader's psychology. As you'll see in the coming chapters, it shows you the key leadership behaviours and the skills underlying them. It also offers a framework to help you develop your presence, knowhow and skill.

- The three levels are Public, Private and Personal Leadership. The first two are outer levels. The third is the inner level and of the three it is the most influential.

- Public leadership concerns the actions you take in a group setting and when trying to influence an organisation as a whole.

- Private leadership refers to your individual handling of group members.

- Personal leadership centres on your psychological, moral and technical development and has powerful effects on your presence and behaviour and, therefore, on how people respond to you. It's the heart of a leader's outer leadership effectiveness.

◇◇◇◇◇◇◇◇◇

3

◇◇◇◇◇◇◇◇◇

Public, Private & Personal Leadership

Public Leadership

Public leadership is about three things. First, creating unity of purpose – often, but not always, around an inspiring vision. Second, getting the group's task done well, on time. And third, building and preserving a sense of togetherness plus group-wide standards of performance, based on trust, mutual respect and dedication to the goals.

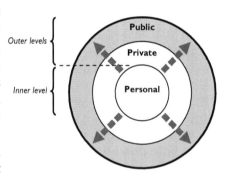

Going back to how I defined leadership, you can see it covers three of the four dimensions (although it shares "task and results" with private leadership). The one it excludes is attention to individuals.

But let's get specific. What are the key public leadership actions? Well, there are thirty four, which we can divide under the headings of *Group Purpose & Task* and *Group Building & Maintenance* – as you see in table 2.[13]

Below these headings, the Purpose & Task behaviours are split by function whereas the Building & Maintenance behaviours are divided according to the leader's visibility. In the five "out in front" behaviours, the leader takes a more visible leadership role, but in the other seven, his behaviour and status would be indistinguishable from others'.

Table 2: Key Public Leadership Behaviours

Group Purpose & Task	Group Building & Maintenance
Setting the purpose, staying focused • *Briefing* – explaining goals or strategies passed down from higher up the organisation • *Challenging* – questioning the "more of the same" attitude, encouraging a shared desire for change • *Navigating* – setting or agreeing a clear, common, motivating purpose or vision with supporting goals • *Prioritising* – focusing on priorities (not overloading the agenda as this impedes the task and frustrates others) **Organising, giving power to others** • *Assigning* – giving tasks and power to group members • *Organising* – planning, finding and granting resources **Ideation, problem-solving, decision-making** • *Co-ordinating* – suggesting how to integrate ideas • *Deciding* – listening, agreeing, concluding • *Elaborating & clarifying* – building on others' ideas, analysing outcomes, removing or lessening confusion • *Evaluating* – assessing ideas, choices and proposals • *Information giving* – providing data, sharing experiences • *Information seeking* – questioning accuracy of opinions, making the group aware of data needs, seeking facts • *Initiating* – proposing a vision, ideas, goals and solutions • *Opinion giving* – stating beliefs, views and feelings • *Opinion seeking* – finding out others' opinions or feelings • *Summarising* – summing up issues and views **Executing** • *Educating* – building competencies across the board • *Energising* – stimulating others to decisions and action • *Doing* – carrying out decisions or plans • *Measuring* – watching and assessing performance • *Following up* – ensuring people have taken the actions • *Tolerating* – accepting occasional failures [14]	**Out in front** • *Gathering* – bringing people together to discuss, decide and do creative work collectively • *Honouring* – celebrating the group's progress and marking individuals' accomplishments publicly • *Representing* – the group to the outside world (and, if needed, protecting individual members) • *Setting an example* – creating a collaborative atmosphere and showing commitment to the group's purpose and standards through your own enthusiasm and behaviour • *Updating* – explaining aims, plans, progress and issues to keep people informed, so they feel involved in something that is worthwhile, bigger than them, and is succeeding **In among the group** • *Compromising* – offering to change position if you were wrong, made a mistake, or there was something you overlooked, or perhaps didn't know • *Encouraging* – praising, affirming and supporting the contributions of others (even-handedly – no favourites) • *Following* – supporting and accepting others' good ideas • *Gatekeeping* – drawing out silent members, ensuring listening and balanced discussion, intervening with members who are trying to dominate • *Harmonising* – resolving differences and reducing tension through mediation or humour • *Observing* – listening, watching and commenting on group members' (and own) feelings, behaviours and functioning • *Standard setting* – making all aware of what is happening in the group, proposing behaviour standards, expressing concerns, pointing out the need for behaviour change

While leaders don't have to memorise all 34 behaviours, they do need to remember the Purpose & Task versus Building & Maintenance balance. Why? Because some are so goal or task biased, they can underemphasise the need to work on group unity, while others are so driven by people's feelings, they can neglect the demands of the task.

Note how the group maintenance side of leadership includes actions some wouldn't consider "leader-like." For example, admitting a mistake (see Compromising). When a leader accepts he or she doesn't know something or admits a mistake, it shows it's okay to seem less than perfect or even vulnerable. This encourages others to be open, tell the truth and cut out hidden agendas – which builds the mutual trust that's a "must" for a high-performance team.

One behaviour you won't see on the list is "listening." That's because a leader listens for a reason; for example, to decide what to do or understand a problem. Thus, a leader uses listening *within* several of the behaviours in the table. However, listening is undoubtedly a key leadership skill and we'll look at it in more depth in chapter 6 (Technical Knowledge & Skills).

Another you won't see is "communicating." Of course a leader must communicate, but it's too broad a behaviour to be useful in this model. Thus, you will see more specific behaviours like "elaborating and clarifying," "information giving," "briefing," "updating" and so on.

It's the leader's role to ensure the public leadership behaviours happen. But while it's true the leader's role carries more responsibility and usually demands more behavioural flexibility from him than his colleagues, *it doesn't mean he has to deliver all the public leadership behaviours himself.*

For example, a team or an organisation does need a commonly shared, motivating purpose to perform well – and usually a plan to go with it. But the leader doesn't have to be the brilliant visionary defining the purpose and building a plan. However, he does have to make sure there *is* a motivating purpose and there *is* a plan. If there isn't, the leader must intervene – for example, by creating and leading a process towards a purpose, vision or plan, or by bringing in an outsider to help the group. Or instead, by playing follower (see Following among the maintenance behaviours) to a more qualified person in the group. But *always keeping responsibility to ensure there is leadership.*

You may like to study the 34 public behaviours to see which of them you need to work on. The following self-assessment exercise (which you can download from the book's website) will help:

Self-Assessment Exercise
Public Leadership Behaviours

So you know the behaviours underlying public leadership. What now? Well, you could do this simple exercise to help you zero in on your learning priorities. Try answering these questions:

- *For each of the purpose/task and group maintenance behaviours, do you perform this behaviour: (a) Often (b) Rarely (c) Never?*

- *And for each of the purpose/task and group maintenance behaviours, when you do perform it, do you do it: (a) Well (b) Poorly (c) Sometimes well, sometimes poorly?*

- *If you answered, "Rarely" or "Never":*
  - *Why is that? Do you avoid it? Does it make you anxious? Do you doubt your ability to do it well?*
  - *Does not doing it affect your team or organisation's performance? If so, positively or negatively?*
  - *Is this something you must improve on – or do you have colleagues who cover your weakness?*

- *If you answered, "Well," how do you know? What is the evidence? Have you asked your colleagues for feedback?*

- *If you answered, "Poorly" or "Sometimes well, sometimes poorly," do you want to improve on this behaviour? What have you tried to improve your effectiveness on this behaviour? Why didn't that work? What else could you try?*

Private Leadership

You may have heard the clichés, "There is no 'I' in team" and "The team is more important than the individual." Well, it's true the team's goals must be at least as important to each person as their own aims and that no individual is indispensable. But teams comprise individuals. And a team is no stronger than the contribution each member makes to its overall purpose.

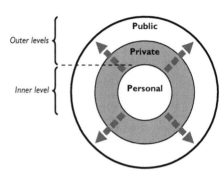

So as well as creating a sense of group identity and atmosphere through public leadership, the leader must treat the individual group members as individuals. For although each person may support the group's aims, their levels of skill, motivation, confidence, experience and mental robustness will vary. Which means they won't see or respond to issues in the same way. Nor will they grow at the same rate. In other words, they are different – they are individuals. So the leader faces the paradox that although the team may be more important than any one person, to lead it to an outstanding performance he must pay attention to the individuals. This is why the leader has to combine public leadership with private leadership.

Private leadership shares with public leadership the Purpose/Task versus Building/Maintenance divide between behaviours, although here we are talking about individual goals, tasks, motivation and feelings. Although it's largely to do with understanding, empowering and inspiring individuals one-to-one so they feel included and play their part to best effect, private leadership is also about the tough side of leadership: making sure individuals do perform against their assigned tasks and taking action if they don't.

Being more specific, you will see the 14 key private leadership behaviours in table 3:

Table 3: Key Private Leadership Behaviours

Individual Purpose & Task	Individual Building & Maintenance
• *Appraising* – giving and receiving honest, effective feedback about the need for behavioural change • *Choosing* – selecting individuals, assigning new or alternative roles, promoting talented people* • *Disciplining* – confronting, reprimanding or removing people who under-perform or under-collaborate • *Goal-setting* – with the individual, for individual performance and career growth* • *Reviewing* – receiving task progress updates, proposals, requests, ideas or solutions and following up individually	• *Assessing & matching* – gauging a person's competence and commitment to know how to flex your one-to-one behaviour and then choosing a suitable approach • *Attracting* – bringing new talented individuals into the group or wider organisation • *Consulting* – conferring privately on sensitive issues that you cannot address in a public forum • *Developing* – agreeing personal growth priorities and actions; helping directly through mentoring or coaching • *Discovering* – learning what motivates each individual, their inner challenges, unspoken thoughts and feelings • *Encouraging* – praising, affirming, building confidence and showing you have noticed individuals' contributions • *Intervening* – noticing and interceding with those who find their role frustrating or are demotivating colleagues • *Recognising* – spotting rising talent • *Understanding* – watching and learning your impact on individuals (how they perceive and respond to you)
* *These behaviours do in fact straddle the Purpose/Task and Building/Maintenance divide even though they are classified on this side for convenience.*	

There are two moments in a team's life when paying attention to individuals rises from "important" to "critical." First, when the team is new and, second, when the team has to shift to a higher level of performance, but is held back by some members. But this doesn't mean the leader can ignore private leadership at other times – even when the group is performing well. For it's possible an individual's personal needs or ambitions may start to diverge from the group; perhaps for career reasons. It's possible too that, as the group reaches higher levels of performance, it will expose one person's weaknesses. Or an individual may face outside problems that interfere with their performance.

The point is this: a leader may be strong on public leadership, but ignore the reality that, however clear the group's purpose and plan, its success depends on skilful, joined-up performances by individuals.

Thus, to ensure lasting high performance, the leader must consider whether people are right for their roles. And he must also pay attention to the motivations of each person – for only then will each member treat the group's purpose as their own and play their part to the full.

I remarked that individuals won't see or respond to issues in the same way. So it makes sense for the leader to vary his style – as what works with one person may not work with another. This is where Hersey and Blanchard's situational leadership model is useful and it's why you see "assessing and matching" among the private leadership behaviours. The idea is for the leader to match his approach to each follower's ability and commitment, using one of four styles. Endnote 15 has more detail on this.[15]

The leader can delegate some responsibility for private leadership if he is running a large organisation. Indeed, the leader must – because he won't have time to privately lead every employee; which is why companies create hierarchies. However, he won't delegate private leadership of those who report directly to him (although an effective leader can, of course, seek help and advice, for example, when it comes to selection, disciplining or learning about his impact on others). If he does, he isn't leading. And a leadership void means a risk to group performance.

Once again, you might like to assess where you stand on the private behaviours by trying the self-assessment exercise below (which you can download from the book's website):

Self-Assessment Exercise
Private Leadership Behaviours

Looking back at the table of key private leadership behaviours, try answering these questions to help you recognise your learning priorities:

- *For each behaviour, do you perform it: (a) Often (b) Rarely (c) Never?*

- *And for each behaviour, when you do carry it out it, do you do it: (a) Well (b) Poorly (c) Sometimes well, sometimes poorly?*

- *If you answered, "Rarely" or "Never":*
  - *Why is that? Do you avoid it? Does it make you anxious? Do you doubt your ability to do it well?*
  - *Does not doing it affect your team or organisation's performance? If so, positively or negatively?*

- *If you answered, "Well," how do you know? What do your team members tell you?*

- *If you answered, "Poorly" or "Sometimes well, sometimes poorly," is it something you want to improve on? What have you tried to improve your effectiveness? If you tried something, why didn't that work? What else could you try?*

Personal Leadership

So far, we have a definition of "leadership," we know the leader's purpose and in outlining the public and private levels, we've seen what he or she has to do behaviourally. Being clear on what leadership is, the purpose of your role and what you have to do are three of the keys to becoming a good leader. But they are not the whole picture.

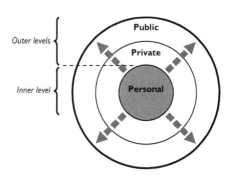

That's because most leaders will have to expand their knowhow and learn new skills – technical and interpersonal – to widen their range of public and private leadership behaviours and make them their own.

But it takes more than knowhow, skills and behaviours to lead well. It demands *presence*. Or rather, the leader's *unique* presence.

What is presence? At its root, it is wholeness – the rare, but attainable inner alignment of self-identity, purpose and feelings that eventually leads to freedom from fear. It reveals itself as the magnetic, radiating effect you have on others when you're being the authentic you, giving them your full respect and attention, speaking honestly and letting your unique character traits flow. As leaders, we must be technically competent to gain others' respect, but it's our unique genuine presence that inspires people and prompts them to trust us – in short, to want us as their leader.

Presence isn't the same as charisma. A person can be charismatic in some contexts by relying on a title, fame or skilful acting. But presence is more basic, more fundamental, more powerful. It is not an act. It doesn't depend on a title or social status. It is, quite simply, who you are.

And it doesn't dissolve when the going gets tough.

Few people consistently radiate their presence (although all have it in them) and we're attracted to those that do. For leaders, presence is the indispensable "something" behind skills, knowledge and the many character traits identified by the research into successful leaders.

Why have researchers found so many different character traits in effective leaders? My view is that it's because *there is no one way of being a leader and no one way of leading*. We each have unique character traits to lead in our own way. In other words, we can be equally effective as leaders, but in different ways, unique to us. So although we can identify the key leadership behaviours and areas of knowhow, the way we express them and how many of them we express will be unique to us, depending on our character blueprint. But – and this is a big point – our ability to express our unique character traits powerfully but wisely and use our skills and knowhow confidently, without fear, will depend on our level of inner integration, of wholeness. In other words, on our degree of presence.

Thus, the key is not to copy the traits of previous leaders or try to reproduce qualities from a list. It is to express your unique combination of qualities by seeking wholeness and, therefore, let your presence flow.

How do you learn the essential knowhow, skills and behaviours – and how do you come to express your presence? This is where personal leadership comes in. Personal leadership is about growing your ability to be a leader and act as a leader, from the inside outwards. It has three elements, as you will see in table 4:

Table 4: The Three Elements of Personal Leadership

- *Technical* – knowing your technical weaknesses and continually updating your knowledge and skills
- *Attitude toward others* – believing other people to be as important as you – or learning to believe it
- *Self-mastery* – committing to self-awareness, self-integration, growth and flexible command of your psyche

---

The first point is the most obvious. A leader must be technically competent – he or she must know how to make things happen. But being competent today doesn't guarantee you will be able to meet the challenges of tomorrow. So leaders must take charge of their technical education and keep learning in a fast-changing world. This starts with self-awareness of our weaknesses. For example, we may need to learn about subjects we're weak on – for instance, strategy – to figure out what questions to ask and how to get things done. Or we may need to become skilled at giving and receiving feedback to drive positive change, learn how to set goals, sell ideas, ask open questions, handle conflict… and so on. Bear in mind that although it's helpful to widen your repertoire of leadership behaviours, *a leader doesn't have to know how to do everything*. So he must not only see his technical gaps, but be discerning in deciding which to work on.

The second facet – our attitude to our colleagues – is a moral one. But it also has a huge effect on your effectiveness as a leader. Why? Because if you see your colleagues as something less than you – perhaps as pawns to be manipulated for your own gain – they will find you out eventually. When they do, they won't follow you – and a leader without followers isn't a leader.

The third part of personal leadership is self-mastery. What is self-mastery? It is being aware of, understanding, taking command of, integrating and transforming the limiting parts of your psychology to overcome inner divisions and become whole, to grow and to express your highest potential as a leader. Self-mastery enables you to be in the mental state that top performers call "being in the flow" – that is, using your skills and faculties freely, with complete focus, minimum effort and maximum enjoyment.

Why do we need self-mastery – why can't we just notice our weaknesses, gain the missing knowhow and learn the skills underlying the public and private leadership behaviours? There are two reasons. First, self-mastery is essential to achieving the inner alignment, the wholeness, I described earlier, because skills and knowhow alone don't lead to presence. Second, because there are usually powerful forces in our psyche that make it hard to see our own weaknesses, overcome old habits and dare to learn new behaviours.

What are these forces holding us back? There are two:

- *Neural patterns:* neuroscientists have found that our physical habits are underpinned by the neural circuits in our brains. Thus, as we repeat certain behaviours, they become our default choices – even if they limit us – unless we work hard at changing them. Without getting technical, you can liken your neural circuits to pathways through a forest. Once a path has been established, we usually follow it every time we walk through the forest.[16]

- *Limiting beliefs:* these block us from learning or applying new skills, leaving us trapped in an inadequate and often unhelpful range of leadership behaviours. One way they do so is by convincing us we don't need to learn something new – that we don't have a problem. Another is to make us feel afraid – usually unconsciously – of learning a new skill or trying a new behaviour.

Thus, even though we may know what to do and how to do it, old habits and limiting beliefs can mean we still don't do it. And this is where self-mastery becomes the key to growth by locating and removing the inner blocks. Self-mastery – or rather, constant attention to self-mastery – allows you to see beyond and let go of your current beliefs and perceptions, enabling you to rise to a higher level of leadership presence and skill.

Returning to the point about being afraid to learn new skills or try new behaviours, have you noticed how many senior people attend training courses to learn leadership and people skills, but rarely change on their return? Have you wondered why? It's usually because what they learned clashed with their unconscious limiting beliefs and the fears they produce.

You see, beliefs are the ideas we hold to be true. They guide us through life. Our most powerful beliefs are around our self-image or self-identity – that is, who we think we are, including our qualities and flaws. They flow through to our feelings about our self-image, which we call "self-esteem." And our self-identity and self-esteem together shape our leadership behaviours.

Now there is a special class of beliefs known as "limiting beliefs." These are negative ideas, especially about ourselves, that we accept as true and they limit our behavioural choices. In short, limiting beliefs reduce our effectiveness and stop us becoming better leaders. They do so by causing fear.

William Schutz's research into interpersonal behaviour shows that many of us fear feeling ignored, powerless, humiliated or rejected – without realising it.[17] These unconscious fears entrap our will, creativity and courage, causing us to learn rigid behavioural habits to avoid experiencing such unwelcome feelings. Psychologists call these habits "defensive behaviours."

For example, if I believe myself to be a successful, but ruthless leader, I'm unlikely to allow others to get close to me. Why? Because they may see what I believe about myself – that I am merciless, unfeeling and will do anything to protect my position. And so they may reject me. And rejection can hurt. So I'll avoid putting myself in a position where I may experience rejection. This is one reason some senior people avoid giving clear feedback in appraisals, even if they know what to do and how to do it. Unconsciously, they avoid being open as it may draw them into an intimate discussion which, they fear, may let the other person see them for what they are – or believe they are – and reject them. And this is too painful for them to allow.

The fear of humiliation, of making a mistake, of failing, of losing others' respect, or of feeling powerless, is another common problem for leaders. So you may see them unconsciously resorting to various defensive behaviours to avoid these fears, including these three examples:

- Trying to be perfect in every task they take on – even if it drives them and others towards stress and burnout.

- Over-controlling – to dominate or even crush opposing views – even if the leader's ideas are flawed or he is ignoring obvious danger signs. And perhaps despite having colleagues better qualified to lead at that moment.

- Avoiding major issues or procrastinating over decisions, even if it puts the business at risk.

Unconscious limiting beliefs and fears not only control our behaviour, they block us from using our self-awareness to examine ourselves and see what we need to change – often by convincing us we don't need to change. That way, we avoid seeing anything that may embarrass us. So returning to the question about training; if something we learn on a course rekindles such fears, we won't use what we've learned – which stymies our ability to apply the new public and private leadership behaviours.

How do we learn to lead if hidden, limiting beliefs are blocking our growth? Through self-mastery! By becoming aware of, dissolving and replacing these beliefs, thus revealing our inner presence and removing the blocks to learning. You see, learning to control and transcend the contents and energies of your psyche – and the limiting mental, emotional and physical habits they spawn – *is* self-mastery.

The journey to self-mastery demands two things of us. First, self-awareness – seeing ourselves clearly, so we know our strengths and what we want to change. Second, will – clarifying what's important to us (our values), having a direction and an intent to grow, knowing the specific results we want and following through with discipline and creativity.

To sum up, personal leadership enables the leader to:

1. Dissolve and go beyond his limiting beliefs.

2. Expand his technical and self-knowledge and master new skills, enabling him to flex his behaviour to connect with and influence others.

3. Allow his inner presence to unfold and express his values and qualities with natural confidence and authority.

Personal leadership therefore makes the "theory" of the two outer levels come alive. Personal leadership is so important that part 2 will focus on it and will include practical steps you can take to develop yourself.

But before we get to part 2, I'll summarise the main points from part 1 in the next chapter because we have covered a lot of ground and the ideas we've discussed set the foundations for what's to come. Chapter 4 will also serve as a "quick reference" source should you want to jog your memory on the foundational ideas as you read part 2.

The Key Points...

- Public leadership is about creating unity of purpose, getting the group task done and building an atmosphere that promotes togetherness and high performance standards.

- There are 34 key public leadership behaviours and they split into two categories. First, group purpose and task. Second, group building and maintenance. You need to attend to both classes of behaviour to lead well in the public domain. The chapter offers you a self-assessment tool to help you spot your public leadership learning priorities.

- Private leadership is where you treat the individuals as individuals. You recognise their differing levels of confidence, commitment, mental toughness and experience and adjust what you do to suit each individual while working on public leadership in parallel.

- There are 14 distinct, key private leadership behaviours. As with public leadership, they divide into purpose-task and building-maintenance related behaviours. Again, there is a self-assessment tool to help you see which private leadership behaviours you need to work on first.

- To be clear, you don't have to memorise the 34 public and 14 private behaviours. But you do have to remember the purpose-task versus build-maintenance balance and decide which behaviours you want to work on. Note: chapter 6 will help you work on your skills.

- You can draw on your colleagues' strengths to cover your public leadership weaknesses. This means you don't have to be great at every one of the 34 public leadership behaviours. But when it comes to private leadership, the challenge is different – you will have to be at least competent on each of the 14 behaviours if you are to be effective.

- Personal leadership focuses on expanding your knowhow to widen your range of behaviours and increasing your skill. But it's also about working on your leadership presence.

- Personal leadership has three elements.

  - Technical: Knowing your technical weaknesses and continually updating your knowledge and skills.

  - Attitude toward others: Believing other people to be as important as you – or learning to believe it.

  - Self-mastery: Committing to self-awareness, self-integration and flexible command of your psyche, enabling you to break old, unhelpful habits and keep growing. This inevitably means becoming aware of, dissolving and going beyond your limiting beliefs.

- You could say the two outer levels (public and private leadership) focus on *what* you do and the inner level (personal leadership) on *how* you do it.

◇◇◇◇◇◇◇◇◇◇

4

◇◇◇◇◇◇◇◇◇◇

Summarising the Foundations

This chapter recaps the main points from part 1 before we get into the details of part 2.

Leadership & The Leader

• Leadership is a process – a series of choices and actions around defining and achieving a shared goal. As the diagram below shows, it has four dimensions: (1) agreeing a motivating, shared purpose; (2) practical management of the group's task to achieve the desired progress and results; (3) building and upholding group unity and team atmosphere; (4) motivating and developing individuals.

Leadership's Four Dimensions

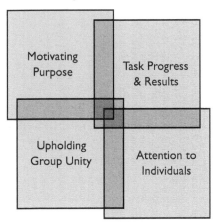

- The purpose of the leader is to make sure there is leadership – which is not the same as having all the answers or leading from the front every time. In reality, leaders don't have to have all the answers. Nor do they have to make all the decisions. Indeed, the leader can delegate the responsibility to lead to others at certain moments. But what he cannot do is give away his responsibility to make sure there is leadership in all four dimensions.

The Three Levels of Leadership Model

- The Three Levels of Leadership model (see diagram) teaches leaders what they have to do to lead effectively and morally, express themselves authentically, and grow in the role.

The Three Levels of Leadership Model

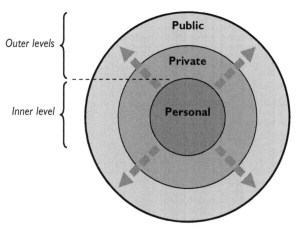

- The model pulls together the findings of previous leadership research while addressing the missing factor: the leader's psychology. It says that to act successfully in all four dimensions, a leader has to work at three levels. Two are outer or behavioural levels: public and private leadership. The third – personal leadership – takes place at inner mental and emotional levels.

- *Public leadership* is what leaders do when they are working with several others, for example, in a meeting, or when trying to influence the wider organisation. It involves agreeing the group purpose, charting the direction, getting the group task done and creating a sense of "us." The three levels model lists 34 key public leadership behaviours.

- *Private leadership* refers to one-to-one handling of colleagues. It involves helping individuals maintain and improve their performance and grow beyond their current roles. But it also pays attention to the performance side of the equation – to individuals' goals, roles and tasks. Thus, it includes selection, heart-to-heart progress reviews, disciplining and firing people. The model includes 14 key private leadership behaviours.

- *Personal leadership* concerns the leader's inner development and its effect on his presence, resilience, behaviour and skill in action – and therefore on the people around him.

We can divide the 34 public and 14 private leadership behaviours into those serving purpose and task and those that build and maintain – whether it's at the group or individual level. You don't have to memorise the many behaviours. But you do need to assess which of them you want to work on so you have some focus when we look at improving your skills in chapter 6.

Thus, public and private leadership is essentially about the leader's behaviour – what he does with and to others – whether in a group setting or face to face with individuals. But the leader's ability to affect others' performance positively depends on *how* he performs those behaviours under testing conditions and the key to this is personal leadership, which is why it's the most influential of the three levels. Personal leadership is the key to growing as a leader, behaving skilfully as a leader and, above all, being a leader deep inside.

The Three Elements of Personal Leadership
No leader can afford to be without technical understanding of his field – whether it is the military, business, government or not-for-profit – or he'll struggle to make things happen. Nor can he restrict himself to a

narrow range of leadership behaviours or he'll limit his ability to connect with and influence others.

Therefore, to become a leader and grow as a leader, most people will have to expand their knowhow, learn the skills underlying the public and private leadership behaviours and practise them to make them their own. So not surprisingly, as the box below confirms, the first element of personal leadership is knowing your technical weaknesses (what you don't know and what you're not good at), expanding your knowhow and behavioural skills, and keeping up to date.

The Three Elements of Personal Leadership

* *Technical* – knowing your technical weaknesses and continually updating your knowledge and skills
* *Attitude toward others* – believing other people to be as important as you – or learning to believe it
* *Self-mastery* – committing to self-awareness, self-integration, growth and flexible command of your psyche

---

But being knowledgeable and behaving like a leader doesn't guarantee effective leadership. You see, leadership isn't just about the leader. Effective leadership needs enthusiastic followership. This is especially true in the twenty-first century when change – in an organisation's results, strategy, skills, attitude, or all four – is usually on the agenda. And when change is in the air, resistance to it usually follows. So to lead successfully, a critical mass of people must want to follow you, even – in fact, especially – when others are resisting change or when results are disappointing. For a leader without followers isn't a leader.

What is it that makes us want someone as our leader and choose to follow them in good times and bad? It is trust. Trust that they know what they're doing, that they can make the right things happen, that they'll tell the truth and put a greater cause ahead of their selfish interests.

And what inspires trust? It's partly a person's record of achievement, but fundamentally, it is presence. Or rather, as I said in chapter 3, the leader's *unique* presence. Presence is that intangible "something" that tells people this man or woman has the qualities to help them meet the challenges they face.

So how does the aspiring leader contact his unique inner presence and let it unfold? This is where the second and third elements of personal leadership come in.

The second element is your attitude towards other people, for it's important to believe others are as important as you – or learn to believe it. And not just because it's the correct moral attitude, but to be effective. If you don't – if you see your colleagues as pawns in your personal game of survival or self-aggrandisement, to be exploited for your gain – they will eventually find you out. And when you can no longer give them what they want, your influence will fade, leaving you high and dry just when you need their support.

The third element is self-mastery: being aware of, understanding, taking command of, uniting and transforming the limiting parts of your psyche to overcome inner divisions, achieve wholeness, grow and express your highest potential as a leader.

In part 2, we'll look closer at each element to see what steps you can take to develop your presence, knowhow and skill as a leader.

Before we do so, we'll deepen our understanding of presence.

Part 2

Personal Leadership

Part 2 – Personal Leadership

In focusing on *personal leadership*, part 2 expands on part 1 and outlines practical ways of developing your presence, knowhow and skill as a leader. It has three main aims.

First, to explain what presence is.

Second, to look below the public and private leadership behaviour headlines and deepen your understanding of them by outlining the key underpinning skills and the choices you have for working on them.

Third, to enlarge on presence, self-mastery and your attitude towards others and explain what it takes for you to develop yourself on these, the subtlest aspects of personal leadership. In so doing, part 2 introduces a new psychological model for leaders and offers more detail on limiting beliefs.

◇◇◇◇◇◇◇◇◇

5

◇◇◇◇◇◇◇◇◇

Presence & Personal Leadership

If presence is a key to being an effective leader, we need to understand it. So what is it exactly? How does it show itself? What is the source of presence?

The Experience of Presence

Presence reveals itself to others when you are being the natural "you" – your true Self. That is, when you're being fully aware and alert; giving others your undivided attention; speaking honestly and respectfully, but without ducking issues; and letting your personality flow, unhindered by hidden fears. When presence flows like this – and it's allied to a strong sense of mission – it has a powerful, magnetic, radiating effect on those around you.

You experience your own presence when you are in the here-and-now (not worrying about the past or future), in the flow, feeling confident and enjoying whatever you're doing – and doing it with ease. When you are in the flow, you are doing what you are doing without filtering your experience. By this, I mean without getting caught in a fixed, prejudiced view of what surrounding events mean or having a set, rigid opinion on how they should unfold.

This is what sports stars experience when they talk about "being in the zone" – they are focused in the present moment, undistracted by thoughts about the past or the future. You see this when a tennis player is on match point and, seeing it for what it is – just another point – plays it like any other, unbothered by its emotional significance. Or when a business leader, faced with a major crisis, deals with it decisively, skilfully and wisely, with no thoughts about the effect on his career or reputation.

Are there distinctive behaviours associated with presence? Well, the man or woman with presence will be attentive and "in the moment" and may speak with disarming honesty. Beyond that, I don't believe one can say that presence shows as "this" or "that" behaviour, for how it displays itself will differ, depending on one's character and the context. After all, leadership is only one context in which to express presence. And, of course, leadership contexts can vary too. For example, in industry the context could be a turnaround, start-up or steady growth.

So one person's presence may be expressed as visionary and charismatic. Another's may be analytical, quiet and contemplative. Yet another's may be both at different times, according to their character and the context. My point is that each person's presence is unique, so it doesn't present itself in one predictable form of behaviour. Yet we recognise it when we meet it.

The Root of Presence

So what is at the root of presence? It is inner wholeness; the opposite of inner division. You see, many of us are unaware of the subtle divisions, conflicts and limiting beliefs in our psyche that lead to anxiety and defensive behaviours when we are around others. However, the man or woman with well-developed presence experiences an inner togetherness, a wholeness. Wholeness stems from – and indeed *is* – a positive inner alignment of one's sense of identity, purpose and feelings about life and oneself. It frees us from limiting beliefs, releases us from fear and expresses itself as a rare combination of inner peace and vitality.

Note: defensive behaviours are action habits we unconsciously create and use to avoid experiencing our fears – most of which are around our self-image. I outlined some of the typical fears faced by leaders in chapter 3 and will say more about them in chapters 7 and 8.

Presence and Charisma

For some people, the word "charisma" includes the quality of presence, but that's not how I use it here. I use it to mean a combination of outer charm, power and persuasiveness. Thus, a leader with presence may or may not have charisma, but then a charismatic leader won't always have presence. That's because *presence is not the same as charisma*. Presence is an inner psychospiritual state with an outer reflection whereas charisma by itself is an outer image lacking a deeper core.

Charismatic people do have something about them that magnifies their impact on others, at least in some settings, so charisma can imitate presence for a while. But I repeat, presence and charisma are not the same. So what is the difference? Table 5 sums up the key distinctions.

Table 5: Charisma versus Presence

Charisma	Presence
• A person can have leadership charisma without inner wholeness, at least for a time, by relying on a high social status – be it fame, reputation, wealth, an impressive title or a large office – to give them an aura of authority and superiority in the eyes of those they meet.*	• Presence comes only from being who you are, the genuine you, comfortable in your own skin, letting your natural character qualities flow from your inner sense of wholeness.
• Another way to gain leadership charisma is to project an impressive image through skilful acting and presentation. For example, by learning to speak well in public, having voice training, talking in memorable sound bites, practising the right body language, wearing the right clothes and learning to evade tough questions.	• Presence is not an act. It doesn't demand social status and doesn't need others to project an image of superiority and power on to us. In fact, presence doesn't need status at all. We can sense presence – that is, something exceptional about a person – on meeting them, even if we know nothing about them, for presence is, quite simply, being who you are.
• It is of course possible to combine both means.	• Presence is therefore deeper, more powerful and more durable than charisma.

Note the words, "in the eyes of those they meet." We often regard people with high social status as impressive simply because we project an image of superiority and authority on to them. The image can stem from our hopes, fears and insecurities or our wish to avoid taking responsibility for ourselves. It can lead us to put the person on a pedestal, rely on him to point the way forward and solve our problems… and to give our power to him.

In the table, I mention that public speaking skill can help a leader appear charismatic. To be clear, I am not suggesting there is anything wrong with learning to speak well in public, as oratory skill can be a helpful accompaniment to presence.

What I am suggesting is that there is a hollowness to charisma. The power of the leader who has charisma – but lacks presence – rests on their acting skills and the power their followers give them, not their true, inner qualities. Deep down, such a leader knows they are living with the constant risk of exposure or abandonment by their followers, so their self-esteem is always under threat. To deal with this, charismatic leaders often create a belief in their innate superiority and use this to feel better about themselves and to reinforce their act, despite the continuing presence of powerful limiting beliefs in their psyche. The trouble is, this is like placing a golden crust on a pie with infected meat. It's a psychological cover-up that merely increases their risk of exposure, especially when events don't go the way they want.

Presence, unlike charisma, doesn't depend on a self-image founded on a fragile sense of superiority offering only leaky self-esteem – a superiority relying on constant success, acclaim or others' relative underperformance to support it. Presence comes from uniting the divisions and letting go of the limiting beliefs in one's psyche to create a durable core that's more robust than a hollow self-image. Founded on a base of positive, healthy self-esteem, it needs little or no outer reassurance and no comparisons with others. Thus, the leader with presence doesn't feel the same degree of psychological threat when the going gets tough.

This contrast between presence and charisma underlies a key difference in leaders' behaviour and decisions under pressure.

If a firm's progress is disappointing or results are poor, the leader who depends on charisma can fear humiliation from what they see as impending failure. Their fear can become self-serving behaviour that hurts the organisation. They may avoid decisions or actions they find difficult or look for, blame and fire scapegoats, even if they have crucial skills or contacts. Alternatively, they may fill their board of directors with cronies; or indulge in ill-conceived initiatives that misdirect the organisation's attention and money, like ego-driven takeovers.

However, the leader with presence can endure rough conditions and navigate with a wiser, cooler head because of their strong self-esteem.

You see, some of the common hazards of leadership roles like arrogance, overestimating one's ability or judgement, oversensitivity to criticism and the fear of failure all stem from an unconscious limiting self-image. And a limiting self-image ("I have this limitation or that flaw") reduces self-esteem. But presence – founded on the rock of robust self-esteem, unlike the sand that charisma stands on – is a natural antidote to these dangers.

Qualities & Degrees of Presence

I'm saying that leadership presence doesn't show up in one predictable set of behaviours – that it bears each person's stamp of uniqueness. Nonetheless, I believe there are seven core, underlying qualities of pure presence, as you will see in table 6.

Table 6: Seven Qualities of Pure Presence

1. **Personal power:** accepting full responsibility for and exercising your will over your life direction and responses to inner psychological forces and outer conditions – giving you freedom to choose how to be and act.

2. **High, real self-esteem:** feeling good about yourself, leading to a sense of empathy with, respect for and positive feelings towards others.

3. **Drive to be more, to grow:** the urge to continually surpass one's previous level by seeing, understanding and rising above the often-hidden limiting beliefs and mindsets behind present limitations and difficulties.

4. **Balance:** A strong sense of purpose and connection with your highest values and the vitality that flows from it, balanced with a concern for others' needs and respect for their free will. Expressed as a drive to serve a cause that's bigger than you.

5. **Intuition:** expressed as creative insight or instead as foresight, vision and perceptiveness in complex circumstances.

6. **In the now:** being fully present to the here-and-now, not limited or distracted by memories, beliefs and feelings about the past or hopes and fears about the future.

7. **Inner peace of mind and fulfilment:** freedom from fear and doubt plus a sense of fulfilment, joy and flow.

Wholeness

Being who you really are, powerfully, wisely, fearlessly, lovingly and creatively as you experience your freedom from inner divisions, while raising yourself and inspiring others

The first quality, personal power, recognises that although we can't always control outer events, including others' behaviour, we can always choose our individual response to them. Note that this is personal power. That is, it's power over oneself; it is not a drive to have power over others. It doesn't spring from a need to have the status, prestige or visibility that power over others can bring or an urge to impose your viewpoint through force. The importance of personal power is this: if you can't direct and lead yourself, you'll find it hard to direct others because they'll sense your lack of inner command. Thus, personal power (as opposed to the power that flows from an impressive job title) is crucial to anyone wanting to be an effective leader.

The second quality is high, real self-esteem. I touched on self-esteem when discussing Personal Leadership in chapter 3, but it's time to expand on it because it's so important. So what is self-esteem? Well, self-esteem flows from your self-image (or "self-concept" or "self-identity," whichever term you prefer). So your self-image is who you believe yourself to be – your qualities, your flaws, your history, your potential and your place in the world – and your feelings about this self-image are what we call self-esteem. If your self-image is positive, your self-esteem will be high and, of course, the reverse will also be true.

A person with high self-esteem will feel they matter, that they're significant, that people notice them. They will also feel they can cope with their lives, that they're competent in their job, that they can make a difference and take responsibility. And finally, they'll like themselves, they'll feel they're a decent person at heart and are worthy of another person's love.

However, we're not just talking about high self-esteem here, but high *real* self-esteem. What does "real self-esteem" mean? It means three things:

- First and most important, it is genuine self-esteem. Some people can appear to have high self-esteem – they can act self-confident, but deep down, they don't feel as good as they pretend. When they are under pressure, you can often see their lack of self-esteem in their behaviour – perhaps through their aggression, indecision, procrastination, nervousness, neediness or, although this can be harder to detect, through their haughtiness towards others. However, people with high, real self-esteem genuinely feel good about themselves, even under pressure.

- Second, real self-esteem doesn't rely on comparison with others. There's no need to constantly feed the belief that you're superior or that you're doing better than others and behave dismissively towards them. You just feel good about yourself as you are, right now, regardless of who you are with. You'll find this makes it easier for you to be natural with others and treat them with respect.

- Third, real self-esteem is grounded self-esteem. Thinking well of yourself is not the same as an inflated self-opinion. It means having a realistic self-view while continuing to feel good about yourself. It means you can admit your weaknesses, mistakes and failings without triggering overpowering feelings of shame, vulnerability, embarrassment or becoming inhibited.

Why is high, real self-esteem helpful to a leader? First, as you'll read in chapter 7, self-esteem is the same as self-appreciation and when you appreciate yourself you'll find it easier to understand, appreciate, connect with and motivate others. Second, as we'll explore in chapter 8, when you feel good about yourself, your fears have less of a grip on you, so it's easier to respond flexibly to events. Finally, leaders who feel good about themselves find it easier to take responsibility and insulate themselves from others' feelings when having to make unpopular choices because their self-image doesn't depend on their followers' opinions.

The third quality is the drive to grow, to become more and renew yourself by penetrating beyond superficial analysis to see and understand what is holding you back within your psyche. It ensures that while others might view someone with presence as superior and having all the answers, the person won't see himself that way. He will recognise his strengths, but won't believe there isn't more to learn. In other words, he will have a sense of perspective, a healthy humility. You could see this quality as an internal dynamo that ensures we don't stand still, giving us the spur to develop and express the other six qualities of presence. At the beginning, it shows as the push for personal growth, to break free of personal limitations. Further on, as your self-esteem and sense of connection with others grows, it can become an urge to lead a fulfilling life, often showing in the leader as a wish to serve – which leads on to the fourth quality.

The fourth quality, a balance of purpose and concern for people – showing as a powerful drive to make things happen in service to others while respecting their free will – is important for three reasons:

- If the leader is too biased towards the mission, he can behave insensitively, which may increase resistance and hinder his ability to get things done. At the extreme end, this becomes fanaticism or an "ends justify the means" attitude. On the other hand, too much bias towards people's feelings and the leader may dodge unpopular decisions or avoid being honest with people who underperform.

- It is the natural antidote to another hazard of leadership – the risk of an otherwise capable leader pursuing harmful or destructive ends. Or to put it more dramatically, it's the inner safeguard against leadership for evil ends. So because this characteristic of presence has a moral value, it is priceless to the organisation and, indeed, to society.

- It underlines a key difference between presence and charisma, for leadership presence is not about charming, impressing or winning power over others, it's about serving a greater cause to the benefit of all.

This balance is hard to get right and it's especially tough for an action-orientated leader. On the one hand, it is about wanting to serve, to make a difference, to make things happen. But on the other hand, it respects others' free will, their right to make their own choices, so it's not about imposing your will by force.

How does a leader steer a path through what seems an unsolvable paradox and attain balance? The answer comes from Gautama Buddha's teachings on non-attachment. The key is to be emotionally unattached to the result of your actions, to not make your happiness, satisfaction or self-image depend on your results or how people respond to you, recognising that while you are responsible for your choices, you are not responsible for others' choices. Note that this is not the same as indifference! The effective leader does care what happens and how others respond and will do his utmost to keep his colleagues on track towards their shared goal. But he doesn't let that preference become attachment. He does his best knowing he has a responsibility *to* others, but that he does not have responsibility *for* them. In this way he avoids the trap of forcing others to do what he wants "for their own good," while retaining a sense of mission.

The fifth quality is intuition, which many people confuse with instinct or their ability to read another person's body language. But intuition is neither of these. Instinct is something we share with animals. It doesn't need learning, it's a pre-programmed danger or survival reaction to outside stimuli telling us something is wrong – often through body sensations (as in "gut instinct") that prompt us to act. So it shares the suddenness of an intuitive thought, but it doesn't have the creative, breakthrough or forward-looking quality of intuition. And our ability to read the facial and body gestures of others and interpret their voice tones is neither instinct nor intuition; it is a social skill.

So what is intuition? It's the ability to connect to truth, grasp a new insight or envisage a new future without conscious step-by-step intellectual reasoning. It's the capacity to see what was always possible, but hidden by old prejudices and fixed mindsets. It's almost as if we mentally seize something whole that was always there, but just out of reach until the moment we engaged our intuition.

Take the example of Albert Einstein. He didn't invent relativity, he discovered it. In other words, he tapped into a truth that was already there. How did he do it? In the same way many scientists, visionaries and innovators do. He educated himself on what we already knew about the subject and concentrated – you could say meditated – on it repeatedly until an idea or solution emerged. Thus, intuition is a process where a person connects through steady attention to what we might call the invisible storehouse of abstract universal knowledge and creative potential, just as Einstein did when he worked on the theory of special relativity. And just as many visionaries and innovators have done before and since; like perhaps Tim Berners-Lee, who dreamt of a "universal, shared information space" and proposed the idea of the World Wide Web.

Thus, intuition is the source of creative insight, of the ability to tap into basic truths and cut through confusing problems to see the issues that matter and envisage a new way forward. In leaders, it often expresses itself as foresight, vision and the ability to choose wisely between alternative directions

The sixth quality is being present to the moment, to what is happening in the here-and-now. But being in the now is something most of us find hard because we can get trapped in our feelings about the past or the future. And yet consider this: neither the future nor the past is real – the only time that's real is the now.

You see, the past has gone. It's a memory and while it may have powerful emotional echoes for you that influence your feelings and behaviour today, you are experiencing them in the now. The only reason the past has power over you is because you're allowing the meaning and significance you put on previous events to exist in the now and limit you. This is living in the past. Equally, the future isn't real either – it's just a mental creation, a new but imagined now. And of course, the future never comes because when you get there... it is the now. And when you think about the future, when are you doing it? In the now. But if you allow your anticipation of what may or may not happen to frustrate you and control your self-image and mental state in the present, you are living in the future. I know from working with clients that living in the future is an issue for many leaders.

Being in the now demands the ability to focus your attention on something – be it a task, a problem or another person – and not let your mind wander, but without becoming fixated on the object of your attention or losing your self-awareness. For many, this takes practice, but with it comes an extraordinary freedom from the patterns and ties of your past – or instead the tension and anxiety you may feel in what you experience as a frustrating gap between the present and the future. Being in the now lets you live in the moment and act without constantly feeling, "If only I can achieve this or that, then I'll be happy, then I can relax, then I'll feel good about myself, but not before." It also lets you respond to a current challenge afresh, without unthinkingly projecting past feelings on to the present experience or the person before you and blindly repeating old, unhelpful behaviours from the past.

This is not to say the past is unimportant or that you should ignore or even deny it. Nor does it mean that you, as a leader, shouldn't envisage or plan for a future. What it does mean is that all you ever have is the now.

So you don't discount the past or the future, but neither do you let past or future-related beliefs and their emotional effects determine or limit your mental state – and thus your effectiveness as a leader. The future never arrives, so if you're always striving to be something you're not now or achieve or have something in the future, thinking *"Then* I'll feel at peace, then I'll be happy," you will never succeed. You will be like a hamster on a wheel, constantly replacing this goal with the next, chasing, forever anxious, never at peace, never realising that all you ever have is the now. And the past doesn't have to hold you in its grip. But you can only change the influence the past has over you by changing the way you look at it and letting go of old limiting beliefs – and you can only do that in the now. Thus, the sixth quality demands that we resolve our limiting past and future-related beliefs. Then we can let go of thoughts of the past and the future whenever they become unhelpful and perform to our highest level in the now.

You may feel this sixth quality seems abstract and philosophical. But it's not. It is instead a matter of facing reality. A reality that many people are not aware of, but a reality nonetheless. A reality that sports champions know well and one every leader would do well to accept.

The seventh quality, you could say, is a result of the first six, yet it also supports them. Inner peace makes it easier to exercise personal power and tap into your intuition, whatever is happening around and to you. And a sense of fulfilment, joy and flow provides the emotional fuel to help the leader both achieve his purpose and continue growing beyond his present level.

The golden thread running through all seven qualities is *wholeness.* Wholeness is being the real you – being true to yourself – fully alive, free from inner fears and conflicts, expressing yourself powerfully, fearlessly, creatively, lovingly and wisely. And in its highest form, it can inspire others to sense and release their potential.

Although these are the seven qualities of presence, I'm not suggesting everyone with presence has them – or that every leader must have them all. But I do suggest they are the seven qualities shared by everyone with *pure* presence. I say pure presence because presence isn't binary – it's not a case of, "You either have it or you don't." There are degrees of presence depending on one's inner wholeness. Few of us are so whole and well balanced that we radiate presence in its purest form, so not every leader with presence has all seven qualities. This explains why there are leaders with genuine presence who are still wrestling with residual psychological challenges. They have some connection with their inner psychospiritual core, but they haven't yet achieved full wholeness.

Winston Churchill springs to mind as an example. He exuded presence and could inspire a nation, but he suffered from depression, which he called "the black dog," and according to historians, he could be haughty and sarcastic around others.[18] Abraham Lincoln also endured depression through most of his life, but he too had presence.[19] Thus, it seems neither man experienced inner peace or joy and perhaps Churchill had a need to feel superior, suggesting a hidden self-esteem issue. Yet both displayed personal power, foresight and a strong sense of purpose balanced by a drive to serve a greater, worthwhile cause. The point to note is that even this diluted form of presence has a depth to it that no amount of charisma can fake.

You may be wondering: has anyone researched the qualities of presence and, if so, does their work support the idea of the seven qualities?

The answer to the first part of the question is, not exactly. However, Abraham Maslow, one of the prime movers in shifting psychology away from a preoccupation with what's wrong with people towards their potential and how to release it, did study what he called "peak experiences" in the 1950s. Peak experiences are sudden feelings of intense happiness, satisfaction and well-being and they're relevant here because they are temporary experiences of presence. If you're interested, read endnote 20, as it lists the features of peak experiences that he found in his research, published in the book, Toward a Psychology of Being. You will notice a correlation between his sixteen attributes and the seven qualities.[20]

Everyone's Potential for Presence

All of us have the potential to exude presence – if we but knew it. To be clear, I'm not saying everyone has the same potential for *leadership* presence nor, as I said earlier, that everyone's signature presence is the same. But I am saying that presence is within us all and that everyone can – with steady effort – release and express their unique presence enough to help them in a leadership role.

How do we contact and express our unique presence? By practising self-mastery and growing our sense of connection to others – the third and second parts of personal leadership, which we'll look at in chapters 7, 8 and 9.

The Key Points...

- Others will experience your leadership presence when you have a strong sense of mission and are in the flow, being the natural you, unhindered by fear, paying full attention to people and issues.

- You will experience your own presence when you are living and working in the now, feeling focused, able to respond flexibly to events, making things happen easily, skilfully and enjoyably.

- Presence doesn't show as any one set of behaviours as each person's presence is unique.

- The root of presence is wholeness – in other words, freedom from inner psychological divisions.

- Presence and charisma are not the same.

- Leaders with presence may be charismatic in style, but not always. However, others will always notice something about them that inspires their trust. Charismatic leaders don't always have presence. A charismatic leader can imitate presence for a while, but there is a hollowness to charisma that you'll often see when he is under pressure.

- A person can display charisma by projecting an impressive image through acting and presentation. We can magnify his charisma if we confer a high social status on him, giving him an image of superiority, specialness or authority over us.

- There are seven qualities of pure presence: (1) Personal power; (2) High, real self-esteem; (3) The drive to be more, to grow; (4) Balance; (5) Intuition; (6) Being in the now; (7) Inner peace of mind and a sense of fulfilment. The thread running through all of them is wholeness.

- A leader doesn't have to display all seven qualities to be effective – he can consider himself a work in progress.

- Everyone has the potential to exude presence although not everyone has the same potential for leadership presence. Nevertheless, everyone has the potential to radiate more leadership presence than they do currently.

- We contact and express our unique presence by practising self-mastery and growing our sense of connection to others.

◇◇◇◇◇◇◇◇◇

6

◇◇◇◇◇◇◇◇◇

Working on Element 1 – Technical Knowledge & Skills

We'll start with technical knowledge, as it will be a relatively brief section. That's because what you need to know as a leader depends largely, but not entirely, on your particular field of work. After that, we'll look at behavioural skills, which are less domain-specific.

Technical Knowledge

There's no way around it – it will be hard for you as a leader to gain others' respect if you don't know your job. To make things happen, you need technical knowhow in your field – be that business, the military, healthcare, government, education or charities – and, of course, in your own specialisation within that if you are a head of department.

Table 7: A Corporate CEO's Technical Knowledge

Functional knowledge: How the main departments run and their key tools, principles and techniques, for example: accounting methods and rules, market segmentation, "lean" manufacturing.

General knowledge: Customer insight (knowing what they want and what they think of your firm) plus a grasp of industry regulations, business planning, budgeting, project planning and negotiating technique.

Strategic knowledge: The principles of strategic thinking and organisational change, that is, how to:

- Understand and anticipate the strategic pressures on your industry.[21]
- Look at the firm's current business model and, working with others, see ways to improve or radically change it. This includes, but isn't limited to, creating new customer benefit.[22]
- Challenge the status quo, tee up the organisation for change and see it through.[23]

But leadership roles broaden as they become more senior, so your technical knowledge must widen as your career develops. It has to become less specialised and more general. The field you are in influences what you need to know as a leader, but to give you an idea what I mean by "general," table 7 shows examples of what a corporate CEO would probably be familiar with.

Beyond domain-specific knowledge, there are three areas I believe leaders should always study, regardless of their particular field or level:

- *Individual psychology and motivation.* How can you master the art of private leadership without being able to understand and motivate individuals? You cannot. So it makes sense for leaders to learn about and reflect on individual psychology and motivation. At present, what's known as the Behaviourist school dominates management thinking on motivation, with its emphasis on the "carrot and stick" approach and financial reward and public recognition to encourage high performance. Now I'm not saying that behavioural theory is wrong. But I am saying it's not the whole story on human motivation and you may struggle to understand some of your colleagues if you limit yourself to the behaviourist model. In chapter 8, I will offer a model of the psyche, but you could also read Toward a Psychology of Being by Abraham Maslow to widen your understanding.[24]

- *Group psychology.* This is an area that few leaders study seriously, in my experience. Yet a working knowledge of group psychology is essential if a leader is to be effective at public leadership. Our understanding of group psychology has improved in the last sixty years, but there is still more to learn – especially about teams. Nonetheless, business leaders can gain from studying "group dynamics" – that is, what we know about groups' behavioural patterns and how being in a group affects an individual's thoughts, feelings and behaviour. Some of what's written on this subject is academic in style and can be heavy going. But one book I would recommend is Working More Creatively with Groups by Jarlath Benson, as it gives you a readable outline of group psychology and offers practical advice.[25]

- *Time management.* How a leader uses his time is crucial because there is never enough of it to do everything one needs to do – and a leader who doesn't use his time well won't lead well. You can find books and courses on the subject, but below are some thoughts of my own.

Time management starts with being clear on the purpose of your role. The question to ask is, "Why does my role exist – what is its unique purpose?" Note that this is different to the question: "What do I have to do in my role?" The second question comes after the first. But I've noticed that some people tackle it before understanding why their role exists and they get lost in a description of tasks and activities. They've missed the point – that's what you do, but why do you do it? And in missing the point, they risk being a busy fool.

Once you know why your role exists, the next question is, "What is my purpose this year… what must I accomplish or make happen this year?" This forces the leader to clarify his goals, his priorities, for the coming period and sketch out what action he must to take – and when. (Note: I'll say more about goal-setting when we look at private leadership skills.)

The final question is, "What am I going to do first?" Many people use a To Do list to remind them what they have to do. And that can be a good way to reduce stress from the fear you'll forget to do something. But as the To Do list lengthens, it can trigger another stressful feeling of having too much to do; a sense that everything seems equally important and that you can't see where to start. This is the "rabbit in the headlights" moment and I have seen it happen with capable, experienced leaders.

How does a leader in a bind like this break out and figure out what to do first? By asking himself:

- Do I need to do this personally or would I do better to delegate it?
- If it is down to me, how important and how urgent is it?

The first question should remove tasks you can and should give to others. The second lets you prioritise the remaining tasks by dividing your workload into four quadrants, based on urgency and importance, as you'll see in figure 3.

Figure 3
Time Management Quadrants

I Urgent & Important	II Less Urgent but Important
III Urgent but Less Important	IV Neither Urgent Nor Important

The four-quadrant approach is a tried and tested technique, but even experienced business leaders overlook it. Not only does it help you separate the wheat from the chaff, it lets you keep an eye on quadrant II (Less Urgent but Important), which is where most of your strategic, goal-driven tasks sit. This helps because these tasks are easy to overlook or postpone as they don't always come with a deadline. They are often the tasks that, if missed, become the leader's errors of omission and these, in the long run, can hit a firm harder than the more obvious errors of commission. The benefit of the quadrants model is that it highlights these tasks, prompting you to set aside time for them each week. Stephen Covey, in his book, The Seven Habits of Highly Effective People, argued that if people spent more time on quadrant II work, their strategic effectiveness would rise.[26] I think he's right – effective leaders make time for quadrant II tasks.

However – and this is a big however – in my work with clients I've found this technique doesn't help if the leader hasn't first set his personal goals down in writing. For if he doesn't have clear goals for himself – in other words, if he hasn't clarified his personal contribution to the future he and his colleagues want to create – it becomes harder for him to judge what's "important." The result? It will seem no task is more important than another. When this happens, task urgency drives the priorities and the leader is like a yacht without a navigator, drifting on the ocean, directed only by the prevailing wind of the moment. At that point, a leader is no longer leading. Can you see why time management is central to effective leadership?

One final point on technical knowhow: being technically knowledgeable today doesn't guarantee your ability to meet the next decade's challenges. So, to stay abreast of changing methods, tools and issues, leaders have to accept responsibility for updating themselves. This demands humility, self-awareness and insight. Humility, because you'll have to accept that sometimes you will need to learn something new. Self-awareness, because you'll need to notice when current and emerging challenges are exposing your technical weaknesses. Insight, because leaders don't need to be experts at everything, so you'll have to discriminate between "nice to know" and "must know" subjects in deciding which to work on.

Public Leadership Skills

There is value in simply knowing what the key public leadership behaviours are because once you're aware of them, you're more likely to apply them. However, if you lack key skills, awareness won't be enough. So the aim in this section is twofold. First, it is to help you look underneath the public leadership behaviour headlines and see the supporting skills below. Second, it is to encourage you to ask yourself, "What am I like on each skill and, given the strengths and weaknesses of my colleagues, which do I need to work on?"

Earlier, I described the four dimensions of leadership. The first is about setting a motivating group purpose. The second is about getting results through practical management of the task at both group and individual levels. The third focuses on building and preserving a sense of togetherness, a group spirit. And the fourth is to do with choosing, motivating and developing individuals. Public leadership addresses dimensions one, two and three – leaving attention to individual task performance and motivation to private leadership. Thus, public leadership is what leaders do when they're interacting with more than

Table 8: Key Public Leadership Behaviours

Group Purpose & Task	Group Building & Maintenance
Setting the purpose, staying focused • *Briefing* – explaining goals or strategies passed down from higher up the organisation • *Challenging* – questioning the "more of the same" attitude, encouraging a shared desire for change • *Navigating* – setting or agreeing a clear, common, motivating purpose or vision with supporting goals • *Prioritising* – focusing on priorities (not overloading the agenda as this impedes the task and frustrates others) **Organising, giving power to others** • *Assigning* – giving tasks and power to group members • *Organising* – planning, finding and granting resources **Ideation, problem-solving, decision-making** • *Co-ordinating* – suggesting how to integrate ideas • *Deciding* – listening, agreeing, concluding • *Elaborating & clarifying* – building on others' ideas, analysing outcomes, removing or lessening confusion • *Evaluating* – assessing ideas, choices and proposals • *Information giving* – providing data, sharing experiences • *Information seeking* – questioning accuracy of opinions, making the group aware of data needs, seeking facts • *Initiating* – proposing a vision, ideas, goals and solutions • *Opinion giving* – stating beliefs, views and feelings • *Opinion seeking* – finding out others' opinions or feelings • *Summarising* – summing up issues and views **Executing** • *Educating* – building competencies across the board • *Energising* – stimulating others to decisions and action • *Doing* – carrying out decisions or plans • *Measuring* – watching and assessing performance • *Following up* – ensuring people have taken the actions • *Tolerating* – accepting occasional failures [27]	**Out in front** • *Gathering* – bringing people together to discuss, decide and do creative work collectively • *Honouring* – celebrating the group's progress and marking individuals' accomplishments publicly • *Representing* – the group to the outside world (and, if needed, protecting individual members) • *Setting an example* – creating a collaborative atmosphere and showing commitment to the group's purpose and standards through your own enthusiasm and behaviour • *Updating* – explaining aims, plans, progress and issues to keep people informed, so they feel involved in something that is worthwhile, bigger than them, and is succeeding **In among the group** • *Compromising* – offering to change position if you were wrong, made a mistake, or there was something you overlooked, or perhaps didn't know • *Encouraging* – praising, affirming and supporting the contributions of others (even-handedly – no favourites) • *Following* – supporting and accepting others' good ideas • *Gatekeeping* – drawing out silent members, ensuring listening and balanced discussion, intervening with members who are trying to dominate • *Harmonising* – resolving differences and reducing tension through mediation or humour • *Observing* – listening, watching and commenting on group members' (and own) feelings, behaviours and functioning • *Standard setting* – making all aware of what is happening in the group, proposing behaviour standards, expressing concerns, pointing out the need for behaviour change

one person, for example, when they are in a meeting, talking to a large group or engaging the whole organisation.

To remind you, there are 34 key public leadership behaviours, as you will see listed again in table 8.

Few people are naturally good at or comfortable with all thirty-four, so the leader will probably have to learn new skills to widen his repertoire. If he doesn't, he may restrict himself to a narrow range of behaviours, limiting his ability to connect with and influence others.

However, there is a balancing act here because the leader doesn't have to do everything. To remind you, the leader's role is to ensure there is leadership – which doesn't mean he has to supply all the leadership personally. But it does mean he must ensure the right public leadership behaviours happen when they need to happen. Thus, he can delegate responsibility for some of the 34 behaviours if he surrounds himself with capable colleagues with whom he can share leadership.

Does this mean he may not have to extend his skills? The answer is, yes, in theory. But in practice, most leaders find their role demands above-average behavioural flexibility even with a good team around them. Why? Either because their colleagues lack certain skills or because they may be reluctant, for personal reasons, to contribute the behaviour the group needs. This forces the leader to widen his behavioural range and learn new skills.

So the question is, what are the main skills underlying the public leadership behaviours and what's the best way to learn them? In my view, four sets of skills support public leadership: Problem solving and planning; Decision-making; Interpersonal; and Group process. Figure 4 shows how they fit the two classes of public behaviours.

The first set of skills, ***problem solving and planning***, supports the Purpose & Task behaviours and is more subtle than it seems. You see, this is not about gaining the mental skills to solve a problem on your own – it's about learning how to lead and take part in *group* problem solving and planning. Breaking it down, there are seven key skills, as you will see in table 9.

Knowing these underlying skills makes it easier to see where you need to strengthen your abilities. It should also help you consider whether reading, private reflection, training, coaching, a change of role, or all five, might best quicken your personal learning.

Figure 4
Four Skill Sets Supporting Public Leadership Behaviours

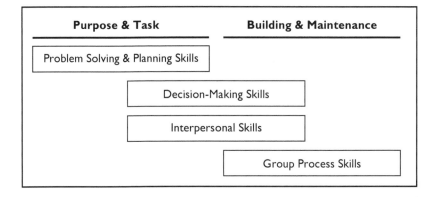

However, whatever steps you take to advance your skills by yourself, you'll still need to learn by experience, in action, by honing these skills alongside your colleagues in real-life meetings.

Table 9: Problem-Solving & Planning Skills

1. Agreeing a common definition of the problem and its negative effects – which leaders often neglect as a step. If the group doesn't have a shared understanding of the problem or share the view there is a problem, it will find it hard to agree on a solution and, of course, on the need for any change.

2. Defining and agreeing an outcome that everyone wants and supports.

3. Uncovering the facts and root causes plus the positive and negative forces pulling for and against change.

4. Surfacing and questioning hidden – often false or out-of-date – assumptions and conventional wisdoms. (Try reading this book's appendix on the Ladder of Inference model to help you develop this skill.)

5. Thinking creatively and imagining different options together.

6. Assessing the pros and cons of each option tactfully and dispassionately.

7. Agreeing a practical action plan with realistic timescales and resources having considered what (a) could go wrong or get in the way and (b) is genuinely actionable amid other day-to-day pressures.

The reality is that some people are better at certain parts of problem solving and planning than others because of natural character strengths. So you as a leader shouldn't put undue pressure on yourself by expecting to be the best in your group on every skill. Instead, you'd do better to remember that leadership involves making the best use of the people around you. The key to doing so is studying the skills, improving your own, seeing where you are still not strong, noticing where others are better and learning how to share leadership by drawing on their talents. The best way to do this quickly is through training or coaching in live problem solving and planning in a group.

Table 10: Decision-Making Skills

1. Ensuring the group hears the views of less vocal members.

2. Sensing information gaps and making sure the group gathers the necessary data in the time available.

3. Exposing and testing unspoken assumptions (a skill shared with problem-solving).

4. Drawing out different opinions and unspoken disagreement and, where necessary, allowing conflict to get the truth out to (a) remove the corrosive effect of hidden, opposing motives and b) reduce the chance of poor buy-in and implementation.

5. Building on or combining others' ideas.

6. Ensuring during contentious issues that everyone listens hard to what each other is saying and, where necessary, that arguing colleagues can explain the other person's point to their satisfaction.

7. Uncovering group members' underlying needs when polarised positions threaten a stalemate.

8. Mediating between members whose disagreement oversteps the line and becomes personal.

9. Reaching a strong enough accord to enable action follow-through.

10. Assessing quickly which of the many decision-making options and techniques to use in the circumstances.

The second set of skills, *decision-making*, spans both sides of public leadership. And when I say "decision-making skills," I'm not talking about your personal ability to be decisive or decide matters on your own. I'm talking about your ability to guide a group to a decision you will all support and carry out wholeheartedly. So we are talking about group decision-making skills. They include the ten skills you see in table 10.

What's the best way to learn them? Well you can educate yourself by reading and seeking training, for example, in handling conflict or chairing meetings. But even after training you're unlikely to be good at everything, which is why the wise leader draws on his colleagues' skills. And that takes us to the key point: as with problem solving and planning, group decision-making skills need live practice in a group setting.

In my experience, few leaders realise that group decision-making demands shared skills. Thus, they don't consider the need to learn how to take decisions together, but the need is there nonetheless. The leader has the choice of bringing someone in to help the team learn together or act as the coach himself. The question for you is: which makes the most sense given your knowledge, talents and personality?

Now I am not suggesting every decision you face must be taken by the group as a whole. Some decisions don't lend themselves to that, which is why the tenth skill is on the list. It involves knowing your seven decision-making options and judging which to use in the circumstances. This is where Tannenbaum & Schmidt's Leadership Behaviour Continuum model helps (figure 5). It explains the seven approaches to decision-making, ranging from leader-based to shared.[28]

Figure 5
Leadership Behaviour Continuum

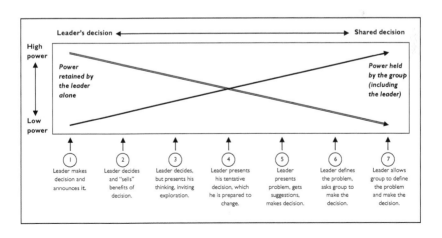

Their model reminds the leader how many decision-making options he has. But it also explains why sometimes it's not right to share decision-making and why, on other occasions, it is. The thinking behind it is that you can choose the best method by balancing three pressures:

- *Decision and time pressures:* The complexity of the problem; the decision's importance; the time pressure.

- *Leader's psychological pressures:* Your confidence in your colleagues' knowledge and experience; how important the decision is to you personally.

- *Group pressures:* Your colleagues' wish to take part in the decision; their willingness to take responsibility for the results; their ability to decide together; their readiness and ability to accept and follow orders.

This explains why although shared leadership is powerful – and indeed the norm in high performance teams – it's not always the best approach. In a crisis, where there's little time, and especially when human lives are on the line, it's sensible for the leader to decide and for his colleagues to carry out the decision without debate. Which explains why surgical, military and fire rescue teams behave at level 1 on the continuum.

My point is that wise leaders flex their approach to decision-making. They know the seven decision-making options. They understand the risks of sticking to only one method – for example, indulging in time-consuming discussions when the business needs a rapid decision, or on the other hand, taking solo decisions when colleagues are desperate to have their say. And they have learnt to quickly assess the three pressures and judge the best way forward in the circumstances. They also know the different techniques of group decision-making if they want to apply levels 6 or 7. You see, there is more than one technique – in fact, there are six. Endnote 29 has more detail on this.[29]

Taking good decisions is not, of course, just about skills and methods. It's also about the readiness to make difficult, perhaps unpopular choices and being robust enough to stand by the aftermath. So the leader has to have strength of character. But his colleagues are not off the hook, for leadership isn't about one person. They too must accept the reactions to an unpopular decision and play their leadership role by standing shoulder to shoulder. The leader's unique part in promoting this spirit is to ensure the group feels that the way they reach decisions is robust, fair and wise. This strengthens the group's sense of unity, which is why the decision-making skills are so valuable to team building and maintenance.

The quality of problem solving, planning and decision-making in groups will also depend on the leader's (and his colleagues') *interpersonal skills*. Good interpersonal skills oil the machinery of a team by contributing to both sides of public leadership. They promote good decisions and cultivate trust, respect and interdependence. You can see the key skills in table 11.

Table 11: Interpersonal Skills

1. Knowing your intent and desired outcome (and why it matters) at the start and, ideally, at each moment.

2. Creating a gap between an outer event and your reaction – amid the dialogue – allowing you to choose your response instead of blindly reacting.

3. Being aware of your own feelings and body sensations and what they may be telling you.

4. Concentrated "clean" listening to the other person's words and the intent and feelings behind them.*

5. Putting yourself in the other person's shoes and knowing what they are feeling (empathy).

6. Asking open questions that don't trigger unintended defensive reactions.

7. Putting forward a persuasive case that appeals intellectually and emotionally (includes presentation skills).

8. Giving effective feedback – one of the most difficult skills of all and crucial if colleagues are to engage honestly and effectively without avoiding helpful conflict of opinion.

9. Responding openly and non-defensively to others' opinions and feedback to you, accepting that the other person's feelings and way of looking at a situation may not be the same as yours.

10. Identifying and testing assumptions about – and psychological projections on to – the other person.**

11. Expressing your true thoughts, opinions and emotions, allowing others to see your limitations and encouraging colleagues to do the same to (a) ensure openness and trust and (b) draw out hidden, opposing motives.

* Concentrated "clean" listening to the other person's words and the intent and feelings behind them means: (1) Centring your attention on the speaker and only the speaker. (2) Not letting your inner dialogue distract you, e.g. figuring out what you are going to say next or wondering what you'd like for lunch. (3) Taking in the person's body language and tone of voice (the way they are saying what they are saying) to receive the underlying emotional "call" in the message. (4) Not filtering the other's message by superimposing your beliefs, values or prejudgements.

** Projection is a psychological defence against self-esteem issues. I explain more about it in endnote 30.[30]

The eleven skills contribute to what's called "emotional intelligence." Daniel Goleman summed this up as "the capacity for recognising our own feelings and those of others, for motivating ourselves, and for managing emotions well in ourselves and in our relationships" and described its five dimensions. If you read his book, Working With Emotional Intelligence, you will find the eleven skills align with all five dimensions: Self-awareness, Self-regulation, Empathy, Social skills and Motivation.[31]

How might you learn the skills? You have several choices. You could:

- Consider training in basic coaching techniques or attend courses on people skills.

- Enrol in a presentation skills course.

- Try experiential training in "sensitivity," "encounter" or "right relations" groups, which I've described in more detail in endnote 32. This will speed up your learning, but I would recommend it only if you find a skilled, experienced facilitator. I make this point because group sensitivity training does help a leader become more effective in leading and interacting in groups, but badly handled, it can lead to emotional wounding. My experience of this way of learning is that it's safe with teachers who have put in years of psychological work on themselves and know what it's like to undergo such training. They have experienced its emotional power and offer secure boundaries, ensuring participants learn without coming to harm. I contrast them with consultants who learn psychology academically, but don't work on their mindsets, feelings and way of interacting with others. Given this "but," I recognise not all leaders will accept training of this kind, but it is a valuable option nonetheless.[32]

- Engage an experienced team coach to help you and your colleagues practise these skills while working on live issues.

- Arrange one-to-one confidential coaching for you (and perhaps your colleagues).

- Read a book on interpersonal skills.[33]

The trouble with the last alternative is that, by definition, interpersonal skills involve two or more people, meaning you will have to try what you've learned in live meetings. Once again, like the previous skills, you need to *practise* interpersonal skills – and for the leader wanting to master public leadership behaviours, that means practising in a group.

It's hard to apply these skills consistently without positive, healthy self-esteem – that is, while being comfortable in your own skin. So leaders with self-esteem issues may wish to consider confidential coaching, as although training is good for learning skills, it won't help when the limiting beliefs (which lie at the root of their feelings about themselves) continue to block progress.

Unlike the skills we've just been discussing, **group process skills** focus not on the content – the issues – the members are working on, but rather, on *how* they are working on them and the atmosphere they create together. So these skills are about helping the group build and uphold their sense of togetherness – the "building and maintenance" side of public leadership.

What the atmosphere feels like to those in the group will show itself in many ways. For example:

- In people's body language.

- In whether there are awkward silences or issues that people avoid repeatedly.

- The degree of trust in the room.

- The extent to which each member has a clear sense of role in the group and feels valued.

- The extent to which each participant feels able to be natural.

- How truthful people are in expressing their opinions, recommendations and feelings.

- How each person feels about the power they have in the group.

- What people feel about the quality of their group decisions and how they make them.

Although this is subtle stuff, anyone who has worked in a group knows the atmosphere has a huge influence on their work together – and their effectiveness. Which is why group process skills are so important to a leader. Of course, how skilful the group are at solving problems, taking decisions and planning together makes a difference to the atmosphere, but there are three extra skills the leader would be wise to learn and practise. You will see them in table 12:

Table 12: Group Process Skills

1. The first – in parallel with following the "content," that is, what others are saying and doing – is paying attention to the "process," that is, how it is happening, and considering what may be going on below the surface.*

2. The second is learning to comment – not hold back – on what you (and they) are seeing, without judging.

3. The third is asking questions – for instance, when the group is going round in circles – to help them examine how you and they are working together, without making anyone a scapegoat.

* This means, for example, noticing others' behaviour; what is said and unsaid; people's degree of comfort with their roles; noting people's interpersonal sensitivity (or lack of it); sensing the degree of trust and openness in the room and what individuals may be feeling when they are together.

How do you learn the three process skills? You could watch a skilled leader at work and then try them yourself with your group. Or you could engage a coach to work with you and your team to practise these skills together, so everyone shares the responsibility of process improvement. This makes sense when you remember that although the leader's unique responsibility is to make sure there *is* leadership, he or she doesn't have to provide all the leadership behaviours personally.

Before we move on, let's be clear that achieving a positive atmosphere isn't just about process skills. There can be other influences on the atmosphere, for example:

- *Shared purpose:* The presence or absence of a clear, shared, motivating purpose will also affect the atmosphere. A positive atmosphere is more likely when members of a group pursue a clear, achievable aim they all care about. But the reverse is true – doubts about the clarity, doability or value of the group's purpose will undermine the group's togetherness and energy. Not surprisingly, the act of agreeing a clear, motivating purpose is among the public leadership behaviours, although it doesn't rely on a single skill.

- *The leader's example:* The example you, as the leader, set through your own attitudes and behaviour also makes a difference. This is why you'll see "Setting an example" under the list of group building and maintenance behaviours. Every leader, whether they like it or not, is an exemplar. The only question is, will the leader choose to behave in a way that supports or undermines the group's ethos? This is a matter of choice, of will, not skill.

- *The leader's inner beliefs:* Limiting beliefs can influence how effectively the leader intercepts group process problems. In fact, they can decide whether he intervenes at all. You see, for some leaders it takes courage to comment on and question the group's way of working because due to their limiting beliefs they may fear people's reaction. For example, if the group isn't working well, they may feel this reflects their leadership ability – or their fitness to be a leader – and be reluctant to open a discussion in case they receive a deluge of criticism. The reluctance is a sign of a fragile self-image built on limiting beliefs and this is what drives their fear of a negative reaction. Which is why the opposite – a robust, healthy self-image – is an asset for any leader and why working on it through self-mastery is so important.

Let's summarise this section on public leadership skills.

Few people step into their first leadership role ready to connect with and influence everyone they meet as even the most talented can find it hard to lead people with different values and attitudes. This is why most leaders have to learn new behavioural skills, especially if they want to reach a senior level.

Now you could decide to gain these skills through trial and error as you face the day-to-day tests every leader experiences. And that might indeed work for you, but it could be a slow process.

If, instead, you choose to take charge of your education and speed up your growth, the question before you is, "Which skills do I need to learn or strengthen?" The answer must, of course, come from you. Using self-awareness – or others' feedback – it's for you to see your weaknesses, gauge whether they hold back the group and decide what you're going to work on first. I say, "... gauge whether they hold back the group" because someone in your team may be able to cover your weakness. As a next step, you could ask yourself the self-assessment questions towards the end of this chapter.

Private Leadership Skills

To remind you, there are 14 private leadership behaviours, as you see in table 13.

Table 13: Key Private Leadership Behaviours

Individual Purpose & Task	Individual Building & Maintenance
• *Appraising* – giving and receiving honest, effective feedback about the need for behavioural change • *Choosing* – selecting individuals, assigning new or alternative roles, promoting talented people* • *Disciplining* – confronting, reprimanding or removing people who under-perform or under-collaborate • *Goal-setting* – with the individual, for individual performance and career growth* • *Reviewing* – receiving task progress updates, proposals, requests, ideas or solutions and following up individually	• *Assessing & matching* – gauging a person's competence and commitment to know how to flex your one-to-one behaviour and then choosing a suitable approach • *Attracting* – bringing new talented individuals into the group or wider organisation • *Consulting* – conferring privately on sensitive issues that you cannot address in a public forum • *Developing* – agreeing personal growth priorities and actions; helping directly through mentoring or coaching • *Discovering* – learning what motivates each individual, their inner challenges, unspoken thoughts and feelings • *Encouraging* – praising, affirming, building confidence and showing you have noticed individuals' contributions • *Intervening* – noticing and interceding with those who find their role frustrating or are demotivating colleagues • *Recognising* – spotting rising talent • *Understanding* – watching and learning your impact on individuals (how they perceive and respond to you)
* These behaviours do in fact straddle the Purpose/Task and Building/Maintenance divide even though they are classified on this side for convenience.	

There is one key difference between the private leadership and public leadership behaviours: while a leader can delegate certain public leadership behaviours to his colleagues, he can't always do the same with private leadership.

To be clear, he can delegate private leadership if he is running a big organisation – indeed he has to, because he won't have the time to offer private leadership to everyone – and this is why organisations have hierarchies. But he can't give away responsibility for private leadership of his own team, his direct reports. He can, of course, seek advice on some of the behaviours – for example, on Choosing, Disciplining or Understanding – but he cannot hand them over to someone else and say, "Here, you do them." If he does, or if instead he ignores them, he is not leading and performance issues are likely to follow.

Interestingly, I have noticed it doesn't follow that if a leader is good at public leadership, he'll be competent at the private level. I have seen well-known CEOs who were strong publicly, but weak privately. This, I've noticed, is the more common imbalance, but I have met one leader who was excellent at private leadership, but neglected public leadership.

He was superb at agreeing goals and following up with each member of his department, but poor at creating a team atmosphere because he saw leadership as a series of one-to-one relationships. He hadn't realised the power and value of promoting a sense of togetherness and couldn't understand why his people didn't work as a unit when he wasn't around. There was no glue between them. They were the spokes of the wheel and he was the hub. But without the hub, there was no wheel and in his absence, they argued and withheld information from each other and their results were poor.

Returning to the more common problem – the leader who is confident publicly, but not privately – he or she will usually avoid certain behaviours, especially Appraising and Disciplining, hoping that any difficult issues will disappear without having to intervene. Why? Partly a lack of skill and partly fear of the one-to-one intimacy of private leadership. You see, the more demanding private behaviours – notably Appraising and Disciplining – can involve strong emotions and a degree of risk, as one can't be sure of the result. Leaders can worry about this for three reasons:

- They may be afraid the meeting will be painful for them. For example, they may doubt their ability to handle the meeting and fear humiliation or feeling inadequate if they perform the behaviour badly or don't get the result they want. Or they may believe unconsciously there is something about them that others will reject if they open up and are seen as they really are. Or – and this isn't uncommon – they may feel the other person's performance issues are due to their poor leadership and fear the meeting will expose this. Whatever the cause, they believe they dare not speak openly and say something displeasing – even if they're more senior – as the other will reject or criticise them or tell them something they don't want to hear. They fear this will confirm their subconscious negative self-view.

- Because of social or cultural norms, they may believe it's bad manners to criticise another's performance or tell them clearly what will happen if they don't change, in case it hurts the other's feelings or causes them to lose face.

- They may be suspicious of others as a rule. For example, they may assume people will retaliate when criticised – even if it's fair criticism – and be reluctant to get into what they expect will turn into a fight.

Can you see that limiting beliefs are at the root of all three problems? The first stems from self-image issues while the second and third come from limiting worldviews.

The point is that a leader's beliefs and self-esteem have a powerful effect on his private leadership behaviour, either positive or negative. If he feels good about himself, he's more likely to be comfortable with private leadership behaviours. If he doesn't, the opposite is true and you can see that avoiding private behaviours like Appraising and Disciplining is a way of defending oneself against limiting beliefs and the fears they produce.

Few leaders have such robust self-esteem that they don't have limiting beliefs. Thus, most leaders will have to learn the private leadership skills *and* work on their self-mastery to address the beliefs undermining their self-esteem. Otherwise, their skills learning may be useless.

So what are the key private leadership skills? The interpersonal, decision-making and problem-solving skills covered earlier all support the private leadership behaviours, but there are two other essential abilities. They are Assertiveness and Goal-setting (see table 14).

Table 14: Skills for Private Leadership

1. The interpersonal, decision-making, problem solving and planning skills listed earlier under public leadership.

2. Assertiveness: putting your point across firmly and honestly, in a way that communicates fully and successfully what you want and feel, while respecting the rights of the other person.

3. Goal setting: agreeing clear, specific performance goals that connect with a person's values (that is, what motivates them) and strike the right balance between stretch and achievability.

The second item, *assertiveness skill*, is essential to effective private leadership. You need it too in public leadership, but the close-quarters nature of private leadership makes it vital.

It includes the listening and feedback abilities under Interpersonal skills. But it goes beyond listening and feedback. It's being prepared to tell the other person what you feel about a situation, or their behaviour, or their performance. It's also valuing what's important to you, being able to say "no" without being apologetic, being firm when faced with a bully – and doing all this while holding your connection with the other person. If you don't hold the connection, assertiveness can slide into anger, accusation and aggression.

Some leaders are unclear on the difference between assertion and aggression. Essentially, it comes down to your attitude towards the other person. Do you see them as a real person with feelings, hopes and values; who can make mistakes, just like you? Or do you see them as an object that's getting in your way? The first of these two attitudes is what I mean by "holding your connection." Here's a simple rule of thumb that may help. If you deal firmly with another person from an underlying stance of "I'm OK and you're basically OK too," you are being assertive. But if your attitude is "I'm OK and you're not OK," you are being aggressive.

You can find many books and articles on the Internet about assertiveness and training is widely available, so I'll only add that it's much easier to be assertive if you feel good about yourself. Yet again, this underlines how important self-esteem is. It also highlights the importance of self-mastery – for in freeing a person of their most limiting beliefs, self-mastery boosts one's self-image and self-esteem.

I find that *goal-setting skill* is a problem for most leaders. In my work with them, one issue recurs time after time. This is the problem of confusing *end goals* with *performance goals*.

Most business people are familiar with the SMART principles of goal-setting. SMART usually stands for Specific, Measurable, Attainable, Realistic and Time-bounded. Those using the SMART principles assume that, if they set goals meeting the five conditions, the targets will drive the change they want. But this isn't always true.

For example, you may see a goal like, "Increase our share of the so-and-so market from 15% to 20% by December 2010." Now, this would meet all five conditions. It's specific – we have clearly defined the market. It's measurable, as we'll know whether we have achieved the goal or not. It is attainable – or at least possible – as we already have a position in the market. It is realistic if we have momentum in gaining market share or have the means to grow it. And it's time-bounded; it has a clear deadline of December 2010.

Yet would it surprise you to know that – in the eyes of a coach – this is not a performance goal? "Why?" you ask. Here's why. In professional sport, coaches and elite performers know how important it is to set goals over which the athlete has a lot of influence or control. You see, an Olympic-class sprinter might set a goal of winning the 100 metres gold medal at the 2012 Olympic Games in London. This would meet the SMART conditions. But an astute coach would know that although it's a good end goal, it's not a performance goal.

An end goal sets the context – the reason for action, the basic motivation. And the gold medal goal does this superbly.

But here's the problem: the performer cannot control the actions or performance of his competitors. This matters, because it can be unhelpful to set goals comparing oneself to others, because in encouraging comparison, it can distract you from your own performance which, of course, is the only thing you can ever control. Thus, it can induce tension, nervousness or irritation – all of which lower performance.

So a sports coach would help the competitor focus on his own performance by defining goals over which he has a high degree of control. In this example, the elite performer might set phased time goals of 9.7 seconds by the end of 2009, 9.6 seconds by the end of 2010 and 9.5 seconds by the end of 2012. These are performance goals. The idea would be to pitch them so, if he performs to this level, he is likely to arrive at the end goal – the gold medal.

But this line of thinking isn't common yet in business. Repeatedly, I see executives focusing on end goals and that can make it hard to judge whether someone has performed well. Imagine one of your colleagues fails to meet a key goal for the year. How would you know if his performance caused the failure or whether it was down to reasons outside his control?

If a leader fires someone because they fail to reach an end goal, he may lose a valuable colleague. After all, the person may have performed well, but was striving for a goal neither he nor anyone else could reach in the time – and with the resources – available. So his replacement may have the same problem. Finding a substitute takes time and can incur severance and recruitment costs, so sloppy goal-setting can carry heavy penalties. This is why I teach clients the *ASPECT* model of performance goal-setting. It meets the SMART conditions but goes beyond to ensure the goals leaders set are wise, motivating, performance-orientated – and likely to drive better performance.

ASPECT stands for: Achievable – Specific and demonstrable – Positively stated – Environmental – Controlled and owned by you – Truly worthwhile to you. Leaders can use this model to set new goals for their colleagues or themselves.

Here are the key *ASPECT* questions to ask yourself in setting a goal (see table 15).

Table 15: ASPECT Performance Goal-Setting

1. Achievable – *Is it possible and achievable?* In other words:

   - Is it possible for anyone to achieve it – that is, is it possible in an absolute sense?
   - Is it genuinely achievable in the timescale you are talking about, considering your current position, resources and competition? Extra questions you can ask include:
     - What resources will be essential? Note: resources may be external, like new products, contacts, technology and money; or internal, such as skills, qualities, or a positive state of mind.
     - Do you have them already? If not, how will you – or could you – get them?

2. **Specific & demonstrable –** *Is it specific and demonstrable?* This has two sides to it:

   - First, how will you, or anyone else, know you have achieved the goal, or are on track to achieving it?
   - Second, it is important to be as specific as possible.
     - Being specific allows you to define contexts in which you do and don't want the goal. For example, a leader might wish to be more assertive and impose his priorities more often than before. However, he may want this in the work environment only, not the home.
     - Being specific allows you to use your power of imagination to picture what it will be like to achieve the goal. This is useful in more abstract or interpersonal behaviour goals as it helps you mentally rehearse.

3. **Positively stated –** *Is it stated in the positive?*

   - Stating the goal in positive language attracts positive mental and emotional energy – it is more motivating over the long-term to move towards something than away from it.
     - The idea is to engage your whole psyche, from imagining the goal to wanting it and it is easier to engage your imagination if you use positive language.
     - The opposite – stating the goal negatively – is just another way of saying what you don't want. So, for example, "To lose 10 pounds in weight" would not be a positively stated goal.
   - As you can appreciate, it's usually easier to plan a route to a positive outcome than it is to figure out how to not do something.

4. **Environmental –** *How well does it fit with what else matters in your world?* The environment angle ensures you choose your goals wisely. It involves two further questions:

   - Will you (or could you) lose or damage something valuable to you – that you want to protect – on the way to the goal, or once you achieve it? If so, how might you redefine the goal?
   - In aiming for and achieving the goal, will you – or could you – unwittingly acquire any side effects or negatives you don't want and won't accept? If so, how might you redefine the goal?

   An example of a poorly chosen goal would be King Midas's choice to have all he touched turn to gold. An example of an environmental goal would be a Logistics Director setting a target of improving stock turns from 4 to 6 turns per year, while stipulating that in doing so, they mustn't damage on-time delivery performance.

5. **Controlled and owned by you –** *Is it under your control and did you set it?*

   - Or at least, is it largely controllable by you? It needs to be a goal that you have a high degree of influence over.
     - Remember the difference between an end goal (win the gold medal in the 100 metres) and a performance goal (run the 100 metres in 9.7 seconds by the end of 2009).
     - End goals are fine for setting the overall context, but only performance goals meet the ASPECT conditions.
   - Is it a goal you have set? Alternatively, is it one you genuinely agreed to – or did someone impose it on you? Do you really agree with it or are you just pretending?

6. **Truly worthwhile to you –** *Is it really worthwhile to you?* Meaning:

   - Is it stretching enough to be interesting?
   - Do you really care about it? Does it motivate you? Or are you just pretending?
   - What will it bring you? What is important about that? Is that attractive enough to sustain your effort?

In stressing how important performance goals are, I do not mean to dismiss end goals. I realise firms will often link bonus schemes to end goals – for instance, an increase in profit. And I understand that end goals often have to be financial to ensure the bonus is self-funding. So end goals are here to stay and that's not a problem. It only becomes an issue if end goals are the *only* goals. For end goals do not provide a guide to action and measurement of a person's performance. But performance goals do.

So how do we meet a firm's need to set self-funding end goals and keep performance goals? The answer is, have both. There is no reason why end goals cannot provide the context for the performance goals. For example, a firm's board might set two overarching end goals for the year: one for profit and one for cash flow. These would apply to every director. However, each would also agree a set of performance goals, representing their personal action agenda for contributing to the end goals. Thus, they would know the answer to the question, "Why am I here this year – what must I do, what must I accomplish, this year to support the end goals?" and this completes the circle we started in the section on time management earlier in the chapter.

Behavioural Skills, Limiting Beliefs & Self-Mastery
I have commented a few times that limiting beliefs underneath a fragile self-image can and do narrow a leader's behavioural range, which is why many of us have to learn and practise new skills. But I want to repeat two other points about limiting beliefs made in chapter 3:

- First, they can blind your awareness to the need to extend your behaviours and learn new skills in the first place.

- Second, they can continue to restrict your behaviour by blocking your readiness to apply new leadership skills even after you have learned them.

Because my experience is that most leaders hold limiting beliefs, I'm stressing the point that attention to self-mastery alongside skills work is the way forward for leaders wanting to leave them behind. Self-mastery is the subject of chapters 8 and 9.

What To Do Next

How do you use this chapter to best effect? Well, of course, that's up to you, but you may find the following self-assessment tool useful in helping you figure out what to work on first. Do bear in mind that it excludes the domain-specific knowhow covered at the start of the chapter.

Self-Assessment Exercise:
Technical Knowledge & Skills Learning Priorities

Technical Knowledge

1. *How much do you understand about individual psychology and motivation? How did you gain your present level of knowledge? Do you sense you need more understanding? What could you do to learn more – what practical steps could you take? So what will you do?*

2. *What steps have you taken to expand your understanding of group psychology? Do you feel you understand enough on this subject? If not, what could you do to learn more? And what are you going to do?*

3. *On time management, do you have a clear sense of what it is important to achieve each week and month? Is what you focus on truly important or is it merely urgent? Have you set clear goals for yourself? Do these guide your view on what is important? If not, what steps will you take to improve your time management?*

Public Leadership Skills

1. *Rate yourself (or ask a colleague to rate you) on each of the seven key **problem-solving** and **planning skills** (table 9) on a five-point scale of:*
   - *A. Poor, but colleagues of mine cover my weakness on this one, so it's not a learning priority for me*
   - *B. Poor and I need to get better*
   - *C. Okay*
   - *D. Okay, but I want to be better*
   - *E. Good*

Where you scored B or D, what could you do about it? Which of the learning options suggested on page 86 do you prefer? Can you think of anything else you could do? So what will you do?

2. *Now rate yourself (or again, ask a colleague to rate you) on each of the ten key* **decision-making skills** *in table 10 using the same five-point scale. Looking at your B and D scores, what are you going to do about them?*

3. *Do the same for each of the eleven* **interpersonal skills** *(table 11). Which of the six learning options suggested on page 90 would work best for you on the B and D scores? So what is your next step?*

4. *Finally, repeat the exercise using the same five-point scale against the three* **group process skills** *(table 12). What will you do about any B or D skills?*

Private Leadership Skills

Rate yourself (or ask someone else to rate you) against the two extra private leadership skills of **assertiveness** *and* **goal-setting** *(table 14) using this four-point scale:*

- *A. Poor*
- *B. Okay*
- *C. Okay, but I want to be better*
- *D. Good*

Where you scored A or C, what could you do to work on these skills? What will you do?

If you have completed the evaluation, you have a list of skills learning priorities and ideas on how to work on them. The question now is, what are you going to work on first and when?

To remind you of what I said in the preface, this is one of the self-assessment tools you can download from the book's website at www.three-levels-of-leadership.com.

The Key Points...

- There is no way to avoid the private leadership behaviours with your direct reports without reducing your effectiveness as a leader because if you do, you will ignore the fourth dimension of leadership: attention to individuals. So performing the private behaviours and mastering the enabling skills is a must for any leader wanting to excel.

- You have more room for manoeuvre on the public leadership behaviours because you don't have to master all of them. Where you see gaps in your range of behaviours and skills, you can legitimately ask yourself, which of my colleagues can I ask to cover me on those? In doing so, you are recognising the practical need to share leadership. Nonetheless, most leaders would be wise to increase their behavioural range because they are likely to face moments when their colleagues won't provide the leadership behaviours the group needs. And as the leader has one responsibility they cannot delegate – to make sure there *is* leadership – he or she will have to step into the breach. So behavioural flexibility is essential to leaders.

- Thus, the first element of personal leadership focuses on growing and updating your technical knowledge, widening your range of public and private behaviours and improving your skill at performing them.

- The field you are in – that is, business, the military, education, healthcare and so on – partially determines the technical knowledge you need. However, I believe there are three non-sector-specific areas of technical knowledge. These are: (1) individual psychology; (2) group psychology and (3) time management. To help with the first, I will offer a leader's model of the psyche in chapter 8.

- The key skills underneath the public and private leadership behaviours lie in the areas of: (1) group problem solving and planning; (2) group decision-making; (3) interpersonal ability; (4) managing group process; (5) assertiveness and (6) goal-setting. I have explained what they involve, suggested ways of working on them and offered a self-evaluation tool to help you see your learning priorities.

- Finally, if you convince yourself you have nothing to learn or improve, even after completing the self-assessment exercise and asking a trusted colleague for advice – or if you find yourself not using newly learnt skills – consider that limiting beliefs may be at work. If they are, attention to self-mastery (see chapters 8 and 9) will help.

◇◇◇◇◇◇◇◇◇◇

7

◇◇◇◇◇◇◇◇◇◇

Working on Element 2 – Attitude Towards Others

The second element of personal leadership concerns your attitude towards others. Thus, it brings a moral dimension to leadership. It's about viewing your colleagues as people with feelings as real as your own, seeing your connection with them and believing them to be as important as you – or learning to believe it. When you take this view your goals are the same as others', their needs matter to you as much as your own and your behaviour reflects this attitude.

Why Does This Attitude Matter?

Why does it matter? Because along with two other factors – your competence and the organisation's direction – it will decide whether people accept you as their leader.

In chapter 4, I asked, what is it that makes us want someone as our leader and choose to follow them in good times and bad? The answer was, "Trust." How much people trust you will affect your credibility as a leader and therefore how they respond to you – in fact, trust and credibility amount to the same thing when we are talking about leadership. And if you want people to trust you as their leader, especially during a time of trial and change, you must meet the three conditions in table 16, the third of which depends on your attitude to others.

Competence is the first condition. No one's going to trust an inept leader for long. We looked at how you can work on this when discussing the first part of personal leadership, Technical Knowledge & Skills, in the previous chapter.

Table 16: Conditions Governing People's Trust in a Leader [34]

1. *Competence:* People must believe you know what to do and how to do it – that you will make things happen. They judge this partly on your style, partly on the actions you launch and partly on results.

2. *Direction:* They must feel the group has a clear purpose and direction that matters to them – whether it stems from your own foresight or your skill at leading people to define a shared inspirational vision.

3. *Genuineness:* This has four aspects. First, people must believe you are *serving the collective purpose*, not secretly putting your personal interests ahead of theirs. Second, they must believe you are *telling the truth* about the group's issues and the progress you are all making – that you are not hiding anything important. Third, they must see you *practising what you preach* and setting an example through the way you behave. Fourth, they must see you *doing what you said you would do*.

The second condition is direction. If you aren't giving direction and communicating progress, you aren't leading and you won't be credible as a leader. People who carry the title of leader, but don't offer direction are not leaders – they are stewards. They look after the organisation's procedures, assets and results, they solve problems and they make the best of current circumstances, but they are not leading. Remember, the first dimension of leadership is agreeing a purpose and direction that people support. So if the organisation isn't going anywhere, if there's no shared purpose, no sense of destination; leadership is missing.

It is the third condition – genuineness – that interests us in this chapter. You see, if your colleagues are important to you; if you feel connected to them; if their needs and the common goal matter to you, they are more likely to see you as genuine and trust you. To see why, let's look at the four aspects of genuineness from table 16:

- *Serving the collective purpose:* You will naturally put the group's purpose first if you have a strong sense of connection to your colleagues' needs, because your interests and theirs will be the same.

- *Telling the truth:* You won't see the point of withholding essential information if the common goal is your top priority, as it will only hurt performance, which slows progress towards the aim – the aim you all want.

- *Practising what you preach in your behaviour:* You're more likely to display the behaviours you want from others if their opinions and the shared aim are important to you. You'll know that failing to set an example – and being a hypocrite – will not only feel bad, it will weaken your ability to lead everyone to the common goal.

- *Doing what you said you would do:* This is a variation on the third point. Because you share the same goal and your colleagues' views matter, in demanding that others be dependable and meet high standards of performance you'll know you must meet your promises and complete your own tasks skilfully, on time.

You may not be surprised to know that the leader with presence, as described in chapter 5, will find genuineness comes naturally, as it's just an expression of wholeness. And wholeness, of course, is the root of presence.

The message is first, that for people to trust you as their leader, they must respect your competence and genuineness and feel they're heading in a direction they want to follow – and second, that their view of your genuineness is influenced by your attitude towards them. To reinforce the second point, consider what happens if you don't believe others are as important as you. If this means your actions become self-serving, if you aren't honest with them, if you say one thing while doing another and if your own performance is sloppy because you don't care about your impact on others, people will lose trust in you. Your credibility will ebb away and you'll find few people prepared to follow you. This is one reason the second element of personal leadership matters.

But people's trust isn't the only thing at risk if you believe people matter less than you. If you see them as disposable assets, there to serve your ends, then however charming you may be and however polished your manner, the chances are that when you're under pressure you will put your needs first and behave insensitively. Others will notice and if it becomes a pattern, you will not only struggle to lead effectively, you may find it hard to keep your job. Here's what the Center for Creative Leadership found when they studied why the careers of promising executives sometimes "derail," to use their word:[35]

- The number one reason was insensitivity to others – being abrasive, showing extreme impatience or neglecting others' feelings and priorities.

- Other key reasons included "betrayal of trust" (not outright dishonesty, but, for example, failing to follow through on promises) and being "over-ambitious" (always thinking of the next job and concentrating on office politics to serve one's selfish interests).

In short, they derail when they put themselves first and don't see others as valued equals.

Am I saying you can never lead effectively if you don't believe others matter as much as you? No, because you can survive with this attitude, at least for a time – either when performance is consistently impressive or there's a crisis and people are desperate and depend on you to drive a turnaround – assuming they believe you are up to the job. But even then, your power will be limited and unstable.

I say "limited" because if you don't feel a connection with your colleagues, if you don't see them as people with needs as real as your own – and especially if you view them as pawns in your struggle for power, popularity, status, wealth or survival – you will find leadership becomes harder and harder. Eventually, your behaviour will betray your attitude, your colleagues will notice your selfishness and their trust in you will fade, reducing your ability to inspire. You may be able to strike fear in some, but fear will never motivate like inspiration. And "unstable" because when your people can't stand you any more or no longer need you, they won't be following – even if you still hold the title of "leader." That's when you enter a game of pretence. You will be pretending to lead when, in fact, you are just a steward and they will be pretending to follow until they can oust you or leave you.

I recall a spectacularly insensitive leader – a CEO of an industrial group. He was a renowned bully and behaved ruthlessly towards his people – even his better performers – yet he beat the odds by lasting seven years. How? He turned around a business that was drifting downward. Financial results in the first six years were excellent and the stock market saw him as a star. But one year of bad results and he was out. He hadn't built relationships to withstand tough times, so his colleagues turned on him and the non-executive directors fired him on the spot, citing their loss of confidence in the CEO.

To summarise, your attitude towards others as a leader matters for two reasons. First, you have to show genuineness to be credible as a leader – especially in tough times – and your attitude to people will determine whether they see you as genuine or not. Second, if you don't see others as important, you may find yourself out of a job.

What This Attitude Involves

We've looked at what can go wrong if your attitude is selfish and negative. But what does the right attitude look like and how does it show as behaviour? Unless this is clear, you'll find it hard to work on the second element of personal leadership.

The effective leader's attitude and behaviour toward others has five characteristics that flow downward, as you see in figure 6.

Figure 6
Five Levels of the Effective Leader's Attitude to Others

Characteristic	Level	Direction of Flow
(1) Interdependence	Mental	
(2) Appreciation	Emotional	
(3) Caring	Emotional	↓
(4) Service	Behavioural	
(5) Balance	Behavioural	

The first attitude is the mental, but practical realisation that without other people, you as the leader can't make much happen. Yes, they need your leadership, but you need their skill, knowledge, contacts, energy and goodwill – and sometimes their leadership input too. The truth is, you need each other. You are *interdependent*.

When you realise this, you can *appreciate* them, which is the second characteristic. The key here is that a thought ("I need these people, I can't do much on my own") must flow through into a feeling. As I'll explain in more detail in chapter 8, thoughts don't drive behaviour until they gain emotional content. Emotions add intensity and direction to our thoughts, creating the desire to act on them. Without desire, a thought stays where it is. You will have met people who had good ideas, but couldn't follow through. Why? Because their thoughts didn't create enough desire to drive their behaviour or because opposing emotions from a more powerful (usually subconscious) belief blocked action.

When the leader's appreciation for his colleagues is strong, it flows through to *caring* about his people – the third characteristic. The leader cares about the conditions his colleagues are working in. He cares about their morale. He cares what individuals are feeling. And he cares how well everyone is working together.

Twenty-five years ago, a book called A Passion for Excellence contained a powerful example of what it's like when a hardened leader cares deeply about his people. It was a speech by Melvin Zais, a U.S. Army General to senior officers at a staff college:

"I will stop providing you with pearls of wisdom and I will elaborate on one. The one piece of advice which I believe will contribute more to making you a better leader and commander, will provide you with greater happiness and self-esteem and at the same time advance your career more than any other advice which I can provide to you. And it doesn't call for a special personality, and it doesn't call for any certain chemistry. Any one of you can do it. And that advice is that you must care.

How do you know if you care? Well, for one thing, if you care, you listen to your junior officers and your soldiers. Now, when I say listen, I don't mean that stilted baloney that so many officers engage in and stand up to an enlisted man and say, "How old are you, son? Where are you from? How long you been here? Thank you very much, next man." That's baloney. That's form. That's pose.

I can remember when I asked my son, when he was a cadet at West

Point, how he liked his regimental commander, and he paused awhile and with that clean-cut incisiveness that most midshipmen and cadets evaluate people, he said to me, "He plays the role." Wow! That was damning! "He plays the role." And I noticed this officer in later life, and he postured a great deal, and he always stood with his knees bent back, and he always turned one toe out, and he always wore special little things around his collar. And, you know, he always turned sideways, and I knew what he meant when he said, "He plays the role." Well, I'm not talking about that kind of stuff. I'm talking about listening... listening ... 'cause the little soldier won't come out and tell you everything's all wrong. He'll be a little hesitant. If you ask him if he's getting along all right and he just shrugs, he's getting along lousy. If he's not enthusiastic in his response, there's something wrong. You better dig a little deeper.

To care, you must listen. You care if you listen to him. Really listen to him! You care if you really wonder what he's doing on his off-duty activities. When you're about to tee-off on Saturday afternoon, when you're at the club at happy hour, if you're wondering, if there's a little creeping nagging in the back of your head, "I wonder, I wonder what the soldiers are doing." Do you do that? What are the airmen doing? What are the sailors doing? Where did they go?

You care if you go in the mess hall, and I don't mean go in with white gloves and rub dishes and pots and pans and find dust. You care if you go in the mess hall and you notice that the scrambled eggs are in a puddle of water and twenty pounds of toast has been done in advance and it's all lying there hard and cold, and the bacon is lying there dripping in the grease and the cooks got all their work done way ahead of time, and the cold pots of coffee are sitting on the tables getting even colder. If that really bothers you, if it really gripes you, if you want to tear up those cooks, you care..."

Speech by Lt. General Zais recorded in A Passion for Excellence,
T. Peters & N. Austin [36]

The point General Zais was making is clear: your effectiveness as a leader depends partly on how much you care about your people. When they know you care as much about them as the goal, they'll respond with the best performance they can give and follow you anywhere.

Now if you have set a group goal that matters to every member and you care about your colleagues as much as the shared purpose, caring turns into *service*, the fourth characteristic. This is when you become a servant-leader - you are helping people achieve something that's important to them.

Robert Greenleaf first coined the term servant-leader for someone who serves others' highest interests by leading them. He tested the quality of a leader's service by asking, "Do those served grow as persons; do they, while being served, become healthier, wiser, freer, more autonomous, more likely themselves to become servants? And, what is the effect on the least privileged in society; will he benefit, or at least, will he not be further deprived?" [37] His point was that servant leadership has a moral dimension – you can't claim you are serving some people while enslaving or harming others. By insisting that leadership has a moral side, Greenleaf reinforced the importance of presence. Why do I say that? Because the fourth quality of presence balances purpose and empathy, expressing itself as service to a cause that's bigger than you.

The progression from interdependence to appreciation to caring and, finally, to service, has an underlying theme. It is love.

Do you feel this is an odd word to use when we're talking about leadership? It's not if you think about it. Consider exceptional leaders like Abraham Lincoln, President of the United States during the civil war, who ended slavery in his country; or General Eisenhower, who, as Allied Forces Supreme Commander in Europe during World War II, was a leader of leaders and had to pull opinionated men like Generals Montgomery and Patton together to form a team; or Mahatma Gandhi, who forced the British to give India independence by leading a campaign of non-violent non-cooperation. They would not have achieved what they did without high, equal regard for others. And "regard" is another, but less emotionally charged, word for love. Love is essential to ensuring that a sense of service to a bigger cause doesn't turn into fanaticism and an "ends justify the means" attitude that leaders can use to excuse immoral behaviour.

Don't misunderstand me. I'm not talking about a soft, gentle, sympathetic, unchallenging love. Nor do I mean a possessive, controlling, demanding-something-in-return kind of love, for the effective leader's love is unconditional. He expects nothing in return (although like anyone else, he welcomes a positive response). It is instead a love that cares about people's welfare, but cares equally about their growth and, of course, the mission. In juggling with these pressures, we come to the fifth characteristic of an effective leader's attitude and behaviour towards others: *balance*.

In action, balance becomes the love that urges others to rise above their current conditions to produce their finest performance. It's the love of awakening people to their highest potential and helping them express it. This love challenges the status quo, people's sense of comfortability and their unwillingness to change in pursuit of a purpose that's important to all.

There is a famous saying in professional sport. It is, "Winning isn't everything, it's the only thing" and the man who first said it was Vince Lombardi. Lombardi is someone many American readers will know. He was an almost legendary American football coach in the 1950s and 60s. Extraordinarily successful as a coach, he was an outstanding motivator with an obsession for winning and a disciplinarian who pushed his players to their limits. Yet he also said this: "…I don't necessarily have to like my associates, but as a man, I must love them. Love is loyalty. Love is teamwork. Love respects the dignity of the individual. Heartpower is the strength of your corporation."[38] This hard, demanding man loved his players and knew it was a key to effective leadership. And his players responded with championship-winning performances wherever he went.

So the idea of leadership as service is no reason to dodge hard-edged decisions for the good of the group. Nor does it exclude an unshakeable resolve to make things happen, insist on high performance standards and take tough action with people who don't perform well and show no sign of improving. Remember, you as the leader are responsible for making sure there is leadership. But, to repeat, this doesn't excuse an "ends justify the means" attitude and the harm it can cause. So being a servant-leader will influence how you deal with below-par performers. It may mean, for example, firing someone, but firing them the way you would like to be fired. This is the balance I am describing. Thus, the effective leader balances power and decisiveness with love for others. We call that wisdom.

Why Don't All Leaders Have This Attitude Toward Others?

If it's important for leaders to realise their interdependence with their colleagues, to appreciate them, care about them, see their role as servant-leader and balance power with love, why don't they all do this? There are two main reasons:

- *Lack of a compelling, shared purpose or vision:*

The first is that not all leaders pursue a clear, exciting purpose or vision that, first, matters to everyone and, second, demands their creativity and initiative.

When there's no clear direction, the leader isn't leading; he is presiding over the status quo and because there is no clear need for change, he's less likely to realise he needs people's skill and energy. So interdependence is less obvious. Even if the goal is clear, if it's dull it won't demand people's initiative and creativity. This can make a leader believe he doesn't need *these* people to make things happen, that he can hire anyone for the job. Thus again, he fails to realise his interdependence. Either way, if the sense of interdependence is missing, it's hard for the right feelings and behaviours to follow.

The problem of failing to agree a clear, compelling purpose or vision is common, by the way. So you may want to ask yourself this: does my group know exactly what we're trying to achieve, did they agree to it, does it excite them and do they think it's possible? Remember, if the group doesn't feel a sense of purpose or destination that matters to all – or at least a critical mass – you aren't leading them anywhere.

- *Lack of self-esteem:*

The second reason is to do with negative feelings about ourselves. Working with leaders, I have noticed their beliefs and feelings about others normally reflect their self-esteem and this is consistent with William Schutz's research into interpersonal behaviour. I will expand on this problem below because its subtlety demands more explanation than the first reason.[39]

Each of us has a self-image comprising beliefs about ourselves – most of which have passed below our conscious awareness. And we have feelings about our self-image. These feelings make up our self-esteem. If parts of our self-image are negative, we can feel bad about ourselves and psychologists would say we "lack self-esteem" or have "low self-esteem." In other words, we doubt our self-worth in some way – we might believe we are insignificant or unable to influence others or perhaps we believe no one would like us if they knew more about our history and motives. Beliefs like these lead to fears of being ignored, feeling powerless or humiliated, being exposed as useless or being rejected. And because we see ourselves this way, we can assume – without realising it – that others see us the same way.

The trouble is, life doesn't stop so we have to find a way of coping with self-esteem issues. So, to survive, we create ways to avoid feeling badly about ourselves – or, more exactly, to avoid reminding us what we already believe about ourselves. We call these "psychological defences."

Now this is a deep subject and I am simplifying to keep the explanation short. We could discuss the childhood origins of these problems and how they lead to feelings of shame and unhelpful neural patterns in the brain, but that would take us off course in a book on leadership. I will outline a model of the psyche in the next chapter to help you understand more and work on self-mastery, but if you want to read about the psychology of negative self-esteem, you could try Understanding Shame by Carl Goldberg.[40]

The main point is that if we don't believe we are significant, capable, powerful, worthy or likeable enough in certain circumstances, or with certain people, we can feel inferior. That's when we usually create subconscious defensive routines to help us smother the unpleasant feeling – the emotional pain – of inferiority while coping with life, especially our responsibilities as leader. These defensive routines include ways of thinking and feeling about others as well as behavioural habits.

One defence is to project our feelings about ourselves on to others and assume they are like us, that we can't rely on them, that they are not important or that we shouldn't trust them. That way we can feel we're no worse than anyone else. This is one way of dealing with a sense of inferiority, but it comes at a price. It means the leader finds it harder to recognise his interdependence and appreciate others if he sees them as unimportant, unreliable or untrustworthy.

Another defence is to strive to feel superior. If you develop the habit of consciously believing you are better than others, it can push away the subconscious fear that you're inadequate, unlovable or so insignificant others wouldn't notice if you were absent. This can drive a leader with deep, unrecognised self-worth issues to use their power and position to uphold the idea that they are above others and feel a sense of pride and entitlement, causing them to suppress people with force or ignore their opinions and feelings. But once again, this defence has a built-in downside. If you believe you are superior, by definition you won't see others as equals, so they cannot be as important as you. Thus, you are less likely to take their needs and advice seriously. And, of course, if your main aim is to shore up your sense of superiority, it's easy to fall into the habit of seeing others as pawns in your game, which can lead to abuse. This, of course, is the opposite of the attitude you need to lead successfully.

A third defence is to learn to ignore your feelings, to numb yourself against emotional pain or anxiety so you either don't notice it anymore or can live with it – in other words, to become insensitive to yourself. But like every other psychological defence, it can come at a cost. For if by numbing yourself you become insensitive to your feelings you will also be insensitive to others – making it unlikely you'll care about their needs.

These are only three examples of the many unconscious defences we use to get by. There are many others. But they illustrate how low self-esteem can make it hard to connect with and care about others.

You can now see why your attitude to others is a key to being an effective leader and that in its most effective form it has five characteristics. You can also see why some leaders don't adopt this attitude. Let's look at what you can do to strengthen your attitude and behaviour toward others by tackling the two main problems. We'll look first at what you can do if your main problem is the absence of a clear, motivating purpose or vision and then we'll see what action you can take to address self-esteem issues.

Working On Your Attitude – *Compelling, Shared Purpose or Vision*

If the lack of a compelling, shared purpose or vision is driving your attitude and behaviour towards others, the obvious answer is to create one.

Difference Between Purpose & Vision

This raises the question: is there a difference between a purpose and vision – and, if so, is it important? In my view, there is a difference and it does matter, so let's address this before looking at how to define your group's purpose and vision.

A group's *purpose* is the same as its mission. It's why it exists. It's what it is there to do. It is its reason for being.

A group's *vision* is the distinctive – ideally unique – way it will achieve its mission. It describes what it wants to become in the future and, perhaps, the impact it will have on its customers or society. Setting a vision is a creative act and inspires a sense of journey, so an existing organisation should be able to say what it is transitioning "from" and "to." The key point is this: two groups or organisations may have identical missions, but very different visions.

But a clear vision is more than just a tool for setting direction; it can make a huge difference to the organisation's results, for two reasons:

- It helps organisations get the most out of limited resources by focusing everyone's efforts. By choosing a particular way to fulfil the mission you also choose what you will and won't do, avoiding wasted effort.

- When the going gets tough – and it always does at some point – a motivating vision provides the essential "glue" that keeps everyone pulling in the same direction. This boosts team spirit. It does so by holding out the promise of a better future – a future that's uniquely yours, attractive and believable. A future that's worth sticking around for.

In short, an attractive vision sets direction, galvanises and channels everyone's energies towards a distinctive, common future. It's invaluable when the opposition have more people and money or when short-term results are disappointing and tension is rising.

To illustrate the difference between mission and vision, here is a real-life example from my first business plan when I set up in 2004:

Company Mission: The purpose of The Scouller Partnership is to inspire and enable transformation at the level of individuals, companies and, indeed, the world of business itself.

Company Vision: The vision – the distinctive way in which we will achieve the mission – is for The Scouller Partnership to become an international force in the transformation of business by: (a) coaching current and future leaders and their teams; (b) writing books on individual and business transformation and, indeed, the transformation of the concept of business and, ultimately; (c) joining with others to open a new generation school for leaders.

Do You Need a Vision and a Mission Statement?

Does this mean you need a mission *and* a vision? Well, it depends. A small group (up to 15 people) formed to deliver something like, say, a project, will need a clear mission, but won't always need a vision. Why not? Because it may be part of a large organisation with its own vision. However, most large groups and organisations need both a mission and a vision if you are to lead them forwards. Note I said "most," not "all" large groups and organisations. Your organisation won't need a vision if:

- It has no need or desire to grow or excel over the long-term; or

- You don't want to be a leader – that is, if you'd rather make the best of current circumstances by managing the status quo, solving today's problems and perhaps improving operational slickness; or

- Its mission is so clear, directional and motivating, there's no need to imagine a new future. An example is NASA's mission in the 1960s to land a man on the moon and return him safely before the end of the decade.

- The circumstances are so stark there's no time to imagine a better future – just an urgent need to deal with the crisis. Think, for example, of the armed forces in times of conflict or a firm needing a turnaround. In both cases, the emphasis will be on a plan, not a vision.

However, if your mission isn't as inspirational as NASA's and you're not facing an emergency, yet you want to lift an organisation to deliver exceptional performance, then yes, a vision is essential to getting a shared sense of direction. A distinctive, exciting vision can give a group the sense of destiny, identity and enthusiasm that a mission often cannot. So in general (but not always) a vision and large group leadership usually go hand in hand.

The Problem with Vision

The problem with "vision" is that it's gained a bad name in some quarters because many so-called visions have basic defects, such as being:

- *Bland* – Some visions are so uninteresting they make no difference to the organisation's action agenda. This can happen when managers confuse a vision with a mission.

- *Superficial* – Some visions are built on sand. The people at the top have put little effort into defining their organisation's future with any imagination or rigour. Witness the, "We wish to be the preferred partner…" style visions. These usually lack the answer to *why* the firm will be the preferred partner. Alternatively, you'll see versions of the, "We will achieve excellence, our customers will love us, so will our suppliers and we'll all go to heaven" variety. I know from experience that these evoke either disinterest or a belly laugh from those in the front line of the business, usually behind the top managers' backs.

- *Too centred on shareholders* – Sometimes you see visions focused on shareholders' concerns. For example, they may stress earnings per share or market capitalisation. But they rarely help to chart direction and don't motivate most employees, especially those outside the top tier.

- *Empty* – When there is no blueprint for action and no determination to follow through, the attractive-sounding vision is hollow. It's revealed for what it is – hot air.

Don't be put off. One of the greatest management thinkers, Peter Drucker, stressed the importance of vision when he wrote: [41]

> "It is futile to try to guess what products and processes the future will want. But it is possible to make up one's mind what idea one wants to make a reality in the future, and to build a different business on such an idea.
> Making the future happen also means creating a different business. But what makes the future happen is always the embodiment in a business of an idea of a different economy, a different technology, a different society. It need not be a big idea; but it must be one that differs from the norm of today...
> ... tomorrow always arrives. It is always different. And then even the mightiest company is in trouble if it has not worked on the future. It will have lost distinction and leadership – all that will remain is big-company overhead. It will neither control nor understand what is happening. Not having dared to take the risk of making the new happen, it perforce took the much greater risk of being surprised by what did happen. And this is a risk that even the largest and richest company cannot afford and that even the smallest company need not run."
>
> *Peter Drucker, Managing for Results*

This may be uncomfortable news for those who'd rather act as a steward than a leader – who'd rather work with "what is" instead of "what could be." But the need for direction setting at some point is inescapable, even if there are people at the top who don't want to admit it. To repeat an earlier point, how can there be real leadership if there's no direction, no destination? A capable steward may cut costs, improve efficiency and solve problems, but he or she doesn't move an organisation forward. I'm not criticising those who wish to act as stewards, merely pointing out that what they offer isn't leadership.

We now know how mission and vision differ and why they are important. Let's look at how to define them in a way that helps you connect with your colleagues and appreciate their value.

Defining the Mission

How do you define a motivating mission or purpose for your group? Well, if you want to lead your colleagues to improved performance I believe your mission statement must meet certain conditions, depending on the size of your group, as you will see in table 17.

Table 17: Conditions of an Effective Group Mission

	Large Performance Groups & Organisations	Small Performance Groups (Teams)
1. Clear	The mission is clear to every member.	Same as large groups.
2. Agreed	All members agree it should be their mission.	Same as large groups.
3. Motivating	The mission matters to everyone in the group.	Same as large groups.
4. Performance	The mission demands high performance from everyone in the group.	Same as large groups.
5. Goals	The mission may or may not be expressed as a performance goal.	The mission is always expressed as a performance goal.
6. Specific	Not applicable.	The mission is specific to them – no one else.
7. Joint work	Not applicable.	The mission demands joint creative or problem-solving work from every member.
Examples	• "To conduct research and generate action to prevent and end grave abuses of human rights and to demand justice for those whose rights have been violated." (Amnesty International) • "To land a man on the moon and return him safely to the earth before the decade is out." (NASA, 1960s)	• "To create and launch a new XYZ product that adds £10 million to sales turnover by the end of 2011." • "To reduce lead-times on our ABC engineering projects from 11 weeks to 6 weeks by the end of this year."

I define a small group as being up to fifteen people. The first four conditions are identical for large and small groups, but from the fifth onward, they diverge. Let's look more closely at the seven conditions and, as we do so, I'll explain why the fifth, sixth and seventh conditions differ:

1. *Clear* – if you asked each member about the mission, they'd give you the same answer.

2. *Agreed* – members believe it's the right mission; that it's necessary. Maybe that's because they feel it's noble or altruistic or because they believe the status quo is no longer acceptable and that something must change.

3. *Motivating* – meaning that the mission is important to the members; it matters to them.

4. *Performance* – members have to contribute and make a difference, otherwise there's no reason for them being there.

5. *Goals* – larger groups will often express their mission in words and agree new performance goals each year. But performance teams won't just back up their mission statement *with* goals; they will usually express their mission statement *as* goals and sometimes they disband when they have achieved them.

6. *Specific* – applies only to teams. A real team has its own distinct mission, expressed as goals that demand results the team members can only deliver by working together. So if it's part of a bigger organisation, a team's purpose won't be identical to the wider organisational mission, although it will, of course, contribute to it.

7. *Joint work* – also applies only to teams. By definition, teams exist to do collective work because their mission demands it. A team always has an output from its own efforts – for example, a football team scoring a goal or an innovation team creating a new product. If the mission doesn't demand joint creative work, a team isn't necessary. (Note: If a small group makes decisions, but doesn't carry them out through collective work, it's not a performance team – it is a directing or supervisory group that passes the responsibility for high performance on to others. For such a group, the first four conditions are sufficient.)

You will see examples of missions for large and small performance groups at the bottom of table 17.

Getting Ready for a New Vision – The Discomfort of Change

We've dealt with mission and purpose. The question now is, how to create a vision?

The first thing you need to know is that defining a vision to change the atmosphere and lead people in a new direction can be harder than setting the mission. Why? Because the organisation must be ready to accept a new vision – a new distinctive way to achieving its mission – which it may not be. As the leader, it's your job to ensure the organisation has a direction and defining a vision of its future is a good way to provide it. However, you shouldn't assume your colleagues are ready for a new vision just because you are.

You see, it's true that if an organisation doesn't renew its sense of direction it will start to drift, but that doesn't mean its people always notice when they are losing momentum and entering a downward spiral. That's because many organisations get comfortable with the status quo or become complacent after years of success, telling themselves, "We're the best." The result is the same: they fail to see the danger signs. Sometimes they only wake up after the rot has set in. Try reading Leading Change by John Kotter if you want to know more about the dangers of complacency.[42]

Why do we resist change? Well, the truth is, most of us don't like it. It feels inconvenient and uncomfortable. It takes away our feeling of security, of being in control. It's hard work – it can force us to learn new things, making us doubt our competence and feel insecure. That's often why it's only when conditions become unsafe or painful that we're ready to consider change – and therefore a new direction. (If you are interested in what neuroscience can teach us about the discomfort of change, read endnote 43.)[43]

Why is this important to a leader? Well, if you push your colleagues into defining a new future or impose your vision when they see nothing wrong with their present circumstances and the current direction, you're likely to meet opposition. The key is this: enough of your colleagues have to believe there's good reason to change before they'll accept a new vision of their future. They must feel concerned about the risks of continuing as they are. They must see the need for a fresh direction and want change before they are ready to consider a new vision.[44]

In the 1990s, I watched the CEO of a multi-billion pound group, a capable man, ignore this principle and impose a new vision involving a shift in values and priorities. He failed, despite being powerful and well regarded by the stock market. His board colleagues didn't argue with him, but nor did they support him. Their comment privately was, "Why do we need to change? We're doing fine as we are." So they didn't follow the new direction with conviction and it fizzled out. Interestingly, I felt the CEO was right, they did need a new direction and I liked what he was pushing for, but it didn't happen because his colleagues didn't agree. The message is that the leader may judge the strategic position wisely, but that doesn't guarantee his colleagues will see it the same way.

So what do you do?

Well, first you should check your motives. It's true that for you to be leading effectively, your organisation must be moving in a direction that makes sense in the circumstances and motivates your colleagues. But that doesn't mean *you* have to set the direction. If the previous leader laid down a distinctive, doable, motivating direction that's underway and it's addressing the main issues, why not stay with it?

This is an important question because setting an organisation's direction is not an exercise in vanity. You don't have to put your stamp on the group's direction just to prove you've arrived. So ask yourself, why do I want a new direction for the organisation? Do I believe in my predecessor's vision? If I don't, why is that? Do I have solid grounds for seeking a new vision or am I being egotistical?

If, after reflection, you are convinced on the need for change, the question is this: how do you stimulate a desire for a new vision, a new direction, when your colleagues see no obvious crisis and believe things are fine as they are?

The answer is that somehow you must arouse dissatisfaction with the status quo and promote a demand for urgent change before you talk about a new vision. Some have called this "creating a burning platform." How do you do this? There's no set answer because this is a creative challenge, but here are some thoughts:

- *Measure the things that matter.* Some organisations measure the wrong aspects of performance so they miss a looming problem. So if you've sensed a strategic problem, but your metrics haven't picked it up, why not change them to make the issue visible?

- *Encourage candour.* You will find that some organisations develop the habit of stifling bad news and not facing facts – and, if someone speaks the truth, shooting the messenger. If this is the case, you can encourage candour by speaking plainly and encouraging others to give you the unvarnished facts.

- *Launch a strategic review.* You might give briefs to your colleagues with questions covering the areas you want to look at and let them get the facts before reporting back to you and their peers. It's best they provide the answers as they are more likely to accept them if the conclusions challenge their preconceived views. Examples of areas to look at include:

  - The truth about your competitive position. In business, for example, that might mean looking at relative costs; market share trends; customer attitudes towards your products or services.

  - The underlying performance trends, so all can see what's happening below the headline numbers. This could mean, for example, analysing your sources of profit and loss.

Creating and Testing a Vision

As I made clear in chapter 1, it's helpful if the leader is a visionary who can express an inspirational future, but that's not the only way to lead. Not every leader joins an organisation with a ready-made vision, so they have to create one with their colleagues. How? Well, there is no one way of doing it, but figure 7 shows a simple model I have used with business clients.

Figure 7

Defining an Organisation's Vision

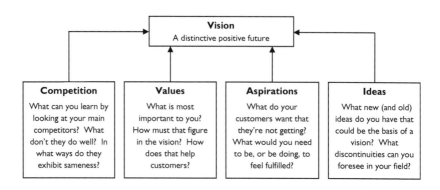

The first step is to look at the competition (however you define them). What are they doing? How do they go to market? How do they habitually operate? What do they do well? What don't they do well? What don't they do that we could do? In what ways do they look the same to customers? What do we and our competitors assume that we all forget to question – in other words, what conventional wisdoms can we unearth and challenge? And how might that contribute to a new vision?

Next, look at your values together. They are the beliefs that matter most to you in life. They define what you care about most. They are your natural motivators. So ask, what's most important to each of us? Why is that important, what will it bring us? Find your common values and ask, how could we include them in a potential vision and, crucially, how would customers benefit?

After that, look at aspirations – customers' and your own. What do customers want that they're not getting enough of – or at all? What issues might they have in using or understanding your product or service that no one's noticed up to now? What could you do about that? What opportunities might that suggest? You can also ask, what is your dream? What kind of difference do you want to make? What could you become? And lastly, what would you have to be, or be doing, as an organisation to feel fulfilled in your work?

Finally, look at any other product, service, customer or technological ideas you already have. Then see what new ideas you can come up with. After that, consider what may change in your industry – what discontinuities or abrupt changes in the customer population or buying behaviour can you foresee and what could you do about that? Can you combine any of these ideas to build a platform for your new future?

The key – especially when you're looking at the competition and customers' aspirations – is to notice the hidden assumptions, beliefs and sacred cows holding you back. Paul Dirac, Nobel laureate and one of the greatest theoretical physicists of the twentieth century said, "The solution to great problems requires the giving up of great prejudices."[45] He was right. If you make the effort to expose your previous blind spots, your prejudices, you can imagine a future that's more than just motivating – it can change the rules in your field.

Armed with perceptive answers, you and your team should have what you need to create an inspiring, motivating vision – a vision you and others will see as worthwhile, distinctive, stretching and possible.

However, to avoid the problem of "groupthink" – where steering clear of conflict is so important to members that they'll agree a course of action without questioning their ideas too closely – I recommend you test your preferred vision against seven criteria: (1) People's readiness for change; (2) Customer benefit; (3) Payoff – which could in some circumstances be the same as the customer benefit; (4) Distinctness; (5) Robustness; (6) Doability; (7) People's commitment. You can use the nine vision-testing questions in table 18 as a tool. They reflect the seven tests, with the last three questions probing different aspects of people's commitment.

Table 18: Testing the Vision

1. Do we accept we need a new vision – what is it about the status quo that makes it unacceptable?

2. How will this vision benefit those we serve and is the payoff big enough to make it worth our effort?

3. What will be distinct – or even unique – about us?

4. Can others easily copy or nullify it, removing our distinctness/uniqueness and will this threaten our success?

5. On what assumptions does the vision rest and are they sound?

6. Is this vision doable – without knowing the details, can we envisage the broad steps we'll have to take, do they feel possible and can we see what we need to do today to get started?

7. Why does it excite us, what will it bring us personally and is that enough to keep us going on the journey?

8. Are we the kind of people who build a business like this – does it fit our self-image?

9. In our hearts, do we truly believe in this vision and do we really want to make it happen?

The result should be a concise, exciting, robust vision statement. It's important to use powerful, vivid language and it shouldn't go on for pages. If it does, you can be sure it isn't clear. But, it shouldn't be so short that it becomes an empty slogan. You need to find a balance: it must be long enough to mean something, but short enough to be memorable.

Grandiose, Self-Serving Visions

There is one potential snag to watch out for when creating a vision: the risk that leaders will try to use the organisation for their selfish ends and set a course that eventually harms it or those it serves. Sometimes, a leader with foresight announces their vision and their colleagues just accept it. Now while this fits many people's idea of the ideal leader – someone powerful, inspiring and visionary – there is a risk to letting one person decide on the vision. Why do I say that? Because one person's vision may be exciting, doable and worthwhile. But another's may flow from their pride, mental rigidity, ignorance, vanity or limiting beliefs about themselves. Thus, the vision they outline may be grandiose, self-serving and foolish, leading the organisation to ignore the search for distinctiveness.

For example, in business, it is not unknown for CEOs to grow their business quickly because they want higher social status or more pay. So they push for takeovers, despite research showing that most acquisitions don't work.[46] Or instead they decide to compete head-on even though this can make companies look and feel the same to customers, turning what were once distinctive products and services into commodities. Few firms do well in that scenario.[47]

The point is that it may be unwise for the leader's colleagues to let him or her blindly dedicate the organisation's people and money to the new vision before they test it. So the senior people should, in my view, get together to screen the potential vision with the questions in table 18.

Working On Your Attitude – *Self-Esteem*

Let's say the group's mission is clear and the vision is motivating, but your attitude and behaviour towards others doesn't reflect interdependence, appreciation, caring, service and balance. Now what do you do?

The short answer is to work on self-mastery – the subject of the next two chapters. But you may be thinking, what has my attitude towards others got to do with self-mastery?

Well, there's a saying that, "To love someone else, you must first love yourself." It's true. To love someone without putting them on a pedestal (thereby diminishing yourself) or being possessive, jealous or needy, you need to feel good about yourself. The same is true for appreciation – to appreciate others, you must appreciate yourself first. It starts with realising that others need you and you need them. That's interdependence. But it's not enough to understand others' importance intellectually. You must go beyond that and *feel* positive about them, for only then will interdependence become appreciation. And for that to happen, you must feel positive about – that is, appreciate – yourself. If you don't appreciate yourself, it's harder to appreciate others.

Why is it hard to appreciate others if you don't appreciate yourself? Well, I touched on this earlier when explaining how self-esteem and our attitude towards others are linked, but the question deserves a fuller answer. Ask yourself, why wouldn't someone appreciate themselves? It can only be because they lack self-esteem due to negative subconscious beliefs and the feelings they produce. Among leaders, these usually fall into three categories:

- *Feeling insignificant.* I have worked with leaders who are capable, who have a great track record and whose colleagues rate them highly. Yet, in a corner of their psyche, they doubt their importance. They believe when they are around certain people or in certain situations, that they are not significant, that their opinions don't matter or perhaps that they don't have the right to voice their opinion. They may believe others aren't interested in them and even doubt their right to be present. Beliefs like these mean they fear being ignored. If people ignored them, it would confirm their sense of insignificance, which would be painful.

- *Feeling inadequate.* In my experience, it's common for leaders to doubt their ability to do their job well even if they are knowledgeable, experienced and have a good record. The fear of failure and humiliation drives many leaders, so they pull out all the stops to avoid this, but it never removes their feeling of inadequacy. It's like pushing a boulder up a never-ending hill; the risk remains that when you tire, it will roll back down again.

- *Feeling unlikeable.* It's not unusual to meet leaders who feel important and capable yet believe, deep down, they're not pleasant people. Some leaders believe their success and importance stems from their capacity to be ruthless, a quality that, although they don't publicly admit it, they loathe in themselves. The classic fear of someone who doesn't like themselves is rejection. Being rejected would confirm how unlikeable they are, which would hurt.

We'll look at these problems in more depth in the next chapter, but the key point is this: if a leader holds powerful negative beliefs about himself, he'll unconsciously defend himself against the fears they produce. And so he develops psychological defences and I gave some examples of these earlier in the chapter.

You may recall that one was to project what we believe about ourselves on to others, leading us to see them as unimportant, unreliable or untrustworthy. Another was to build a sense of superiority and pride, which automatically means we see people as beneath us. The third was to become insensitive to our own feelings – with the side effect that we can become insensitive to others too. Yet another, that I didn't mention, is to criticise others and, by pulling them down, feel better about ourselves by comparison. There are many more such defences and they are all coping methods to ward off uncomfortable feelings like being ignored, feeling humiliated or powerless, or being rejected. The more we use them, the more they become ingrained. Once they become habits, we're usually unaware of them.

Can you see that while they help you avoid your fears, these defences have an unhelpful effect? They cause negative behaviours that may corrode your connection with others, which is the opposite of what the second element of personal leadership calls for. The greater your fears, the stronger and more rigid your defences will be. And the stronger your defences, the harder it is to see others as significant, to appreciate them, to care about them and get things done while balancing power with love.

Thus, leaders with low self-esteem can unwittingly create defences that warp or numb their feelings towards other people, making it harder to appreciate them. What this means is that if you as a leader are to appreciate your colleagues, even when you're under pressure, you need enough real, healthy self-esteem. So how do you come to appreciate and love yourself, how do you develop high healthy self-esteem? Through increased self-awareness and letting go of your negative self-image beliefs, which is a feature of self-mastery. So let's return to the question I asked at the start of this section, "What has my attitude towards others got to do with self-mastery?" The answer is that self-mastery addresses self-esteem issues, freeing you to appreciate and care about others and lead with balance.

The road to self-mastery is not quick and easy, but its rewards are huge. However, you can take steps to make shorter-term gains on this, the second element of personal leadership, while starting on self-mastery. You can:

- Become more aware of your current attitudes and behaviours towards others.
- Take better care of your body.
- Practise remembering people's names.
- Improve your ability to read people's feelings.

We'll look at these four steps before moving onto self-mastery in the next two chapters.

Become More Aware of Your Attitude and Behaviours

The first step is to understand your present attitudes and behaviours towards others and yourself because you can only deal with your most limiting negative beliefs if you know what they are. So you might reflect on the questions in table 19:

Table 19: Reflective Questions on Attitude to Self & Others

- Do I believe I'm significant? With everyone I meet? Do I think others believe I am significant?

- Do I really believe others matter? How does that show in my behaviour?

- Do I pay attention to others, for example, to what they say and how they say it?

- Do I seek out contact with others? Do I avoid contact with others? What does this tell me?

- Do I trust others to do a good job? Do I think others trust me to do a good job?

- Do I trust my own ability?

- What am I like at delegating? Do I over-control? Do I allow others to influence me?

- Do I feel close to others? Do they feel close to me?

- Do I like people? Do they like me? Do I like myself?

- How open am I with others? And how open are they with me?

- Do I choose my behaviour and express myself naturally when I'm with others, or do I feel limited with certain people or in certain circumstances?

Alternatively, you could have a conversation with a psychologist or coach qualified to use the FIRO Elements B (Behaviour), F (Feelings) and S (Self) series of tools to understand your attitude to yourself and others.[48] I found they helped me understand my beliefs about myself and other people.

Take Care of Your Body

It's easier to feel good about yourself if you feel good physically. While this may seem obvious, many leaders don't pay attention to diet and exercise, which can take them into a negative spiral. You don't have to be fanatical, but it makes sense to pay attention to your physical needs. Eating a balanced diet with enough fruit and vegetables, exercising moderately each week, getting out into the sunshine and avoiding junk food all help.

Practise Remembering Other People's Names

This may seem a small point, but when someone says our name, we feel recognised and important. So one practical way to raise your attitude towards people's significance is to concentrate on remembering people's names when you meet them for the first time. You will find tips on how to do this on the Internet.

Practise reading others' feelings and point of view

Empathy is understanding another person's feelings, needs and point of view. An empathetic person can put themselves in the other's shoes and sense what's happening inside them emotionally.

You will naturally become more empathetic as you gain in self-mastery. But you can practise putting yourself in the other's shoes before that happens. If you are in dispute with a colleague, there's a technique you can practise to understand them better. In private, get out of your chair, move to another seat or part of the room and play the other person like an actor in a role. For example, say aloud what you believe they're thinking about you and what their rationale would be. Or try presenting their arguments from their angle. You can also use this technique with someone else playing you and let the dialogue develop naturally while you play the other person's part. You will be surprised what insights you gain from this method.

Another technique is to pay close attention, not only to what the other person says, but how they say it. You can make it a drill you practise two or three times a day until it becomes a habit. Note the words and tone they use. Then ask yourself what this tells you about their feelings and needs. Finally, if you have time, jot down some notes on what you have learnt – this helps to lock in what you've learnt.

These suggestions will help, but they won't be as powerful as working on self-mastery. Self-mastery focuses on inside-out transformation – in other words, renewal from your centre outwards. In my experience, this is a more powerful route to change than the outside-in approach of skills-based work. Why? Because learned behaviours can break down under pressure from inner, negative beliefs whereas self-mastery addresses the heart of the problem.

Take note that I'm not saying skills work is useless. On the contrary, it can be invaluable, but it's better to combine it with work on self-mastery, which we'll turn to in the next chapter.

The Key Points...

- The second element of personal leadership is your attitude towards others. It addresses the moral side of leadership – the way you treat others and the aims you pursue as leader. Thus, we've widened our focus on "good leadership" to include "leadership for good."

- Your attitude towards other people (along with your competence and the direction you set) will influence how much they trust you as a leader.

- If you feel a sense of connection with your colleagues and if their needs and the group goal are your top priorities, they are more likely to trust you. If the opposite is true, they are unlikely to trust you. Without their trust, you will find it hard to lead.

- The right attitude will drive the right behaviour. The right attitude and behaviour has five characteristics: *interdependence, appreciation, caring, service* and *balance*. Thus, the leader wanting to become the best leader he can be will see himself as a servant of those he leads.

- Some leaders don't display these characteristics. There are two main reasons:

  - The *absence of a compelling, shared purpose or vision*. When this is missing, it's harder for a leader to realise his interdependence because it's less obvious to him.

  - The leader's *self-esteem*. If he lacks self-esteem, his defensive attitudes and behaviours usually mean it's hard for him to see others as equally important.

- The rest of the chapter focused on what you can do about these issues.

- Purpose (mission) and vision:

  - There is a difference between a purpose (or mission) and a vision. A group's mission is its reason for existing; it's what it's there to do. A group's vision is the distinctive, motivating, and, ideally, unique way it will achieve its mission – it sets the direction, galvanising and channelling everyone's energies towards a common future.

— You won't always need a mission statement and a vision if (a) your group is not looking to excel (b) you prefer to be a steward (c) your mission is unusually motivating or (d) your group is facing an emergency. In these circumstances, a clear mission is enough.

— To lead people to improved performance, your mission statement must meet four conditions if it's a larger group or organisation and seven if it's a (smaller) team.

— A group must be ready to accept a new vision of its future. If it's not, if it prefers the status quo, it will reject a new direction. Thus, the leader may have to create a "burning platform" before broaching the subject of a new vision.

— The leader can offer his own vision or help the group define one, perhaps using the model offered here. It's important to test the new vision with the questions in table 18.

- Self-esteem:

   — It's hard to care about and serve others if your self-esteem is low as you'll be too busy defending yourself against your fears. It's hard enough in ordinary life, but it becomes doubly difficult if you're in a leadership position where your visibility means you cannot hide. The key to working on self-esteem is self-mastery.

   — Although self-mastery is transformational, it's neither quick nor easy. You can speed your progress by (a) becoming more aware of your attitudes and behaviours towards others (b) taking better care of your body (c) practising remembering people's names and (d) improving your ability to read people's feelings.

◇◇◇◇◇◇◇◇◇

8

◇◇◇◇◇◇◇◇◇

Working on Element 3 – Self-Mastery: A Leader's Map of the Psyche

We turn now to the third element of personal leadership: self-mastery.

What is self-mastery? In chapter 3, I defined it as "being aware of, understanding, taking command of, integrating and transforming the limiting parts of your psychology to overcome inner divisions and become whole, to grow and to express your highest potential." But what is the "you" that's being aware of, understanding, taking command of, integrating and transforming its psychology? The answer is Self. And so another, simpler definition of self-mastery is this: it is the Self's mastery of the energies and contents of its psyche.

This invites three questions. What is Self? What is the nature of the psyche it is mastering? And how does one work on self-mastery? This chapter answers the first two questions by introducing a new model of the human psyche. The next chapter uses the model as a foundation to address the third question. The answers to the first two questions are important because without understanding Self and the psyche, you will make only limited progress towards self-mastery. However, if you understand what you are and how your psyche works, you can quicken your progress towards self-mastery, benefiting your leadership and those you serve.

How does self-mastery help you as a leader? The answer is scattered among the previous chapters, but it's time to pull the threads together. It enables you to:

- Dissolve your limiting beliefs, shift your self-image and raise your self-esteem, letting you:
  - Recognise your weaknesses, take action and grow beyond them.
  - Control your mind's reactions to outer events, enabling you to choose your response, including your behaviour – not blindly react the same way every time.
  - Connect with and appreciate others more, thus shifting your motive from personal ambition to service and balancing others' needs with the demands of the task.
  - Know what is important to you and assert yourself confidently and skilfully.
  - Admit your mistakes and not take yourself too seriously – even laugh at yourself.

- Sense and express your unique presence; the presence that makes others want to follow you.

- Focus and direct your energies better, enabling you to achieve more in less time.

- Handle pressure, to be "in the flow" as you lead, giving you a sense of ease and enjoyment.

How this happens will become clear as this chapter unfolds. In writing it, my aim has been to keep technical justifications and detours to a minimum to avoid losing the thread or obscuring the key points. It has enough detail for you to understand and apply the model in your work as a leader, but if you want to know more you will find extra commentary in the endnotes.

Because the model is new it needs a few words of introduction.

About The Model
My first comment is that we need a new model of the psyche for leaders to use in their push for self-mastery. You see, there are many theories on *facets* of human psychology; for example, Maslow's hierarchy of needs (his theory of human motivation) and Bowlby's work on attachment (his study of how our earliest experiences drive our behaviour towards

others). But I know of only three models of the *whole* human psyche and they date from the first half of the 20th century – their originators being Sigmund Freud, Carl Jung and Roberto Assagioli.

Now there are two drawbacks to their models. First, all three were trained doctors working as psychotherapists who wrote with patients' treatment in mind, so they didn't shape their ideas to suit an audience wanting to become better leaders. Second, most of their work pre-dated new, crucial ideas and discoveries in psychology and neuroscience. For example, Albert Ellis's Rational Emotive Behaviour Therapy (a forerunner of cognitive behavioural therapy), William Schutz's Fundamental Interpersonal Relations Orientation (FIRO) theory, Abraham Maslow's writings and what we now know about neuroplasticity, mindfulness meditation and its effect on the brain. So it's time we had an updated model to serve people in positions of leadership – and indeed anyone else who has to work with and influence others. [49]

My second point is that there's a lot to say on the psyche, but here the model takes up only a chapter because this is a book to help leaders grow themselves, not a treatise on psychology. Thus, the description of the model you will see later in figure 9 is incomplete, but it will serve our purpose in this book. Nonetheless, in a different context, it deserves fuller examination; especially the games of what I call the False Self and the effects of the Collective Unconscious. This may be possible in the future, if readers find the material helpful and want more detail.

Third, I shall say something about the model's origins as although I'm not writing for psychologists and executive coaches, some readers will, understandably, have questions about its provenance and soundness. So to be clear, I am drawing on three sources. First, my own experience as a leader and user of the self-mastery practices I describe in chapter 9. Second, what I've learnt in my executive coaching practice, both in training and from working with clients, most of whom are leaders. Third, a synthesis of the research and writings of many authors and schools of thought in the fields of psychology, neuroscience, medicine, epigenetics and both Christian and eastern mysticism, which I list in endnote 50. Within these I would give a special mention to the work of Roberto Assagioli, as I had some training in the approach to psychology he founded (Psychosynthesis) and the ideas of William Schutz and Albert Ellis. [50]

While noting this mixture of sources, you may still be asking yourself; can I trust it, is the model right? Well, is any model "right"? As I wrote in chapter 2, a model describes reality in a simplified way, but it's not reality itself. Thus, for me the question is not, "Is it right?" but "Does it fit the facts available to us and is it useful?"

The reason I'm offering it is, firstly, that although it's not perfect, I do believe it fits our inner experiences and what we know about human psychology and, secondly, that both clients and I have found it useful. It's worth noting that many of the key advances in applied psychology came from practitioners in the field drawing on their experiences (like Freud, Jung and Assagioli) rather than scientific researchers. So what I'm doing here in offering a new model from my practical experience and reflections as both leader and coach isn't unusual.

The real test of the model will come from you. Ask yourself at the end of the chapter, does it resonate with me? Does it clarify my own challenges and experiences? Do I sense it will help me grow as a leader? If the answer in each case is "yes" or "maybe," then use it (or at least try it) and if it's not, discard it.

Love & Power

Before going into the detail of a human psyche, we'll start with the big picture because at the root of this new model is the view that there are two primal psychospiritual forces driving all of us throughout their lives. We can call them Love and Power.[51]

Love and Power are the psychological equivalents of Yin and Yang, symbolised in the famous image on the left. In Taoism, they represent the two basic forces of life. Like Yin and Yang, Love and Power are not polar opposites. They are contrasting forces with complementary qualities, like masculinity and femininity. When they are in harmony, they drive sustainable progress, innovation, growth and unity. They are two sides of the same coin, working to the same end. This is why the symbol has a white dot in the dark half and a dark spot in the white area, meaning that in the heart of one lies the seed of the other.

Love and Power show up in many ways – often with distortions because of the self-image issues we looked at in the previous chapter – as you see in table 20.

Table 20: Expressions of Power and Love

	Pure Expressions	Distorted Expressions
Power	• Drive to grow, to assert, to be distinct, to take responsibility, to make a difference, to create, to express our uniqueness • Will, energy, determination, intensity • Intent, vision, choice, values-based action • Achievement, creativity, freedom, discipline	• *Selfishness, ruthless ambition, fanaticism* • *Rigid control of and imposition on others* • *Separativeness, superiority, pride* • *Aggression, violence, unhelpful competition* • *Feelings of inadequacy or powerlessness* • *Seeking independence to avoid rejection*
Love	• Drive to nurture and be nurtured; to be part of something bigger than us; to raise all, not just self; to connect with others • Action in service or support of others • Compassion, acceptance, intimacy, affection • Harmony, unity, order, joy, co-operation	• *Dependency, passivity, inertia, resignation* • *Feeling unlovable, unworthy, un-nurtured* • *Conformity, fear of standing out* • *Over-concern for others' opinions* • *Love of status quo, fear of responsibility* • *Loneliness, fear of rejection, shyness*

In short, Love and Power together supply the drive for everyone to live, grow, connect with and care for others, assert ourselves, create and be everything we have the potential to be.

They underpin, for example, Maslow's theory of human motivation, in which he outlined a "hierarchy of needs." He argued that we strive to meet our needs and, eventually, to "self-actualise" – in other words, to become everything we can be, to realise our full potential. He developed a five-tier model, as shown in figure 8. Working from the bottom upward, Maslow argued that as we fulfil enough of our lower needs, we turn our attention to the next highest need in the hierarchy. So he reasoned that a person's chief motivating force is his next highest unfulfilled need.[52]

Figure 8
Maslow's Hierarchy of Needs

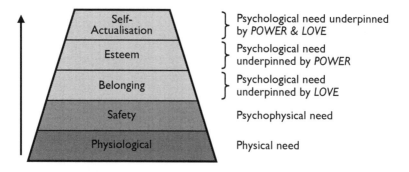

Self-Actualisation	Psychological need underpinned by POWER & LOVE
Esteem	Psychological need underpinned by POWER
Belonging	Psychological need underpinned by LOVE
Safety	Psychophysical need
Physiological	Physical need

Our physiological needs (food, water, shelter, sex, clothes) are lowest in the hierarchy. Then comes a partly physical, partly psychological need: safety. This includes protection from physical danger and emotional safety – for instance, financial security. After that are three psychological needs: belonging, esteem (of self and others) and self-actualisation.[53]

- *Belonging*, the need for social contact, to feel part of a group (a family, a tribe, a nation) and experience friendship and romantic intimacy, is driven by Love.

- Power is the force behind the search for *Esteem* (both self-esteem and others' esteem for us). It pushes us to feel capable and achieve recognition.

- And finally, Love and Power together impel *Self-Actualisation* – the drive to fulfil our potential in a balanced way. Power provides the thrust to understand more and to create or do something beautiful, original or exceptional. Love gives the impetus to respect, appreciate and help others, offer unconditional love, respond without judging people and feel comfortable in our own skin (or in other words, to love ourselves).

So Love and Power are basic principles in our psychological life. How they link with our individual psyche will become clear as I outline the model.

Overview of the Model

The multi-layer circle you see in figure 9 represents the individual human psyche. Outside the thick dotted line is the *collective unconscious*. This holds the world's widely held ideals, values, norms and beliefs – the shared ideas we take for granted, that we rarely think of challenging. It's also the psychological holding ground for our society-wide emotions and the way we interpret history. This gives it the power to affect our individual and collective behaviour.

Think for example, of a lynch mob, where individuals will commit acts they wouldn't do alone; or the reaction in Britain to Princess Diana's death. Consider too, that for hundreds of years people thought the Earth was the centre of the universe, with the Sun and other planets orbiting around it. This was untrue, but it was dangerous to say anything different. When Galileo agreed with Copernicus and said the Earth orbited the Sun, the Catholic Church denounced him as a heretic, forced him to recant and kept him under house arrest for the rest of his life. This shows the power of the collective unconscious to make people believe in false ideas and cling to them so tightly they'll limit others' freedom to think and act as they choose.

Figure 9
Model of the Human Psyche

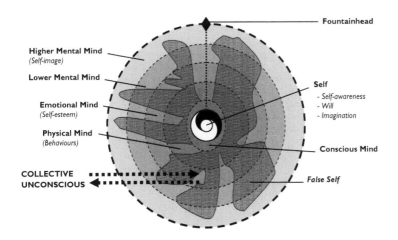

You will notice the human psyche has a dotted line between it and the collective unconscious. Why? To show that although each of us is distinct, we're not separate from each other. So while a group's unconscious beliefs, thoughts and feelings can affect the individual psyche (and its behaviour), it's also true that the individual psyche contributes to and affects the collective unconscious. Leaders, of course, are people who try to influence the collective unconscious in a certain direction.

Within the circle, you have the Fountainhead, the Self, the conscious mind, the four levels of unconscious mind (higher mental, lower mental, emotional, physical) and the False Self. We'll look at each in turn.

Fountainhead

The diamond at the top of the circle represents the Fountainhead. As its name might suggest, it is the wellspring, the source of your life force. If you have a spiritual outlook on life, you can see the Fountainhead as spirit. If you don't, you can regard it as the unnamed source of energy that animates every human being and withdraws when it dies, leaving a physical shell to decay. You can hold either attitude and still find the model useful. But the Fountainhead is more than an energy supply.

It is, first of all, the source of your self-awareness, your ability to know you are alive, to say "I am." Thus, the Fountainhead is the font of both your life force and consciousness – in fact, this model considers life force and consciousness to be one and the same.

Second, it's where the two universal forces just discussed – Power and Love – enter your psyche. To give you a mental picture, imagine them as two shafts of light and your Fountainhead as a crystal-like structure, unique to you, acting as both a lens and prism. As you know, when light shines through a prism, it splits into a rainbow-like spectrum of colours. Now imagine the Fountainhead acting as a lens-prism, focusing and then splitting the combined stream of light to form a unique rainbow – a lifestream that is you. Thus, the Fountainhead individualises the two primal energies, giving you:

- The unique starting blueprint for your individuality. This is your potential contribution to the world and the signature character strengths marking you out as the distinct, unique being you are.[54]

Note that I say the "starting blueprint." It's the role of the Self, which I'll describe next, to detect and build on it.

- Your urge to grow and experience a sense of purpose and fulfilment in your life. When we connect this urge to our talents and what we care about most (our highest values), we can feel a sense of mission or devotion to a greater cause. This can lead us to serve; perhaps, but not necessarily, in a leadership role. Or instead to heroic action; to self-sacrifice; or towards a creative project – whether it's inventive, artistic or scientific – despite sometimes difficult outer conditions. It's the same urge that leads some to seek spiritual enlightenment. However, if this urge is strong, but unresolved, we feel uneasy. That's when we can experience a crisis of purpose and meaning, which sometimes shows up as a "midlife crisis."[55]

Third, it's our source of connectedness with other people and the basic truths of life because the streams of love and power flowing through us also run through everyone else. Thus:

- It's why we care about other people. And it's the wellspring of conscience and moral guidance (which, by the way, is not the same as the norms and expectations we absorb from our parents and society – what some psychologists call superego).[56]

- It's also the source of creative insight and breakthrough thinking when, having soaked our mind in data and after prolonged attention, we trigger our intuition – just as Einstein did when he discovered the theory of special relativity. I touched on this in chapter 5.

- It's what allows us to experience oneness with others and individuality at the same time. This may sound mystical and at one level, it is. But at another level, it's something we can run into in everyday life. For example, have you been in a team with a clear motivating purpose, where you and others happily subordinated your personal interests to the team's success, where you felt you made a difference, supported your colleagues and enjoyed the experience? If so, you've experienced simultaneous oneness and individuality.

Fourth, it is the still, pure ground of your being before you form any beliefs or self-image, think any thoughts, feel any emotions, experience any sensations or take any action. Most people who have practised mindfulness meditation for many years will have sensed this stillness in their daily practice and know it's real. What they have sensed is the source of their unique presence – the presence so valuable to a leader.

Does the idea of the Fountainhead seem distant to the practical concerns of a leader? If so, consider this: without it, we'd struggle to explain the source of presence. And if there was no Fountainhead it would be harder to explain human beings' longings, extraordinary achievements and behaviour. For example, their desire for excellence, innovation and beauty. Or their exceptional sacrifices, devotion to abstract causes (think of Nelson Mandela and Aung San Suu Kyi) and difficult missions, and their genius-level attainments. Or so-called peak experiences – the sudden feelings of intense joy, satisfaction and well-being that are another name for temporary experiences of presence. And finally, our longing for growth, purpose and fulfilment in our lives. The last of these – the drive for growth and fulfilment – is a force that you as a leader can tap into as you develop yourself, motivate others and create a vision for your organisation.

The Self

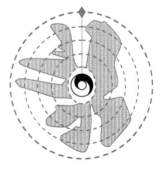

The black and white icon at the centre of the circle represents the Self. It is what you refer to when you say "I," "me," "myself." We could equally call it the "I." When I refer to "you" in the rest of the book, I am referring to the Self.

You, a Self, are a centre of self-awareness (or self-consciousness), will and imagination. It's the blend of these three faculties that makes a human being "human."

- Self-awareness gives us our continuous sense of "I" through time and the power to be aware that we are aware, to turn our attention inward and look at the contents of our psyche. Animals, as far as we know, don't have this ability. They are aware, but not aware that they are aware; unable to think "I am..." and assess themselves.

- Will is the power of intent, independent of the bodily or survival instincts. It is also the power to choose, to decide and to take responsibility. Its role in the psyche is to direct our psychological energies, enabling us to follow through with skill and determination.

Comments on the Will

1. The role of the will is to direct and integrate the rest of the psyche, but it's not all-powerful. Other forces can block, distort or sidetrack the will. Endnote 57 has more detail.[57]

2. I am not suggesting every decision we take needs a conscious act of will as many everyday repeated actions happen unconsciously. Nor am I saying everyone uses their will. I am instead saying that all of us have the capacity of will.

3. There are clear phases to the act of will, which involves more than just making a choice. You will find further detail on this in endnote 58.[58]

4. Benjamin Libet led some ground-breaking experiments on free will and consciousness in the 1980s. The results led many scientists to infer that there is no such thing as free will. His research has been a major scientific talking point since then. As the model outlined here puts will at the centre of the psyche, you may want to know how it fits with Libet's findings. If you don't want to know the detail, the headline is this: the model does tally with his results. But if you do want to know more, see endnote 59.[59]

- Imagination is our power to envisage something new, not just for survival or physical needs, but in pursuit of beauty, progress, innovation or growth. It's not the same as intellectual or problem-solving ability, which is something we share to some degree with animals. No animal has yet proposed the theory of special relativity or the idea of the World Wide Web and it's partly because they don't have the faculty of imagination.

Your three faculties – self-awareness, will and imagination – are entangled. If you think about it, one of a human being's distinguishing characteristics beyond its ability to experience, learn and grow is its power to transform not only its environment, but also itself. This comes through the interplay of the three faculties. You envisage possibilities, choose between them, hold your attention on one and act through your imagination and will. And you experience your sense of learning and growth, plus the results of your choices, in your self-awareness. And of course, in growing you open yourself to new creative possibilities, leading to more choices, new experiences and a sense of further growth. And so on, in an upward spiral.

Your will and imagination together – plus a medium for giving form to the imagined idea, which is mind – are the basis of creativity. Thus, you create in the mind by envisaging (imagination) something you cannot physically see and by holding that idea in the mind through attention (will). How does mental form-building turn into physical action and results? This will become clearer when we look at the four levels of mind.

Although the Self has individual self-awareness, will and imagination, it doesn't have individual characteristics. In fact, it would be better to say the Self *is* pure self-awareness, will and imagination and that you, the Self, are a centre of potential, not of content.[60] Thus, you need a sense of identity through which to express yourself, gain experience, grow and connect with others in the world – and this you create in your psyche. You can therefore see your psyche as a container for the psychological contents – for example, your beliefs, knowledge, memories and habits – that you, the Self, create and use to live in the physical world. This leads to one of the keys to mastery: *you, the Self, are distinct from the contents of your psyche.* In other words, you *have* thoughts, feelings and habits but you *are not* those thoughts, feelings and habits – you are more than them.

The Self draws the foundation of its identity from the Fountainhead. In ideal circumstances, once you have discovered your unique strengths and talents – or at least some of them – your role is to build on them. You do so by first defining and then shifting your self-image as you face the challenges of infancy, growing up and going out into the world. I'm therefore saying that alongside the ideas of "nurture" and "nature" in psychology, there's a third force at play. This is the creative, self-determining potential of you, the Self. To be clear, I'm not discounting the environment's importance as an influence on our self-image. It is significant because life often provides less than ideal circumstances in which to detect our underlying strengths and unique potential. But what decides how we interpret our circumstances? What decides how – or even if – we let those circumstances affect our self-image and attitude to life? It is the Self. That's why not everyone growing up in difficult circumstances lives a grim life as an adult.

The Self doesn't just exist. It has a purpose. Its direction is towards mastery of its psyche, wholeness, growth and fulfilment by expressing its creative powers to raise all life, not just itself. In fact, the enlightened Self doesn't see itself as a separated being. To use the earlier sports analogy, it experiences itself as an individual *and* as a team member – seeing its own fulfilment and the team's success as one and the same.

Relation Between Fountainhead & Self

The Fountainhead and Self are two facets of the one unique lifestream that is you, linked by the stream of consciousness shown by the vertical dotted line in figure 9. However, if you are finding it hard to understand their complementary roles, these points may help:

- Self-awareness has two sides to it: "awareness" and "self." The "awareness" part is our ability to experience, to be conscious of events and to sense we exist – leading to our ability to say "I." "Self" is what the awareness focuses on – our identity, our self-image. Now an infant hasn't developed much of a self-identity in the early months, but its potential for self-awareness is always present via the Fountainhead. So the Fountainhead is the source of pure "awareness" and the Self – through its use of will and imagination – builds a sense of "self" to hold in that awareness.

- Thus, the Fountainhead *gives you the ability to know,* "I am, I exist." But the Self *decides how to use that opportunity.* It's the Self that says, "I am..." and decides what words come after that. Therefore, the Self is the creator of your sense of identity. You can view the Self as the projected agent of the Fountainhead, using will and imagination around its core of self-awareness to build an identity, learn, grow, create and contribute to life.

- When the Self achieves full mastery of its psyche – that is, when it has gained control over its mind, when it realises its identity is something it has created and it knows it's a centre of pure self-awareness, will and imagination – and it opens itself to the flow of energy from its source, then it's all the Fountainhead is plus the gains of its experience and growth. This is when the Self lets its unique presence flow and you will see the qualities I outlined in chapter 5.

- The difference between them is most obvious when you, the Self are asleep or under a general anaesthetic. At those times, the conscious "I" seems to disappear, but the Fountainhead goes on providing life, enabling you, the Self to reawaken.

The Self's Greatest Problem

You can see from this that you, the Self are – as this model describes you – a unique purposeful, creative lifestream with the faculties to grow and create a satisfying life for yourself and others. If every Self knew its potential, surely it would understand its strengths and opportunities, create a sense of direction, use its powers of will, imagination and self-awareness to live a fulfilling life and enjoy being alive... wouldn't it? But if we look around us, it's clear not every Self knows its true potential because not everyone lives a happy, satisfying life. So why don't we always know our potential?

The answer is that – as a centre of imagination, will and self-awareness – *you, the Self can imagine being something less than your potential, choose to accept that limited view of yourself and then experience the results.* What might you imagine yourself to be? You can imagine yourself to be the False Self – a construction of subtle, negative or limiting beliefs. I'll explain more about this and how it affects us after outlining the conscious mind and the four levels of unconscious mind.

Conscious Mind

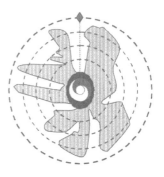

This you'll see as the oval around the icon of the Self at the centre. The conscious mind is your field of conscious awareness. It is the ever-changing flow of body sensations, feelings, desires, ideas, thoughts and images that you, the Self, are aware of at any moment. It's also the outer world – including the words on this page – you are consciously experiencing, seeing, feeling, hearing or assessing right now. And it's where you bring the unconscious material in the four levels of mind into current awareness. So it's not consciousness itself – that's the Self – rather, it's the *contents* of conscious awareness.

The conscious mind is a subset of physical mind, which we'll look at in the next section. This model says that – except for the conscious mind – the contents and workings of the four levels of mind are unconscious. In other words, you're unaware of their action, contents and effects at the time they are running. However, the Self can, with effort, bring some of the previously unconscious contents into this, the conscious portion of mind. The model also accepts there are different depths to the unconscious, meaning some contents and mental habits are more easily accessible to the Self than others.

Many of us don't realise how much our unconscious mental processes influence our aims, feelings and habits. But this isn't necessarily a problem. After all, as you leave your house and walk to your car, you don't want to be thinking, "Left foot forward, right foot forward, left foot forward..." and so on. That would drive you mad. But you do need to recognise there are hidden mental, emotional and physical "software programs" running inside you, outside your field of conscious awareness. Many of them result in behavioural habits. Some of them are instinctual drives. But others were created by you. Some are near the surface and others lie hidden in the depths. You can become aware of these programs and what impels them, but only by making an effort to bring them into the conscious mind.

Four Levels of Mind

As I've already said, the Self is a creative centre of potential, but not of content. Through the faculty of mind you, the Self, create and hold such content – including a sense of identity – and with the help of your physical body, express yourself in the world.

Yet there's a hierarchy to mind; a hierarchy that psychology has begun to realise with the rise of the Cognitive Behavioural school of psychology.[61] You see, this model says there's more than one level of mind; four, in fact. In figure 9, they are the four concentric circles. You can think of them as being like a set of Russian dolls, with each level nesting within the next. The outermost circle is the highest level and the innermost circle – the one lying just outside the oval representing conscious mind – is the lowest level.

At the top of the hierarchy is what I've called *higher mental mind*. It's here that you, as a Self, hold your most invisible, fundamental and unchallenged beliefs about:

- Yourself.
- The world and other people.
- How you, other people and the world affect each other.
- Abstract ideas like "success," "beauty" and "leadership."

It's at this level you store your sense of self-identity, which is crucial to your leadership behaviour. Higher mental mind also enables you to think abstractly – to generalise, to connect ideas and see patterns, to explore philosophical arguments. So if I asked you to define "free will" or "love," you'd have to use your higher mental mind. Higher mental mind is also the field in which imagination begins to take form, although to be clear, it's not imagination itself. The imagination is an aspect of Self; it uses mind to give shape to ideas.

The next level down is *lower mental mind*. This is the faculty you use to analyse, plan, compare and classify. It's also where you wrap more detail around the abstract thoughts you develop in higher mental mind. You could say that higher mental mind deals with the abstract and lower mental mind deals with the concrete. Sometimes we use only lower mental mind in problem solving. At other times, we combine it with higher mental mind if the problem is complex or new.

Below lower mental mind is *emotional mind*. This produces your feelings and desires. The key to understanding emotion is in the word itself, "e-motion." You can think of it as standing for "energy-in-motion." By adding feelings, emotional mind gives movement, intensity and direction to your beliefs, thoughts and ideas flowing from lower mental mind. The feeling (for example, fear, anger, enthusiasm, excitement) leads to a desire to act – or avoid acting – and the intensity of your emotion decides the firmness of your action or inaction. Creating the desire to act is emotion's primary role. Thus, emotional mind acts as the bridge between lower mental mind and physical mind. Its secondary role is to add texture and quality to your mental life by adding feelings, giving you the sense that what you're experiencing is real and "in here," not "out there" and therefore matters to you. Crucially, for leadership behaviour, emotional mind is where you hold your feelings about your self-identity; what psychologists call self-esteem.

Physical mind is where the rubber hits the road as it's linked to the physical body. It's where mind meets brain. So the energy from emotional mind flows into physical mind, sparking neural activity in the brain and emerging as behaviour – either as action or avoidance of action.

Unlike the three higher levels, physical mind includes unconscious and conscious activity, because as I mentioned earlier, the conscious mind is a subset of physical mind. So it's in the conscious mind that you are aware of body sensations and it's where you consciously think, feel, assess choices, decide and take action. It's also where you can examine your beliefs, thoughts, feelings and previously unconscious content – if you make the effort to draw it out. The unconscious part of physical mind governs your physical drives (for example, the need for sex, food and water). It also runs the body's autonomic nervous system (governing your heart rate, breathing, digestion and other physical processes running automatically in the background).

> Note: this isn't the place to discuss the science around the mind-brain connection because it will interrupt the flow. If you want to know more, endnote 62 outlines the latest research and thinking from neuroscience, quantum physics, epigenetics and a key medical study into near-death experiences.[62] Endnote 63 comments on whether the hierarchical flow can work in reverse.[63]

Now here comes a key point: *the conscious part of physical mind, being the lowest in the hierarchy, can only work with choices allowed by the higher levels.* In fact, every level sets the boundaries for what the level below can work with. The choices you consider in physical mind are controlled by emotional mind, which is limited by boundaries set in lower mental mind, which is subservient to the limits set in higher mental mind. What sets the limits at every level? The answer is your beliefs.

Figure 10
Four Levels of Mind – The Hierarchical Flow

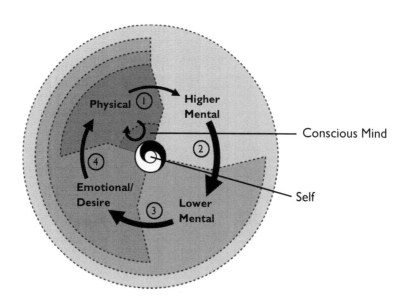

So when you consciously mull over a decision in physical mind, you simultaneously – but without knowing it – refer it to the beliefs and workings of your higher mental mind (see figure 10). This sets the boundary for what you consider is possible. The energy spirals down to lower mental mind, where it's further limited by your knowhow and skill and whether you believe you can see a way forward. Then it enters the two lower levels. Here it meets beliefs about what's morally right and wrong, feelings that inhibit or support certain choices and beliefs about the impact on you and others of trying each alternative. All these reduce the choices further by telling you what is possible, wise and right for you to take on. Thus, you experience a limited range of choices (or only one) when the spiral ends in physical mind. This is why you may hear people say, "I had no other choice," in explaining their behaviour. They don't realise their lack of choice flowed from higher-level, unconscious thinking.

This is why it can be difficult to change long-standing negative habits by *only* applying one's will. You see, if you say to yourself, "No, I won't do that any more, I will do such-and-such instead," this self-talk takes place in the conscious mind – the lowest level in the hierarchy.

Now it's possible to change your behaviour by applying your will without addressing the higher levels of mind, but it's not easy. That's because the feelings and desires in your emotional mind are still present and they remain because beliefs in both levels of mental mind live on. So a person may use their will consciously and apply intellectual reasoning ("if I keep putting off this appraisal I'm frightened of doing, I'll be a poor leader because I'm not giving feedback") to help them suppress their unwanted habits – in this example, avoiding appraisals. But this often won't work as the old higher-level beliefs still feed the emotion and desire behind the habit, causing it to overcome the will and break through into behaviour. So leaders who dislike doing appraisals with their staff – and there are many in my experience – may avoid them altogether. Or they might manage to push themselves into going ahead with the appraisal, but their fear may drive them to do it superficially just to get it over with.

Now it's true there are exceptions to this. Using your will alone can sometimes overcome a habit (for example, drinking alcohol) at least for a time, but you often have to struggle against the old desires and endure an inner battle, which is draining. So this model says that while a decision to change an old habit starts in the conscious mind, you must dissolve and replace the unconscious higher-level beliefs causing the habit if you want to avoid an inner tug-of-war.

Let me give you an example of the hierarchical flow in action. Let's say the owner of a company decides his business should enter a new market and asks his directors to make it happen. They consider the alternatives, including developing new products, buying a competitor, licensing someone else's technology, alliances and so on. In doing so, they weigh up the pros and cons of each route. Let's say they choose to develop new products.

They pass their decision to the marketing and research and development (R&D) people. They set targets and budgets, draw up action plans and get to work. When the new product is ready, they brief their salespeople, who go out to see customers. Now the individual salesman may or may not believe in the product or like the advertising behind the launch, but he'll feel there's little he can do about it. That's because the product and the promotion plan came from higher-level decisions. If something's going to change, it has to happen above the salesman's level.

As you can probably guess, the owner represents your higher mental mind. The directors are the thoughts stemming from your lower mental mind. The marketing and R&D people are your emotions and the salesman is the conscious part of your physical mind.

So we form initial ideas, at the outline abstract level, in higher mental mind. This is where, for example, Einstein would have begun to form his theory of relativity. Once the outline design is ready, the thought passes to the lower mental mind, where we give it more detail, in the same way Einstein would have used mathematical equations to prove and refine his idea. However, a thought, if it's to result in a physical act – for example, writing the theory of relativity – must gain intensity and direction and this is where emotional mind comes in. Emotional mind is there to infuse the static idea with desire; the desire to act. In this example, the desire to write and communicate the idea. From there the idea flows into physical mind and the brain where it ends as behaviour; in this case, as writing.

The same hierarchical flow is true for self-image and self-esteem. Your feelings about yourself stem from your self-image – your view of your qualities, your faults, your potential, your ability to influence your environment, your limits and so on. And these feelings trigger behaviours which, repeated over time, become unconscious habits. Can you see that your self-image – stored in higher mental mind – will affect your leadership behaviour? So anyone working on self-mastery should start with the beliefs in their higher mental mind. Research by Will Schutz supports this idea. He studied the effect of self-image and self-esteem on behaviour for over 40 years, and developed the FIRO (Fundamental Interpersonal Relations Orientation) theory. I've drawn on some of his ideas in the rest of this chapter.[64]

Before we move on to the False Self, let's summarise what we've covered so far. This model says that two fundamental forces, Love and Power, affect everyone. Together they supply the drive to grow, connect with and care for others, assert ourselves, be creative and become all that we have the potential to be. They flow through the Fountainhead, which is the source of our awareness, unique presence and starting psychological blueprint. However, it's the Self that decides where to go from this starting point using its three faculties of will, self-awareness and imagination. This is what you are, a Self, a centre of psychological potential – but not of content. You create a personality by allowing beliefs and habits into your psyche, but you remain more than these contents. The Self interacts with the world through four levels of mind, the lowest level being conscious mind. Its greatest problem is that it can unwittingly use its powers to believe it is the False Self.

False Self

If we had no limiting beliefs our intuitions, thoughts, feelings and behaviours would flow naturally. So would our presence. The trouble is, most of us do have limiting beliefs. And with our three core powers – self-awareness, will and imagination – we can identify so closely with limiting beliefs about ourselves that we not only believe we *have* them, we believe we *are* them. We can imagine and accept the beliefs are true and then experience the limiting results in our self-awareness. That's why you can find yourself immersed in a mass of beliefs that block or distort your natural thoughts, feelings and behaviours – especially the way you behave around other people. These limiting beliefs comprise the False Self.[65]

In figure 9, it showed as the dark blob-like shadow.

Before saying more about limiting beliefs, let's first be clear on *beliefs*. Beliefs are ideas we think are true. We need beliefs because no one can experience everything in life. So they act as useful proxies for truth. For example, I don't know from personal experience that if I jump from an aeroplane at 20,000 feet without a parachute, I'll die when I hit the ground. But I believe it. And it's a helpful belief. It ensures I don't put  myself at needless risk. If you think about it, some of what you "know," you have indeed experienced. But much of what you "know" is stuff someone told you, or taught you, or that you read – and you accepted it was true. Or it stems from your interpretation of events, even though you may not have known all the facts. Whatever its origin, much of what you believe helps you navigate your way through life. But not all of it… which takes us to limiting beliefs.

Limiting beliefs are negative, often unconscious ideas we have about our identity, our abilities, other people and the world, that we believe are true. They exert a huge influence over the psychological well-being and behaviour of the world's population. They control how we interpret and experience life, they can block us from achieving our goals and they affect how we get on with other people.

An example of a limiting belief would be, "I'm not an attractive person, so if I ask that person out on a date, she will reject me and that will feel so terrible I must never let it happen." A limiting belief usually has a section that seems true ("I'm not attractive, so if I ask that person out she will reject me") and a section that judges the first part ("that will feel terrible"). The judgemental bit is always negative, which is how limiting beliefs rule by fear.

Your most powerful limiting beliefs concern your self-image, your view of the purpose and nature of life, and how life affects you. They exist in higher mental mind. In line with the hierarchical flow described earlier, the limiting beliefs affecting your self-image lead to self-esteem issues. In other words, they leave deposits of fear in your psyche. They in turn drive psychological defences (defensive attitudes and behavioural habits) to protect you against your fears. But the defences have four side effects:

- First, they restrict your behavioural choices and therefore your ability to lead when circumstances demand that you flex your approach.

- Second, they can cause you to behave in ways that help neither you nor the people you lead.

- Third, they block the flow of your unique presence.

- Fourth, as I've remarked in earlier chapters, they can either make you unaware of your need to change or stop you learning new skills.

These beliefs also spawn or connect with other limiting beliefs in the lower levels of mind. This leads to a network of limiting beliefs and associated fears in your psyche. But at its core is a set of identity and worldview-related beliefs. This network is the False Self. The model in figure 11 shows its four layers and the types of limiting beliefs it contains.

Figure 11
Structure of the False Self

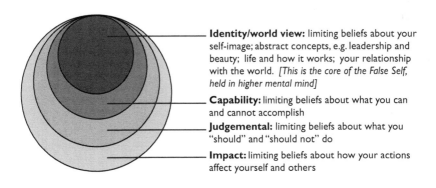

Identity/world view: limiting beliefs about your self-image; abstract concepts, e.g. leadership and beauty; life and how it works; your relationship with the world. *[This is the core of the False Self, held in higher mental mind]*

Capability: limiting beliefs about what you can and cannot accomplish

Judgemental: limiting beliefs about what you "should" and "should not" do

Impact: limiting beliefs about how your actions affect yourself and others

The False Self spans all four levels of mind and builds up over many years. At first, it acts as "psychological protector" of the Self when it's young and therefore at its most vulnerable. You see, a child has little sense of self and not much experience with which to understand and assess what's happening around and to it. So our world can and does appear threatening at times. Therefore the Self needs beliefs in the form of a self-image and ideas of how the world works to make sense of what is happening, to feel safe and, indeed, to survive.

So the Self takes on several beliefs. Many will be useful, nurturing and accurate, but not all. Those that aren't are the limiting beliefs. As we grow older, some of our limiting beliefs will be challenged by events in life, proven to be false and replaced, but again, not all of them. And so a set of limiting beliefs centred on our self-identity and how we see the world will usually take hold alongside more helpful beliefs. How do limiting beliefs develop? They come from:

- Drawing negative conclusions from behaviour we receive from influential people – for example, parents, peers and teachers.

- Giving a negative interpretation or meaning to our own or others' life experiences.

- Absorbing limiting or negative interpretations about the world or ourselves from the collective unconscious. For example, from what we read in newspapers, hear on the radio or see on television. Or by comparing ourselves unfavourably with high profile people, based perhaps on our appearance, intelligence or natural talents.

We can develop limiting beliefs at any age. But many of them form in our first two decades of life when our self-image is changing quickly and is less robust and, of course, when we have fewer mastery experiences on which to fall back on. By "mastery experiences," I mean those periods when we've coped or achieved in the face of resistance and obstacles. They give us positive memories to lift us in times of trial and help us interpret events more objectively.

Table 21: Limiting Beliefs: Impact On Interpersonal Behaviour

	Significance	Competence	Likeability
Core personal desire	To feel significant, worthwhile, to feel that you matter.	To feel competent, intelligent, influential and reliable.	To feel likeable, to give and receive affection.
Interpersonal drive	To have contact with people, to belong, to be noticed, to feel distinct and significant, to feel included.	To direct the course of our life, to influence decisions that affect us, to exert power over other people.	To have intimate or close relationships, to be liked and trusted.
Classic limiting belief	*"I am insignificant and worthless and if I experience this by people ignoring me or taking no notice of my opinion, that will be awful."*	*"I am not good enough and if I'm found out or make mistakes, I'll be humiliated and that will be dreadful."*	*"I am an unpleasant person, so if others get to know me they will inevitably reject me, which will be horrible."*
Interpersonal fear	*Being ignored, feeling insignificant or invisible.*	*Being humiliated, feeling powerless or useless.*	*Being rejected, feeling unlovable or unlikeable.*
Examples of defensive behaviours	*Not raising certain issues, giving in too easily, staying away, being a loner... OR ... being ultra-visible, being the "life and soul."*	*Over-controlling, dominating, perfectionism, criticising others, rebellion... OR... avoiding responsibility, being passive.*	*Keeping others at arms length... OR ... disclosing too much about self, being clingy, trying to cause early rejection.*

From William Schutz's research, we know there are three common limiting beliefs around our self-image that cause major self-esteem issues and limit our behaviour with other people. We touched on them in chapter 7. These three concern our sense of significance, competence and likeability and they create our fears of being ignored, humiliated or rejected. You will see them summarised in table 21. Given its importance, the table is worth studying.

If these fears dominate us, they drive us to avoid exposing ourselves to the unbearable "truths" – or rather, the beliefs masquerading as truths – lying behind them. So we cling to certain ways of protecting ourselves, without knowing why we are behaving as we are. These are defensive behaviours. You will see classic examples in the last row of table 21.

For example, take someone with a strong belief in their insignificance – who, deep down, feels that although they're a CEO, they aren't worthy to be around people they see as more important. (Note: this isn't an unusual problem for a leader.) Their defence might be to make themselves visible by taking the credit for others' work, exaggerating their achievements or making themselves the centre of attention, even if others find this annoying. Their unconscious idea is, *"I'll make myself so visible, you can't possibly ignore me."* Another example would be a leader with deep doubts about his professional competence or innate power to lead people, who fears being exposed as inadequate in his job. His defence may be to criticise others, even when it doesn't help the organisation. Underlying his behaviour is the belief that, *"If I belittle you, I raise myself by comparison and feel better about my ability."* Finally, take someone who believes, at heart, they're a ruthless, callous leader and that if anyone got close, they too would see it. They might insist on keeping their relations cool, distant and businesslike, even when it would help them to be more open. The idea behind their defence is that, *"If I keep you at arms length, you won't get to know me well, so you'll be less likely to reject me."*

To be clear, I'm not saying the behaviours listed in table 21 are always defensive. They are only defensive when three conditions are true:

* First, the unconscious motive behind them is to prevent us experiencing our worst fears about ourselves.

* Second, we don't choose them, they are just reactions.

* Third, we find it hard to behave any other way and use them even when doing something else would be wiser for us and others.

They become a problem if we rely on them so much we become rigid in working with others, hurt our relationships and perhaps build a deep-seated, unrecognised frustration with ourselves.

Now I am not suggesting the three limiting beliefs in table 21 are the only ones affecting leaders. But because they tie in closely to leadership behaviour they – or variations of them – are among the key limiting beliefs I meet in working with clients. Nor am I saying the defensive behaviours in the table are the only ones leaders use. I mentioned others in the previous chapter: projecting beliefs about yourself on to others and seeing your flaws in them, but not yourself; building a sense of superiority and pride, for example through the people you mix with, your possessions and your manner; and learning to ignore your feelings.

I should add that limiting beliefs don't usually affect leaders in every situation. So a leader with unconscious feelings of insignificance won't feel like that with everyone. It's only when he's with people he judges more powerful, more important or more worthy than him that his old fear will rise to the surface. And a leader with doubts about his ability to do his job won't always feel them – only certain circumstances, like a crisis, a high-profile setback or making a mistake will set his inner alarm bells ringing.

Finally, sometimes we can have a limiting belief without a defence. Some leaders I've worked with believe this: "I can't do public speaking – I'm dull, if I give a talk to an audience, they'll be bored and that's so awful I don't want to go there." The trouble is, being leaders, they often have to speak in public. Most have had training in giving presentations and they become okay at public speaking, but no more than that. Their limiting beliefs block their presence from flowing, making it hard for them to be enthusiastic and inspire their listeners.

My main point is that limiting beliefs around our sense of identity, our worldview and our place in the world sit at the core of the False Self, in higher mental mind. Over time, we justify them, give them emotional significance and they emerge as unhelpful behaviours around other people. As we give them attention and repeat them, they become habits. They will remain habitual unless we change our limiting beliefs, especially those in higher mental mind. Such limiting habits are common among leaders in my experience because there's nothing like a leadership role for bringing the fears of the False Self to the surface.

Despite using the word "self," it's important to understand this: the False Self has no self-awareness at its core. It's just a mental creation, a formation of false beliefs, a scaffolding of limiting ideas that you have built – or at least, allowed to build up and remain from previous years. It's one big illusion, in fact. But an illusion that will go on deceiving you unless you expose the false beliefs and replace them with truer, more helpful alternatives.

You see, the Self can identify with the False Self, its limiting sense of identity and its associated fears and habits – and trap itself. At this point, it thinks it *is* the False Self. How? Through its powers of will and imagination. You, the Self, have the power to imagine you are this false identity and surrounding beliefs – and the power to choose to accept these ideas about yourself as real. And so self-image and self-esteem problems will emerge if you identify yourself with – and indeed *as* – the False Self, with negative effects on your leadership presence, happiness and behaviour with other people.

Although it's not self-aware, the False Self has an animal-like survival instinct. Indeed, survival was the reason it developed. You see, whatever the first trigger was, an idea representing a threat formed in our (young) higher mental mind. Perhaps the world seemed hostile or uncaring. Or perhaps the young Self, began to experience itself as worthless, useless, powerless, unattractive or unlikeable. This was the origin of the False Self: a major negative belief that effectively said, "You have a big problem because *you* are the problem and you're on your own." A belief like this is painful. It spawns further, lower-level beliefs about how best to protect yourself from the pain and survive. And these beliefs breed strong feelings that drive behaviours. Over time, they become automatic, gain a momentum of their own and reinforce the False Self.

So the False Self builds and protects a limiting, often-wounded self-image ("I'm insignificant/alone/useless/unlovable") and an associated worldview ("It's a dog-eat-dog world"). But it doesn't just build it; *it is* this identity and worldview. So its own protection and survival – not the Self's – becomes its chief motive. After all, if the Self discovers and lets go of its limiting beliefs, the False Self will be no more.

How does the False Self support the limiting beliefs and therefore survive? In several ways:

- Above all, by staying invisible. This way it doesn't even occur to you that you are looking at yourself and the world through the filter of beliefs. And so the possibility of transforming your life by changing your beliefs doesn't arise. This is the False Self's master strategy. But if this fails and you, the Self, become aware of limiting beliefs, it has two other defence strategies.

- The first is to make you afraid to look inward and examine your beliefs for fear of seeing and experiencing something shameful, humiliating or painful about yourself. Now of course, these are the beliefs of the False Self, against which it has created defences. But if you believe you are the False Self, you will believe in these terrible flaws.

- The second is to make it difficult to dissolve and replace the limiting beliefs, by various means:
  - One way is to lead you to focus on information and interpretations that support the limiting beliefs and ignore or disparage data and opinions that challenge them. The Ladder of Inference model (described in the appendix) explains how this works.
  - Another is to create habits you find hard to break.
  - Yet another is to create several layers of beliefs that are so hard to unpick, you put off dealing with the False Self and focus on everyday tasks.
  - A subtle, but common method is to make it seem your problems are "normal," that you are "normal" and that you should go on living a "normal" life. And therefore, any effort to reduce the False Self's grip would be abnormal and eccentric.

You can perhaps see there's a certain irony to the False Self because it develops to protect itself from beliefs that are... itself! So the False Self is founded on a contradiction. It's under threat from itself and is therefore fighting itself! This is why anyone strongly identified with their False Self finds it hard to enjoy inner peace and let their leadership presence flow.

To summarise, the False Self limits a leader's effectiveness and development. Unfortunately, sometimes the behaviours a leader has learned to protect himself from his fears are those that got him to his present position, so it's hard for him to change. That's when his problems become more visible.

Reclaiming Your Will & Imagination

The message is this: you are a Self expressing yourself through an identity, intellect, feelings and body. We each *have* an identity, a mind, and thoughts, feelings and body sensations. But we *are not* that current identity – nor are we our minds, our feelings, our bodies or our behaviours. We are more than them. They are, instead, our means of expression in the world. Thus, you are not the unhelpful by-product of your mind, the False Self, with its limiting worldview and sense of identity – and its associated emotional and behavioural habits. However, you do remain responsible for your limiting beliefs, thoughts, feelings and actions.

Most leaders (in fact, most people) identify themselves with – indeed as – the False Self to a greater or lesser extent. But once you understand your psychological constitution, you can begin to disidentify from and rise above the beliefs of the False Self to achieve self-mastery.

Why is disidentifying from and transcending the False Self important? First, it gives you the chance to reclaim your will and imagination and choose who and how to be in the world while appreciating that other people matter too. You can let your natural presence unfold, focus on your strengths, grow and enjoy your life instead of letting unconscious, fear-inducing beliefs dominate and limit your potential. Second, it allows you to connect with others better. And for leaders, it allows them to lead powerfully, wisely and authentically; which can bring fulfilment and inspire others to give their best. For great leadership – and, indeed, living a fulfilling, effective life – starts and ends with being who we are.

We will look closer at the art of disidentification as we study the techniques and tools of self-mastery in chapter 9.

The Model, Presence & Self-Mastery

I have said repeatedly that self-mastery leads to presence. But now we have this model, one final question remains: how does that work? What does the model tell us about the practice of self-mastery and how it helps you develop your unique presence?

Well, as I explained in chapter 5, the root of presence is wholeness. I said that wholeness stems from "a positive inner alignment of one's sense of identity, purpose and feelings about life and oneself." And so it does. But at that stage of the book I hadn't outlined the new model of the psyche. Now, having introduced it, I can use the model to explain wholeness from another angle. Now I can say that the process of becoming whole (which is another way of describing self-mastery) has two aspects:

- Healing of inner psychological divisions, leading to integration of the Self.

- The union of the integrating Self with the Fountainhead.

How do you heal your inner divisions? By taking three steps. First, you gain command over your mind's habit of creating random, distracting thoughts, feelings and urges – which you will know well if you have ever tried meditating. Second, you stop automatically identifying with these unbidden thoughts and impulses that often take you (unhelpfully) into your past or future and learn to concentrate on the here and now. Third, you see and dissolve your False Self, thus freeing yourself from its limiting beliefs. (Note: it is important to understand that limiting beliefs are different to the passing thoughts and feelings addressed in the first two steps – they are more long-standing and less visible.)

These three steps help you realise that you are a centre of pure self-awareness, will and imagination looking out at the world through an identity you have created and can change. They give you command of your mind (both your beliefs and ability to direct your attention at will) and your responses to outer events. Thus, instead of being a slave of your False Self you can begin expressing yourself as a Self and spend less time defending yourself. That's when three of the seven qualities of presence – personal power, self-esteem and empathy with others, and being in the present – begin to flow. How do you take these steps? By practising the techniques of self-mastery outlined in chapter 9.

The second part of wholeness is the union of Self and Fountainhead. How do you, the Self, unite with your source, the Fountainhead? You do so when you begin to access the faculty that both parts of your psychological constitution share: pure awareness.

To remind you, the Fountainhead is the *source* of your self-awareness while you, the Self, *decide how to use* that self-awareness with your faculties of will and imagination. Now it's possible for the Self to pollute its self-awareness with passing thoughts, feelings and urges and semi-permanent limiting beliefs, but the awareness of the Fountainhead remains pure. The awareness of the Fountainhead is two-directional: "down" to the Self and "out" to what I would term the universal field of abstract knowledge and creative potential. This wider field surrounds and connects all of human life and holds the truths and creative possibilities that scientists and inventors like Albert Einstein, Isaac Newton, Thomas Edison and many others have accessed through intuition. Its defining feature is attentive, alert stillness – the stillness that is pure self-awareness at rest before use of the will or imagination and before any mental activity of the three higher levels of mind. (I say the three higher levels because I am excluding the unconscious body regulation activities of the physical mind.) Many seasoned meditators have experienced this stillness and it's something anyone can know for themselves if they practise meditation. In fact, I include three forms of meditation among the techniques I suggest in chapter 9. So when the Self enters the stillness of pure awareness it is experiencing its source and that's when it can begin to unite with the Fountainhead.

What does uniting with the Fountainhead do for your presence? First, it strengthens your urge to grow and feel fulfilled by sensing, using and building on your unique character strengths to serve others, perhaps (but not only) through leadership. Second, it boosts your sense of connection and empathy with others, leading you to realise they are just like you – a unique Self sharing a common source – and to feel this bond with them. Third, through the power of intuition, it improves your ability to access truths and new insights previously hidden by old prejudices and mindsets. Fourth, as I'll explain in chapter 9, the experience of stillness lets the hidden sense of joy and freedom within you begin to flow. Thus, it allows you to develop the other four qualities of presence, while deepening the three listed earlier.

In the next chapter, which is on the practice of self-mastery, you'll find techniques for experiencing pure awareness, strengthening your intuition and uncovering the values and strengths that are key to having a fulfilling experience as a leader.

In short, when the Self is in full command of the psyche and is connected without impediment to its source, the Fountainhead, the seven qualities of your unique presence flow unhindered.

The Key Points...

- This chapter introduced a new model of the human psyche.

- The individual human psyche stands within the collective unconscious, so while a human being is distinct from another, it is not separate. Therefore, a group's unconscious beliefs and feelings can affect you and your behaviour. It's equally true that you contribute to and affect the collective unconscious – which is what all leaders aim to do.

- There are two primal psychological forces: love and power. They affect all of us. They supply the drive to live, grow, connect with and care for others, assert ourselves, express our potential and achieve a sense of fulfilment in our lives.

- The source of your life, consciousness and presence is what I have called the Fountainhead.

- You are a Self – a centre of self-awareness, will and imagination. While the Fountainhead gives you the ability to know yourself, to say "I," it is the Self that decides what to say about itself and how to use this awareness. The Self is pure self-awareness, will and imagination; meaning that it is (or in other words, you are) a centre of life and potential, but not of content. The only thing you can say about Self is that it *is*. You can experience yourself as a Self at rest – as pure awareness – during meditation if you can hold an alert state in which your mind becomes silent and you are aware you exist, but you are not holding specific thoughts.

- Self needs a sense of identity to express itself, gain experience and connect with others. This it creates in the psyche.

- Your psyche acts as a psychological container. You, the Self, fill the container with content: beliefs (including, above all, a sense of identity), memories, feelings, desires and habits. But you are not these contents. You have beliefs, thoughts, feelings, desires and habits, but you are not them. You are more than them.

- The good news is that what you have created in your container – or accepted into it from the collective unconscious – you can uncreate and replace.

- You have four levels of mind. Most people are unaware of much of their contents and activity. There is a hierarchy to the four levels, with the lowest being physical mind. Conscious mind lies within this lowest tier.

- Beliefs are the ideas you think are true. The problem is, many of them are not true – these are the limiting beliefs. Your most powerful limiting beliefs are to do with your self-image; notably your beliefs around your significance, competence and likeability. Negative self-beliefs create fear; like the fear of being ignored, humiliated, powerless or rejected. These fears lead to many (but unconscious) defensive behaviours that limit your ability to lead effectively.

- Over time, the number of limiting beliefs in your psyche usually increases and forms what I call the False Self.

- Because your core powers are will, imagination and self-awareness, you can choose to imagine yourself to be the False Self. This is most people's and indeed most leaders' greatest problem.

- So the False Self limits your possibilities, confidence, creative expression and ability to connect with and influence others through fear. It works hard to survive, mainly by remaining invisible. If that doesn't work, it has more than one plan B. One is to make you afraid to look inwardly for fear of what you will see. Another is to make you notice or look only for data that confirms its beliefs. Yet another is to ignore or discredit anything that challenges its beliefs.

- Self-mastery is the process and challenge of recognising and freeing ourselves from the False Self (and indeed the limiting effects of the collective unconscious) and uniting with our source.

- Self-mastery enables you to meet four conditions necessary to let your unique leadership presence flow. First, it helps you realise that you are a centre of pure self-awareness, will and imagination looking out at the world through an identity you have created and can change. Second, it gives you the tools to gain command of your mind (both your beliefs and ability to direct your attention at will) and your responses to outer events. Third, it leads you to realise that everyone else is just like you – a unique Self sharing a common source – and to feel this bond with others. And fourth, it unites you with the stillness at the source of your being from which flows the love and power giving you the drive to grow and serve as a leader.

- A leader who has walked some distance on the road to self-mastery:

  - Can recognise his weaknesses and do something about them without being caught in overwhelming feelings of guilt or shame as he knows they are just the defences of the False Self. Thus, he quickens his rate of growth.

  - Gains control over his inner reactions to outer events, enabling him to choose his behaviour.

  - Feels a sense of connection with others, a connection that leads him to put service above personal ambition.

  - Knows what matters to him, has a sense of purpose and asserts himself skilfully, while respecting others' free will.

  - Feels good about himself and can admit failings and mistakes and laugh at himself.

  - Handles pressure, knowing that what he experiences as "pressure" is just the False Self at work.

  - Displays a blend of power and love that shows as the aura of confidence, enthusiasm and genuineness – of wholeness – that others respect and choose to follow.

- It's hard to imagine anything that could help a leader's growth and effectiveness more than self-mastery.

◇◇◇◇◇◇◇◇◇◇

9

◇◇◇◇◇◇◇◇◇◇

Working on Element 3 – Self-Mastery: Principles, Obstacles & Techniques

The aim of this chapter is to help you start and stay on the road to self-mastery, the third part of personal leadership. Self-mastery, as I've already explained, is the key to freeing yourself from limiting beliefs, seeing others as equally important, letting your leadership presence unfold and gaining the freedom to learn new skills.

We will build on the model of the psyche from the previous chapter by outlining the key principles of personal change, the obstacles you may face (plus how to deal with them) and techniques to develop self-mastery. This chapter will give you enough detail to create a personal action plan, but where space is limited I will suggest sources of further information.

One chapter isn't sufficient to take you to full self-mastery, but it's enough to set you on the path, allowing you to learn more and chart your own course as you gain experience and insight. However, you need to know that it will be your efforts – and your efforts alone – that will decide your progress. You see, knowledge from a book stays in a book until you experiment with it, apply it and make it yours.

Seven Keys to Progressing Towards Self-Mastery

There are seven keys to making progress on the path to self-mastery. Understanding them will help you lock on to the path, making your progress faster, surer and more enjoyable.

Key 1: Know the usual pattern of personal change

You may want the inner change that brings self-mastery, but the experience of changing can be uncomfortable at times. This is because growth involves stepping outside your comfort zone, which means you'll experience what you don't know or don't understand or aren't currently good at. Many people find this experience unpleasant. That's usually because they judge themselves harshly for their ignorance, lack of effort, mistakes, so-called failures, inability to learn quickly or for what they see and dislike in themselves. It's possible that you may do the same. But if you know about the normal pattern of change, you can be ready for the possible inertia and feelings of confusion, embarrassment, frustration and discouragement that you may face along the way.

However – and this is good news – there will come a time on the road to self-mastery when you understand the process of learning so well that discomfort melts away. Why? Because you'll realise that it's not you, the Self, experiencing the unease. It is the False Self. We can experience discomfort in growing only when we are so identified *with* the False Self that we believe we *are* the False Self with its fear (and sometimes pride). By disidentifying from the discomfort (I'll explain disidentification later in the chapter), you may still feel some unease but you'll have more power to choose how to respond to it and what's happening around you. The even better news is that as you progress further, you'll learn to observe your thoughts and feelings without passing judgement on yourself, which will take the discomfort away.

The point I'm making is that you will inevitably meet inner psychological forces and old habits that will try to deflect, delay or block your progress. These psychological forces are the games, the defences, of the False Self. If you know that in advance, it's easier to anticipate and work around them until the time comes when they can no longer sabotage your progress.

Key 2: Move towards, not away from

Dissatisfaction with the status quo is usually the origin of a person's push for change. However, you will find that the motivation you feel from avoiding (moving away from) a state you dislike will not carry you as far as the motivation you'll get from moving towards a goal you value, especially when you encounter the obstacles I described under key #1. So it's helpful to tap into your values – the ideas and beliefs that motivate you most – to craft a personal mission-vision statement defining who you want to be in terms of qualities of character and the contribution you want to make to the world. We'll look at how to do so in this chapter.

Key 3: Concentrate on what you can control

This starts with setting an aim or a mission over which you have great influence (the "C" of the ASPECT model in chapter 6). In other words, your personal mission-vision statement must centre on what is going to change in you and what you are going to do. It cannot focus on changes in other people's attitudes or behaviour because you don't control them and never will.

This attitude of focusing on what you control extends beyond your mission to how you respond to daily events. You see, many people believe their experiences in life are determined by other people or physical events. Thus, you may hear someone say, "You made me angry." But the truth is, no one *makes* us angry. Like it or not, getting angry is a choice – an unconscious choice perhaps, but a choice nevertheless.

Let me explain what I mean with an example. Imagine you're relaxing in your sitting room at home and you hear the doorbell ring. And imagine the moment it rings, you are furious. You get out of your chair and stride grimly towards the front door, opening it aggressively. What would you have to be thinking when the doorbell rang for you to be so angry? Perhaps you believed this was someone who was two hours late and had disrupted your schedule, making you late for another event, so you walked angrily towards the door to complain to that person. Now wipe this scene and emotion from your mind and imagine again you're in your sitting room and that once again you hear the doorbell. This time, imagine you smile broadly, jump out of the chair and rush to the door excitedly. The question again is, what would you have to be thinking to react like this? Perhaps you'd been looking forward to special visitors and you assumed this was them arriving.

The key point is this: the trigger in both cases – the sound of the doorbell – was identical, but your emotional and physical reactions were different. Why? *Because your perception of the event, the doorbell ringing, was different.* And perception is simply awareness coloured by your unconscious beliefs. Thus, your beliefs led you to feel and react differently – you were responsible for your reaction. So the principle of focusing on what you can control extends beyond your personal vision to taking command of your responses to events, including other people's behaviour.

Key 4: Remember the mental hierarchy

Many self-help authors have written about the benefits of positive thinking and the use of willpower to cause personal change. Positive thinking is certainly healthier than negative thinking, but it won't guarantee change and self-mastery. That's because positive thinking – for example, in the form of affirmations or self-talk like, "I can do this..." takes place in the lowest level of the mental hierarchy, conscious mind.

I explained in chapter 8 that we subconsciously refer decisions (for example, a decision to change an old habit) to the beliefs and workings of the higher, unconscious levels of mind. These will allow or block the decision, making the change easier or difficult. This means that if you are to take command of your responses to events you must uncover and remove the most powerful limiting beliefs in the deeper recesses of your psyche. To be clear, this doesn't mean you have to remember what originally caused them, but it does mean seeing what those beliefs are today and how they are limiting you.

By the way, I'm not criticising the usefulness of positive affirmations and self-talk. Indeed, I regard them as useful tools, but their usefulness will be limited without first identifying and undermining old, powerful limiting beliefs in the higher unconscious levels of mind.

Key 5: Keep an open mind

This is the key to continual growth because we stop growing when we believe we know all the answers or think we don't need to learn any more.

In Zen, they call this fifth key "beginner's mind." Beginner's mind is one that is free of fixed expectations, prejudgements and mindsets and always accepts there is more to learn. It is the mind that's not already made up, that's comfortable with saying, "I don't know" and letting go of previous beliefs, replacing them with a wider or better understanding.

There is an old story illustrating this principle. A learned man went to see a well-known Zen teacher. As the teacher began to serve tea, the learned man lectured him on the purpose and practices of Zen. The teacher filled the man's cup and kept on pouring until the tea overflowed on to the table. "Stop!" shouted the learned man, "It's overflowing, you can't pour any more into the cup." "Indeed you are right," said the Zen teacher, "but if you do not first empty your cup, how can you taste my tea?" Thus, to learn and grow, we must *be willing* to learn and grow. And this means behaving as though our mental cup isn't full, which the learned man didn't do.

This is not to say that you shouldn't appreciate your existing expertise, act with confidence or have beliefs to guide you in your choices. But it is to say that your beliefs should never be fixed; that you should never believe you cannot go beyond them and learn more.

Key 6: Have the humility to ask for and accept help

As you grow towards self-mastery, you will feel more and more self-sufficient. Yet don't kid yourself; you will sometimes need others' help. That's because the great benefit of another person's knowledge and perspective is that they stand outside your mental box – that is, the personal set of beliefs controlling your perceptions.

This is why another person can often see what you cannot. So a teacher, a mentor, a coach or a wise friend can be helpful and even essential at times – especially, but not only, at the earlier stages of the path to self-mastery. I say "not only" because talking to someone outside your mental box can help you get moving again when you find yourself stuck for reasons you can't see, even if you've already gained a degree of self-mastery.

However, it pays to be discerning about whom you consult. I suggest you look for someone you trust and respect, who can respond to you without prejudice, without projecting their psychological issues on to you and your circumstances. Often, this will mean looking for someone who is also working on self-mastery and has perhaps been doing so for longer than you. But not always. For sometimes, what we need to hear from another can come from the most unlikely sources – for example, someone we think knows less than us, including a child.

Key 7: Understand the psychological laws governing habits and change

If you understand the psychological causes of habits and the key to changing them, your chances of staying on the road to self-mastery are higher.

Nearly forty years ago, Roberto Assagioli, founder of Psychosynthesis psychology, outlined what he called "the ten psychological laws" in his book, The Act of Will. Eight of them explain how we unwittingly create and preserve old unhelpful habits and they offer clues to psychological change. In table 22 you will see a summarised updated version of these eight laws.[66]

Table 22: Eight Pychological Laws Governing Habits & Change

1. Mental images, ideas and beliefs tend to produce matching behaviours and physical conditions.

2. Playing a role, making certain movements or adopting certain behaviours can evoke matching images and ideas.

3. Ideas, beliefs and images will tend to awaken matching emotions.

4. Emotions tend to awaken and intensify ideas, memories, images and desires that correspond to them.

5. Needs, urges, drives and desires tend to arouse matching images, ideas and emotions.

6. Urges, drives, desires and emotions normally demand to be expressed.

7. Repeating an action makes it more likely you will do it again and makes it easier to perform until eventually you can do it unconsciously.

8. Paying attention to and affirming ideas, beliefs and images will reinforce them and the emotions and behaviour springing from them.

The question is, how do these laws explain how we trap ourselves in limiting habits and show the way to breaking out of them? The best way to answer this is with the help of a diagram, which you will see in figure 12. We'll start with the left-hand chart, the Maintaining Cycle.

Figure 12
The Eight Laws, Habit Maintenance & Breaking the Cycle

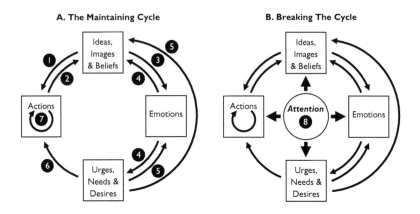

A. The Maintaining Cycle   B. Breaking The Cycle

- Law #1 says that your mental images, ideas and beliefs will produce matching behaviours and physical conditions. The arrow marked "1" in the black circle represents this law. An example of it in action would be a psychosomatic illness.

- Law #2 explains that if you play a role or behave in a certain way, you can evoke matching ideas and images which in turn, according to Law #3, awaken matching emotions. This, of course, is what many actors do to get in character for their roles.

- Law #4 states that your feelings can awaken and intensify thoughts and desires associated with them. This can lead you to create expectations that cause you to see only what you want or expect to see, thus filtering and often distorting reality – making it impossible to discern truth. Thus, for example, a scientist who is rigidly attached to a certain theory may find himself noticing only data that supports it while ignoring facts that contradict it. This, by the way, is one of the False Self's typical ways of surviving.[67]

- Law #5 says that your desires and urges will arouse matching emotions, ideas and thoughts, which explains why you may find yourself intellectually justifying your urges to yourself, making you feel better about them.

* Law #6 is the least surprising, explaining that your desires and urges usually (but not always) come through as behaviour, either in private or around other people.

* Finally, Law #7 tells us that if we repeat certain actions, not only are we more likely to do them again, they'll become easier to perform until eventually we can carry them out unconsciously. In this way, we form behavioural habits.

Now each law is important, but look at the overall effect they create. You will see the left-hand diagram in figure 12 forms a closed, self-reinforcing circuit that makes it difficult for new ideas, feelings, desires or behaviours to enter and break the cycle. This is what locks us into habits we find hard to change.

Current thinking in neuroscience supports this idea of a self-reinforcing cycle. Neuroscientists have a saying, "Neurons that fire together, wire together." A neuron is a brain cell and the saying means that if neuron A repeatedly stimulates neuron B, the connection between them will strengthen and become a neural circuit that we hold in our memory. In essence, repetition and reinforcement (driven by the first seven psychological laws) create and prolong the neural circuits supporting our habits. The process is much like the way a footpath forms in a forest. One person is the trailblazer, walking through a forest for the first time A second person follows her tracks, the third does the same and eventually there's a well-worn path that everyone follows without thinking.

To give you an example of this cycle at work, imagine a national leader with a strong urge to dominate his colleagues so he can feel secure and unthreatened in his power. Let's say he justifies this urge by telling himself, "It's a tough situation, so I need to be harsh and tolerate no opposition for the sake of my country." This leads him to push through laws that, at other times, his fellow citizens would see as unacceptable reductions in their freedom. Imagine the leader repeats this dominant behaviour at meetings with his ministers by refusing to listen to opposing views and when one dares to speak out, he assumes this is a rebellion against him and flies into a rage. The rage – which stems from his fear of losing power – only strengthens his urge to feel secure and unthreatened so he fires the dissenting minister. The fear, anger and controlling behaviour reinforce his sense of threat, making it more likely he will do the same again... and so the cycle continues. Thus, a maintaining cycle can lock us into mindsets, feelings and behaviours that aren't always helpful.

That's how habits form and stay in place, but how do we change them? How do we grow beyond our habits? Law #8 offers the key and you will see this illustrated in the right-hand diagram in figure 12, Breaking the Cycle.

Law #8 says that if we focus our attention on and affirm new ideas, beliefs and images, not only will we strengthen them, we'll also reinforce the emotions, desires and behaviours they cause due to the mental hierarchy I described in the previous chapter. The reverse is also true. If we become uninterested in certain old ideas, beliefs, thoughts, feelings, desires or behaviours and starve them of attention, they will weaken. In other words, *where we place our conscious awareness and attention is the key to change and growth.*

Note that the diagram shows you don't have to intercept the maintaining cycle at the level of ideas (higher and lower mental mind). You can also intervene at the level of feelings and desires (emotional mind) or behaviour (physical mind). Focusing attention on your emotions and actions can change your mental images and ideas because the seven laws are entangled, but as I explained in chapter 8, only if there are no higher-level limiting beliefs in the way.

Here's a real-life example of this law in action. A young man I knew once had a bad interview experience. For several years afterwards, he believed that if he had an interview for another job he would feel the same humiliation he'd experienced the first time. So he decided to forgo all interviews and stay in his low-paying job. But, as the years went by, he felt increasingly miserable as his job gave him no satisfaction and he felt his life was going nowhere. So he asked an older family friend for help. The friend helped him anticipate the interview questions he would inevitably face and taught him to rehearse his answers. As they practised role-plays, the young man's confidence began to rise and he realised the reason he did so badly years earlier was that he hadn't prepared for the interview at all. As his confidence grew, his self-image began to change, reducing his nervousness to the point where he could attend an interview and do himself justice. In the end, interviews no longer frightened him and a well-known company offered him a job he wanted. Can you see that although the intervention focused on behaviour, the interconnectedness of the seven laws meant that his improved interview skills changed his thoughts and feelings about himself and went on to break his pattern of avoiding interviews?

Bear in mind that while attention is the key to change, it can also keep a habit going because focusing your attention on an old way of thinking, feeling or behaving only maintains it. Note that "focusing your attention" includes resisting habits as well as indulging them. Does that surprise you? Have you heard the saying, "What you resist persists" and wondered what it meant? If so, consider that when you pay attention to a habit – by either doing it or fighting it – you are accepting its power and thus reinforcing it. And when you do that, you let it persist.

So now you may be asking yourself, how do I get rid of an old habit – by simply ignoring it? No, that doesn't usually work either. The solution is to gain insight into the old habit, then shift your attention to the new habit you want to create and substitute the old habit by repeatedly practising the new one. Note that – you substitute the old habit rather than resist it. Gaining insight has three aspects. First, understanding the roots of the old habit and why you let it persist – and by the way, there will always be a reason. Second, seeing in detail how it limits you. And third, realising that it's just something you created and has no more permanence than you choose to give it. With these insights, it's easier to let it go as you focus on the new habit.

Studies by neuroscientists have confirmed that repeated, conscious, willed attention to a physical action, an image or an idea can remodel an adult's brain circuits – the circuits representing habits in physical mind. Scientists call this effect "self-directed neuroplasticity." What's interesting is that it doesn't matter if your attention is in the form of repeated physical practice, mental rehearsal, meditation or intentionally adopting new thinking patterns. All four methods create new neural circuits and strengthen old ones – and can even change the thickness of parts of your brain. In this way, your conscious attention can overturn old mental, emotional and physical habits, build new skills and create new habits.

For example, Jeffrey Schwartz, a research professor at the UCLA School of Medicine has worked with sufferers of Obsessive Compulsive Disorder (OCD). As is typical with OCD patients, they had unwanted, intrusive thoughts that forced them into unhelpful habits such as obsessive cleaning, checking or counting. For them the thoughts and habits were distressing and impossible to stop. Indeed, so difficult is it to change these patterns that for much of the twentieth century, psychiatrists saw OCD as untreatable. But Schwartz proved with the help of PET scans that his patients could use the fourth method – adopting new ways of thinking – to change their brains' neural patterns and remove or at least reduce most of their symptoms.[68]

The techniques in this chapter use your core faculties of will, imagination and self-awareness, thus drawing on law #8. So if you understand the principle behind these techniques, it may give you more confidence to try them and, indeed, keep on using them.

Typical Obstacles & How to Deal With Them

There are six obstacles you may face in working on self-mastery: inertia, fear, doubt, discouragement, pride and believing that pursuing self-mastery is selfish. If you can recognise and understand these hurdles, you'll improve your chances of avoiding them or lifting yourself above them. We'll look at them one by one except doubt and discouragement, which we'll handle under the same heading.

Inertia

Inertia is the inability to start working on the challenge of self-mastery or, if a start is made, a failure to persist. It's the condition of non-will. Non-will is, in effect, a denial of Self because each of us is a centre of will (and, of course, imagination and self-awareness).

Now you may be wondering why leaders – men and women of action who presumably gained their leadership position by using their will – would experience inertia in working on self-mastery? Well, it depends what drove them to succeed and get to the level they have. For some, it may indeed have been their will, showing as a strong inner sense of direction based on their values. But for others, it may have been desire born of fear, not will. Why does this matter? I'll explain.

Will is one of the three fundamental aspects of Self. As I outlined in chapter 8, will is the power to set a purpose and direction, to intend, to choose, to decide, to take responsibility and to follow through. Now for an act of will (that is, the use of your will) to be successful, it needs motives that create an intent and a desire powerful enough to carry you to your goal. And what shapes your motives? Your values – the ideas that matter most to you. Your values are therefore your natural motivators. Thus, a person's will and his or her values are bound together. The Self draws on its values to generate a powerful intent that stirs emotional mind to create the desire to act, as I explained in the previous chapter. So when the will is in control, desire is its servant.

But the will isn't the only force that can drive a desire to act. Fear can also trigger desire. For example, a fear of failure, of being exposed as not being good enough, of not "getting it right," or of not being noticed or admired by colleagues. This can lead to a powerful emotional attachment to the need to succeed, to reach a certain career goal, to have power over others or to achieve whatever recognition we think we need to feel more complete, more at ease. An emotional attachment always has a powerful limiting belief behind it – a belief that says we're lacking in some way, that we must prove ourselves or have something (like a promotion or other people's admiration) to push away this sense of deficiency. It's not unusual for successful people, including leaders, to have a limiting belief like this and build their record of achievement, not with their will, but through the fear of not achieving.

Note: you can read more detail on how powerful emotional attachments can replace the will's role in driving desire in endnote 57 and point 4 under endnote 59.

The problem for leaders who depend on public achievement and recognition to feel better about themselves is that self-mastery can be too private, too hidden, to inspire them. For them, it doesn't bring the reward that public recognition offers. So self-mastery may attract them briefly, but often they won't have the drive to stay on the journey for long, as other more public, fear-driven priorities will distract them. They may tell themselves they are too busy or that they'll make a start when "this busy period is over," but that time never arrives. So can you see that one of the chief causes of inertia is losing contact with your most motivating values while becoming caught in the deepest fears of the False Self? In this way, we can become insensitive to what we care about deep down, making it hard for us to move in a new direction.

Another cause of inertia is the False Self's drive for survival. I mentioned in chapter 8 that one of the False Self's survival defences is to make it seem unnecessary and indeed eccentric to try and loosen its grip. "Just be normal like everyone else," it says, "Look at others, are they all working on self-mastery? No, they're just concentrating on living their lives. You should do the same." And of course, the False Self is right; most people are not working on self-mastery because the collective unconscious doesn't (yet) put a high priority on it.

Sometimes inertia in leaders can also be caused by a deep-seated, often unrecognised feeling of unworthiness. This is the feeling that you don't deserve to be a better leader – or indeed to be a leader at all. You can sometimes see this when a leader has inherited his position, perhaps if one of his parents founded the organisation – for example, in a family business. This can leave the inexperienced successor feeling vulnerable, believing the only reason he has the job is because of his surname. Now while this may act as a spur to self-improvement for some, for others a sense of unworthiness can be enough to cause inertia.

One clue to overcoming inertia lies in the heart of the most common problem: the loss of contact with one's values. If inertia proves to be a problem for you, I recommend you focus on uncovering your values. This won't stop the negative pull of the False Self, but it may give you enough of a boost to give you lift-off. I will offer a tool to help you detect your values, but if you find it hard to use on your own, it might be best to engage a coach to help you. The problem of unworthiness is more troublesome and if you sense it could be a block for you, I'd recommend talking to someone you trust, preferably one who has had psychological training.

Fear (of guilt or shame)

As I hope I've made clear, self-mastery involves liberating oneself from limiting beliefs. But to be free of limiting beliefs you must first be aware of them for it has rightly been said that you cannot give up what you do not already own. This means you will have to face your limiting beliefs and the feelings they have deposited in your psyche on the road to self-mastery. Some of these feelings are strong enough to trigger a fear of going too far with self-mastery. The feelings most likely to do so are guilt and shame, especially the latter.

Few leaders I've met understand the difference between guilt and shame or realise that shame is often a leader's greatest obstacle. I certainly didn't when I was a leader. So let's define guilt and shame and explain why the latter in particular is so toxic and so relevant to leadership.

Guilt stems from an action or a failure to take action. So we feel guilty about something we've done or failed to do. Guilt is painful, but shame is worse. You see, shame isn't about something we have done or neglected or forgotten to do; it is instead about who we are – or rather, who we *believe* ourselves to be. Figure 13 sums up the distinction between them with a simple example.

Figure 13
Guilt & Shame

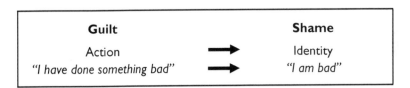

You could argue that guilt is useful and healthy if – and only if – it gives a person the motivation to change and not do the same in future. But guilt can sometimes penetrate the higher levels of mind and the sense that we have done something wrong can become a belief that there's something wrong with us. In the example above, we no longer think we have *done* something bad, but that we *are* bad.

However, shame doesn't always start as a distortion of guilt. Many people grow up with low self-esteem not because of things they have done wrong, but because they drew negative conclusions about themselves when they were young, often based on how they perceived their treatment by other people. Thus their self-image, their sense of identity, became infected with shame. That's more difficult to deal with than guilt. Why? Because a shame-based belief sits at a higher level of mind (higher mental mind) than a guilt-based belief (emotional mind). This makes it not only more powerful, but more invisible too.

Now I explained shame with the statement "I am bad," but shame is more subtle than this in real life, although no less painful. You see, shame is just the overall heading for the negative feelings we discussed in chapter 8 – powerlessness; feeling unlovable or unworthy of love; feeling incompetent, useless or irresponsible; feeling invisible or insignificant. They are all expressions of shame, they lower our self-esteem and expose us to the fears of being ignored, being humiliated or being rejected.

A leader who identifies with his False Self will inevitably harbour some feelings of shame, usually unconsciously. Why? Because identity-related limiting beliefs are the core of the False Self and the feelings they produce are just variations of shame. Now when the leader decides to work on self-mastery, he is putting the False Self's survival in question because it can no longer hide in the shadows and eventually its limited beliefs will be exposed as illusions. So one way for the False Self to neutralise the threat is to send the subconscious message, "Oh no, you shouldn't look too closely for you'll only see what you've always believed about yourself and that will be too painful. Don't go there, it's unsafe – it's better to stay as you are."

So can you see that the fear of looking inward and experiencing either guilt or shame – but especially shame – can be so powerful that a leader may be reluctant to work seriously on self-mastery? In my experience, variations of shame are common among leaders. To be clear, I'm not saying they experience shame all the time or in every circumstance. But I am saying there are subconscious pockets of shame in the psyches of many leaders that can limit their growth, effectiveness and flexibility under certain conditions and indeed their preparedness to work on self-mastery.

How can you deal with this fear? Well, it's not straightforward and at the earlier stages of the path it's hard to address on your own. Not impossible, but hard. If the fear of looking inwards is strong enough to stop you working on self-mastery, you could ask a qualified professional (perhaps a psychotherapist or a coach) to work with you for a while. But if you are determined to work on your own I suggest these steps:

- Ponder on what it will be like if you do not change, if you do not grow. This can sensitise you to the unacceptability of status quo, giving you the "away from" motivation I touched on earlier in the chapter.

- Find out what your values are as knowing them may give you enough "towards" motivation to move beyond the discomfort of guilt and shame. (I offer you a values tool later in the chapter.)

- Know that what you are feeling, although uncomfortable, has no truth behind it. It is just a tactic of the False Self to stop you looking too closely at its distortions of reality. Behind it is just a belief, a mental construction of your own. You created it and can also uncreate it.

- If you are burdened by guilt, learn to forgive yourself. This will demand honesty and fearlessness on your part. Consider that although you feel bad about what you did, you don't have to let your past actions define your self-image today. What you did happened in the past, so it's a fact and it was your responsibility. But it's also true that the past is gone. It's now a memory. The only time that's real is the now, as we saw in chapter 5 and the past has no more power over the now than you choose to give it. You see, what you did in the past doesn't mean you're going to do the same in the future. You may still feel painful emotional echoes from your history, but that's not caused by the past. It's caused by you allowing the meaning that you (or others) gave to your past actions to limit you in the now. In other words, you are letting your past actions control your current self-identity. The reality is that although you can't change the past, you can change how you think, feel and act in the now. However, you can't do that if you base your self-image on your past – or more specifically, on your past actions.

So what can you do? You can reflect on and identify what led you to do what you did without denying it, defending your decision or pretending it wasn't your fault. Then you can look for and examine the limiting beliefs behind your actions. I'm not saying this will be easy and indeed it may be painful, but if you want to move beyond the guilt, it's necessary. Then ask yourself, are the beliefs I held true? And are they helpful? When you know the beliefs are false, when you understand how they limit you, when you are sure you have let them go and know you won't make the same mistake, that's when you can move on. That's when you can forgive yourself and start living in the now, knowing you are a different person, regardless of what others may think or say about you.

Doubt and discouragement

Doubt stems from fear. Either the fear that although the material about Self and the psyche resonates with you, it may not be true and so you will be stuck where you are. Or the fear that's it true, but for some reason *you* won't be able to gain from it. Discouragement can follow on from doubt if you create unrealistic expectations about your progress to which you become emotionally attached – and fail to meet them. Either can stop or slow your progress.

Here are three thoughts that may help.

First, the problem of doubt and discouragement highlights the need for "stickability," the ability to persevere. Stickability is essential and it's wise to accept from the start that self-mastery is a marathon, not a sprint. You are unlikely to get instant results as the limiting beliefs in your higher levels of mind will provide resistance and it takes time to remove them. Just think, how long have you spent creating and reinforcing your mental, emotional and physical habits and building a False Self? Thirty years? Forty, fifty, sixty years? Let's say it's 45 years. That's 394,200 hours. Why would you expect to invest any less than 450 hours (roughly 0.1% of this time) before seeing significant results? I know from my own development and from working with clients that sustained work on self-mastery will take less time to produce results than it took for you to create your False Self, but it nonetheless takes time. To be clear, you need to see your self-mastery project in terms of years, not months.

So like it or not, you must be prepared to take the first steps and try the techniques outlined here without seeing an instant payoff or immediate evidence that you're on the right track. I'm not saying you won't see immediate evidence, just that you can't guarantee it. But the results *will* come. I can't say how quickly because everyone is different – it depends on your existing blocks, your willingness to try and your diligence.

This takes us on to the second thought: the need for faith. Now I'm not talking about blind faith, but informed faith born of understanding. Understanding, that is, at two levels: of intellect and intuition. This is why I offered the new model of the psyche in the last chapter and added scientific data in the endnotes. If you feel the model makes intellectual sense in that it explains many of the challenges you've faced as a leader and is backed by convincing scientific data – and if it also intuitively feels right – you're more likely to trust it and try the techniques I suggest in this chapter. You're also more likely to hang in there and keep going.

You need faith not only to get started and keep going, but to make best use of the techniques and avoid becoming discouraged. Ideally, you'll have no doubt they work because of what you've read here and in the endnotes. Now complete faith may not be possible, but you will need *enough* faith that the techniques will make a difference. You see, if you doubt they will work, you will be working against yourself and you will neutralise the power of these techniques. I explained in chapter 8 that all change starts in the conscious mind, but the limiting beliefs in the higher, unconscious levels of your mind can block progress. Thus, if you don't believe in the techniques but persist with them through gritted teeth, your imagination will be working against your will. In a battle like this, the imagination wins every time. For you can't will yourself successfully to do something you cannot first imagine. Nor can you achieve something you can't imagine yourself being able to do, even if you can imagine others doing it.

So to repeat, you don't have to work from blind faith, but with a faith based on an intellectual and intuitive understanding of what you are (or at least what you may be) and how your psyche works. So the key is to set aside your doubts and get to work with confidence and enthusiasm. But if you cannot do that, what do you do?

This leads us on to the third idea – you could accept something Albert Einstein said, "No problem can be solved from the same level of consciousness that created it." In other words, if you try to strengthen your faith in the techniques while staying in the mental box defined by your limiting beliefs – the same beliefs causing your doubts – you won't get anywhere. So you could use the self-enquiry technique explained later in the chapter to surface the limiting beliefs lying behind your doubt and discouragement and challenge them to see if they are true. If that's too hard for you, doesn't work or isn't practical, you might consider working with someone who – because of their own experience and example in working towards self-mastery – can help you strengthen your belief in the change process.

Pride

Pride is probably the greatest obstacle to self-mastery as it's the hardest to overcome. Pride is the sense that you know all you need to know, that you are above others, that you know better, that you don't need to change or improve, that you don't need to look at your flaws, admit your past mistakes or understand why you made them, or that you're never wrong. Thus, pride will question the need for self-improvement and can halt any work on self-mastery before it begins.

Being realistic, a leader with a personality founded on pride is unlikely to read this book. But it's possible that someone wanting to develop their leadership ability will have pockets of pride in their psyche holding them back. In other words, pride has some hold over them, but isn't completely dominant. So if this feels like your challenge, how do you break through?

The key is to understand the source of pride. It stems from ignorance and fear. "Ignorance" because the most prideful people don't understand that although everyone has different talents, every human life has equal value and we all need each others' skill, knowhow and goodwill. Thus, the idea of superiority and inferiority is just foolish. "Fear" because pride is often a sophisticated but unconscious defence against the dread of "not being good enough."

Let's take a closer look at the fear issue. There are two broad False Self responses to the fears of not being good enough. At one end of the scale – the more passive end – the defence is to avoid responsibility. You see, if you aren't responsible, no one can blame you for making mistakes and you won't feel a sense of failure. The opposite form of defence –

the more active approach – is to strive for success and superiority. Now there are two levels to this. The first is to compare yourself against others and compete with them, striving always to look and feel superior. This means raising yourself and perhaps suppressing others. But it never fully succeeds because the fear of failure is always present – you will always be open to envy and anxiety because other people may improve and overturn your feeling of superiority. So the False Self can go one step further and create an extra layer of illusions to give you the feeling that you no longer have to *strive* for superiority because you *are* superior – you no longer have to compete with others. You now believe it's impossible for others to catch up with you. This higher-level defence is pride.

What can you do with this understanding? Well, first you can realise that if you look at your leadership role through the lens of superiority and inferiority you will always struggle to see others as equally important and therefore fail on the second element of personal leadership. Second, you can ask yourself, "Am I being the person I want to be, am I enjoying my role, am I enjoying my relationships with colleagues, is my leadership as effective as I want?" Then you can ask, "How might pride have entered my psyche, perhaps through my family background, my time at school, my wealth, my position or my fears?" The aim is to see what you have come to believe and detect whether those beliefs have sown the seeds of pride. The third thing you can do is to reread the earlier key 5, *Keep an open mind* and cultivate beginner's mind which, being free of fixed ideas and prejudgements, is a natural antidote to pride.

Believing that the path of self-mastery is selfish

Does part of you feel that focusing on self-mastery is self-centred – and therefore selfish and wrong? If so, even if it's not a strong feeling, it may be enough to put the brakes on your progress by discouraging you from spending enough time on self-mastery. The key to dealing with this feeling is to realise that it rests on a false assumption.

Why do I say that? Because although self-mastery *is* Self-centred, it is not False Self-centred. If it centred on the False Self it would indeed be selfish. But in achieving self-mastery as a leader, you shift your attention away from the concerns of the False Self – survival, defence against inner fears and personal gain – towards service to other people. You aim to inspire them to greater heights; perhaps even to follow your example.

What this means – if you stick at it – is that you'll find self-mastery is not just about you.

It may seem to be about you in the beginning, but your sense of connection with people will grow as you begin to appreciate their importance to the common goal. And as your preoccupation with defending yourself against the fears of the False Self starts to wane, you'll sense you're not as different from others as you may once have thought. You'll realise the challenges you face (which perhaps you thought were unique to you) are shared by many of the people around you. Their problems may have features unique to them, but the underlying issues will be similar. This will strengthen your feelings of empathy and caring for others and it will dawn on you that leading others towards a common goal is an act of service.

This means the definition of self-mastery at the start of chapter 8 is incomplete. The full definition is, "being aware of, understanding, taking command of, integrating and transforming the limiting parts of your psychology to overcome inner divisions and become whole, to grow and to express your highest potential *in the service of others*." Thus, your work on self-mastery is an act of sustained unselfishness.

Overview of Self-Mastery Techniques

Having laid the foundations, let's move on to see what you can do to work on self-mastery. We'll start with an overview of the self-mastery techniques organised under two headings: core and extra (see table 23).

Table 23: Overview of Key Self-Mastery Techniques	
Core	**Extra**
• Disidentification and centring	• Mental rehearsal and affirmation
• Mindfulness meditation	• Knowing your values
• Self-enquiry	• Personal mission-vision statement

You will see there is a division between core and extra techniques. Core techniques are the ones that, in my view, are "musts" – the unavoidable essentials for anyone working on self-mastery. The extra techniques are optional depending on your needs. Mental rehearsal and affirmation is a combination method that builds on self-enquiry; the idea is to use it when replacing especially old, stubborn limiting beliefs with new, more useful beliefs. You won't always need it, but of the three extra techniques, mental rehearsal and affirmation is the one you will probably call on most. The other two techniques will be relevant to some readers, but not all. Use them if you feel they will help and ignore them if you know your values and already have a clear personal sense of purpose and direction.

We'll look at the techniques by category, starting with the core methods. I'll explain how to perform each technique and the benefits you can expect. Listing a technique means that you can do it on your own, but it doesn't mean it's straightforward. In my view, the self-enquiry technique is the hardest to carry out successfully on your own, so (at least at the beginning) you may find it helpful to combine it with support from a qualified coach or psychotherapist.

I will discuss how you might organise these methods into a programme for yourself towards the end of the chapter.

Core Self-Mastery Techniques

Disidentification & Centring

Disidentification is the starting point, the foundation of self-mastery work. It draws on the central feature of the model in chapter 8 – that you are a Self with thoughts, beliefs, emotions, desires and habits in your psychological container, the psyche, but that you are not them, that you are more than them. It's a technique first described by Roberto Assagioli in his book, Psychosynthesis.[69]

The aim of disidentification practice is to free yourself from the habit of unknowingly identifying with your mind, feelings and body and bring you into contact with your centre, your Self. From there you can more easily direct your thoughts, feelings and actions, thus taking greater control over your life and responses to events.

How do you learn to do this? By practising disidentification (from what you are not) and centring (on what you are, a Self). You will be disidentifying from your mind, thoughts, feelings, desires and even the physical body that, until now, you may have assumed was "you."

You see, you have a physical body; it's essential for expressing yourself in the material world, but you are not your body. You are more than your body. If for example you think you are your body, then when it ages or changes in appearance you may feel your identity is at risk. Look at what happens to some celebrities as they get older – they feel obliged to seek cosmetic surgery to protect their public and self-image. But we can take charge of our sense of identity by refusing to identify with our physical body. This is not to say we don't value or look after it, just that we recognise we are more than the body.

We can also disidentify from our emotions. Our language often leads us to identify with our feelings. For example, when we say, "I am angry." Note the words "I am…" This is different to saying, "I sense anger within me." Both statements recognise your current state, but the first identifies you with anger. The second puts an all-important distance between you as the Self and the anger. This is disidentification. You do have emotions and sometimes they can overwhelm you with their intensity, but they are not you. They are constantly changing, but you, the Self, remain. As you learn to recognise and disidentify from your emotions, you will strengthen your sense of your centre, your experience of Self. So you don't deny or repress your emotions; you simply note them from the inner observer's position and then decide how you wish to act or respond to events. This gives you choice instead of being swept along by your emotions. This is will in action – leading eventually to mastery.

Similarly, we can also disidentify from our mind and its changing contents. For many people, especially leaders, this can be tough. Leaders often live in an internal world of ideas, thoughts, beliefs, judgements, plans, problems and analysis and can – and often do – experience themselves as their minds and their contents. But as the model of the psyche makes clear, the mind is only a tool for Self to express itself.

Here's a quick way to experience that you are not your mind. Choose an object. It could be your watch, a pen or anything small. Place it before you. Now fix your gaze on the object and command your mind to pay attention to the object and only the object. See how long you can hold your attention on it. Try it now.

How did you get on? Did you find that you started with the best of intentions only to suddenly notice you were thinking of something else without realising it? Did you find, as most people do, that the same happened after you had dragged your mind back to the object and tried again? If so, consider what just happened. You commanded your mind to focus on the object, but instead it did something else. Can you see that both the act of commanding (which requires a distinction between Self and mind) and the disobedience shows that you are not your mind?

As you practise disidentification and you have experienced feeling centred as a Self, you will gradually find that you become more sensitive to knowing when you are or are not centred, enabling you to re-centre yourself when you need to. And as you experience a sense of centre, you will feel more stable within, but not rigid. This enables you to engage more powerfully, wisely, creatively and flexibly with the changing world around you.

Before outlining the technique, it's important to be clear on the difference between disidentification and disassociation:

- *Disidentification* is about stepping back and becoming aware of – and recognising – the energies within you, giving you the choice to identify with them or not and therefore the chance to regulate and direct them. Disidentification is not about denying these energies, refusing to accept responsibility for them or practising emotional numbness. You may still feel anxiety, anger, shame and other emotions, but you won't have to identify with those feelings; which means they won't automatically take charge and limit your choices. Instead, you can disidentify from your feelings or thoughts, centre yourself and act from a position of personal power, which is one of choice. So disidentification is about experiencing your inner energies and choosing whether to let them run the show. This leads to a key point: if you cannot come into contact with your thoughts, beliefs and feelings, you cannot practise disidentification because to disidentify, you first have to notice and accept that the energies are present.

- *Disassociation* is different and unhelpful. Disassociating is about denying or repressing uncomfortable thoughts and emotions – and, in extreme cases, splitting them off. It can also extend to denying responsibility for your thoughts, feelings and urges. But all that does is to push the energy deep into your unconscious where it continues to affect you ever more subtly, usually negatively, and beyond your control.

The point is that disidentification is not the same as disassociation and the latter is an obstacle to the former. With that clear, here is a description of the technique:

Disidentification & Centring Exercise

The exercise takes five minutes (or less if you want) and it's good to do it at the beginning, middle and end of every day. I recommend you practise it sitting down with your back straight in a comfortable, firm chair with your eyes closed.

1. *First, become aware of your breathing. Notice your in-breath, then your out-breath, your in-breath, then your out-breath and keep following your breathing for perhaps 30 seconds. Don't force your breathing, just let it flow and enjoy it.*

2. *Then examine how you are in your body. Become aware of the pressure of the chair on your legs, buttocks and back. Then carry out a mental scan of your body and ask yourself, where do I feel good? And where do I feel stiff or tired? Consider how your body has carried you through life and indeed through this day so far. And then affirm to yourself, "I have a body, this body. It carries me through life. And yet I am more than this body. I am not my body. My body may be energised or tired, but I am not my body. It is a tool that I treat well, but it is not me. I have a body, but I am not my body. I am more than my body."*

3. *Then turn your attention to your feelings. What are you feeling, right here, right now? Name the emotion precisely – find the descriptive word that sums it up. Don't say "nothing" because you will be feeling something. If, for example, you are tempted to say "nothing," ask yourself, is that numb, serene, empty, drained, relaxed and alert? Be specific. Don't accept vague descriptions like "nothing" or "fine." Note your feelings with interest and accept them. Don't judge them, push them away or censor them. Realise that whether you like your present feelings or not, they enhance your sense of contact with the world and act as the bridge between thoughts and action. And then affirm to yourself, "I have feelings, these feelings, but I am more than these feelings. I may experience the feeling of being excited or sad or tense or anxious or [current feeling] and yet although I have feelings – my feelings, feelings that I am responsible for – I am not my feelings. My feelings change, but my essence does not change. I am more than my feelings."*

4. *Now turn your attention to your mind and the thoughts within. Watch them as they change. Note them without judging them. If it helps, see them as though on*

a cinema screen or as clouds moving across the sky. If or when you find yourself getting lost in them (i.e. identifying with them), stand back and watch them again. Then after a minute or two, affirm to yourself, "I have a mind and I have thoughts within my mind. Yet I am more than my thoughts and mind. Behind my beliefs and changing thoughts I am the one who is aware, who chooses, who thinks. Sometimes I command my mind and it refuses to do what I want – therefore it cannot be the Self. It is a tool of knowledge and understanding, but I am not my thoughts and beliefs. Nor am I my mind. I am more than my mind."

5. *And finally, moving on from disidentifying with your mind, imagine yourself moving into a quieter, still place deep inside. Identify with Self by affirming to yourself, "I am a Self; a centre of pure will, self-awareness and imagination. I express myself in the world through my mind, my feelings and my body. And yet behind them and above them I remain the Self – a centre of pure will, self-awareness and imagination – able to choose who I am and how to be in the world. I choose to remain aware of this fact throughout today. I am a Self, a centre of pure will, self-awareness and imagination." Now pause for a few moments and try to hold and experience this state of knowing you are a Self.*

6. *To close, redirect your attention to your breathing and watch and experience the in-breath and the out-breath again for a few seconds. Then become aware again of the pressure of your buttocks on the seat of the chair and the feeling of the back of the chair. Become aware too of the soles of your feet on the ground and any sounds you can hear inside or outside the room. This has the effect of grounding you, reconnecting you to your normal world. And when you are ready, open your eyes. You have completed the exercise.*

Questions & Answers

How often should you do this exercise? And for how long?

There's no straightforward answer. But repeating this exercise often and regularly is the key. I suggest you try it two or three times daily for at least six months, but you can practise it for years if you choose.

The idea is to use this exercise often enough to start shifting your psychological centre of gravity away from the False Self towards the real Self that you are. This will help you disidentify from negative overpowering emotions or unhelpful thoughts and habits under pressure – making it easier to understand the causes of your problems, figure out your aims and see your options. The result? Increased effectiveness as a leader.

Mindfulness Meditation

Mindfulness meditation is the next step beyond disidentification and centring after you have been practising it for several months. Disidentification is great preparation for practising mindfulness meditation. You can do both in parallel, but as you become a daily mindfulness meditator, you can let go of the disidentification exercise because the new technique covers the same ground and goes beyond. It helps you move from affirming that you are a Self to experiencing that you are a Self. You no longer see "Self" as a concept, you begin to know it as a reality.

You see, it's one thing to see the Self as an idea to play with and another to take it on board as your working truth. Intellectual understanding is not enough because self-mastery is not an academic exercise. It is intensely practical. Only when you accept – at least as a working hypothesis – that you are not your mind, psychological contents and habits can you separate yourself from them, giving yourself the chance to master your psyche. Only then can you not only sense that you may be a Self; you can begin to act from this sense, enabling you to live and work while mastering your psyche.

So what is mindfulness and what is meditation? Let's start with meditation and what it is not. First, despite what many think, it's not a relaxation technique. It does usually have a relaxing effect, but that's not its purpose. Second, it is not an escape from reality. It's the opposite of that. It is learning to see and accept what's in your psyche because only then can you change it.

So what *is* meditation? It is work, hard work. You can also view and indeed use meditation as a spiritual tool, but that's not the only way of looking at it. Another is to see it as one of the most powerful creative and psychological development techniques available. In essence, it is conscious use of the four levels of mind under the direction of the will, which is one of the three facets of Self. This is the one thread running through the many forms of meditation. Now I realise that doesn't tell you much, but it's hard to say any more than this without explaining the different types of meditation, so let's do that. We can split the forms of meditation into three groups and explain mindfulness at the same time:

- *Concentrative meditation* is the first group and within it there are many variations. The common theme in all but one of them is intense focused thinking on and around an object; be it a mental image, a statement, a question, a problem, a puzzle, a habit or a limiting belief. It strengthens the Self's ability to hold the four levels of mind on the subject of focus through the power of will and leads to a clear, deep and sometimes breakthrough understanding of the subject or problem you are meditating on. The self-enquiry technique listed in table 23 is one example of this form of meditation. An advanced version of this form, known as contemplation, aims at achieving the same focused state, but without the object and the thinking. Contemplation takes the form of a concentrated, alert waiting; it is a method of stilling the mind to clear the ground for an intuition or creative insight. It is not a technique I include in this book.

- *Creative meditation* blends the power of imagination with concentration to help you build specific qualities of character, strengthen certain skills or handle upcoming outer events better. The mental rehearsal technique in table 23 comes into this category.

- *Mindfulness meditation* also draws on the power of concentration, but it is joined by the discipline of mindfulness. This form uses concentration as a launching pad for building mindfulness. Mindfulness is your ability to pay attention, your awareness of what is happening in the present moment, but without judging or adding meaning to what's going on. Mindfulness allows you to be in the now and experience the changing contents of your psyche without getting trapped in them, setting you free from the idea that your thoughts, feelings and impulses are all that you are. This loosens the grip of your False Self, allowing you to experience yourself as a Self and giving you the freedom to choose how to be and act as a leader.[70]

Without realising it and without calling it meditation, many businessmen, academics, scientists, inventors and composers use the first form. And many professional sports men and women, often working with a sports psychologist, practise creative meditation although they'd call it mental rehearsal or mental simulation. So meditation is more widely used than you might have thought.

We are now going to focus on mindfulness meditation in more detail. The best way to do that is to outline a basic mindfulness meditation exercise so you can see what it looks like in action. After that, I'll provide further explanation on what mindfulness can do for you.

Mindfulness Meditation Exercise

Note: For the first two or three months it's best to build up your power of concentration before extending this work to become a full mindfulness exercise. Thus, steps 1-5 should be your focus in that period. Only add the later steps once you have gained some experience in holding your mind fixed on your breathing.

1. *Choose a quiet place to sit and make sure you are ready to work on this exercise for up to 15 minutes. Sit in a comfortable firm chair, ensure your back is upright, your hands are resting on your legs and your feet are flat on the floor. Now close your eyes and relax your body, allowing it to settle in to a natural position that's comfortable for you.*

2. *Then, as in the disidentification exercise, become aware of your breathing. Simply notice how your breath feels as it goes in and out naturally. Don't force your breathing, just let it flow and enjoy it.*

3. *Notice any differences between the in-breath and the out-breath. Don't think about the differences, in other words don't describe them mentally in words, just notice them.*

4. *When your breathing has settled into a natural relaxed rhythm, focus your mind on your breathing and notice the breath flowing freely in and out. And just keep your focus there.*

5. *Sometimes – and indeed often as a beginner – you will find your attention has wandered and you are no longer focusing on your breathing. Instead, you find you have been remembering something that happened the previous day, or you've been thinking about a task you have to complete, or perhaps you've been wondering if this is all a waste of time. Whatever you were thinking, you'll realise you were absorbed in (or identified with) your thoughts and didn't notice you had let your attention wander. This is normal. Don't worry about it. The four levels of your mind have a momentum of their own – especially the lower three – and aren't used to the discipline of being held in one place. So you will face resistance. That's why some people compare the mind to a wild animal. When this happens, gently bring your focus back to the in and out flow of your breathing. And if it happens again, do the same; gently bring your attention back to your breathing. Just keep repeating this sequence: focus on the breathing and when you notice you have wandered off, return to the breathing.*

6. *Now you add mindfulness to your concentration. To do that you simply have to notice whatever arises in your mind while you are concentrating on your breathing. It may be a thought, perhaps in the form of an idea, an image or a memory. Or instead an emotion. Or a body sensation. Or an urge to do something. When that happens, feel pleased that you've noticed you're no longer focusing on your breath because that's mindfulness. Whatever it is that's deflected your attention just note it kindly or on some occasions, with gentle amusement, and look through it to the space – the pure self-awareness in which the thought arises – behind it. So unlike step 5, you temporarily turn your attention to this mental event. But you don't think about it; meaning you don't describe it in words, get caught inside it, classify it or scold yourself for failing to concentrate on your breathing, you just observe. Nor do you judge, censor, deny or push away what arises; you just let it be and note it. Notice too how, having risen, it usually fades after you have noticed and looked through it. TIP: In the act of noticing the event you may find it helpful to mentally note it with one (and only one) neutral descriptive word such as "thinking," "feeling," "image" or "sensation." I have found this helps develop mindfulness in the early months of practice without getting caught in the mental event.*

7. *Once it has fallen away, gently return your attention to the in and out flow of your breathing. And when another inner event arises, note it without becoming absorbed in it, look through it to the pure awareness behind and watch how it fades away. And again, return your attention to your breath. Keep repeating this process for the rest of the meditation: concentrate on the breath, note any random thought or feeling, look through it, watch it fade and return to the breath.*

8. *Occasionally you may find a thought that doesn't fade automatically. Don't worry. Note it, look through it and even if it hasn't faded, simply turn your attention back to your breathing. That usually causes it to go. If it doesn't, repeat the cycle of noticing it, looking through it and returning to your breathing.*

9. *At the end, become aware of the pressure of your buttocks on the chair, the feeling of the back of the chair and the soles of your feet on the floor. Then open your eyes. You have completed the exercise.*

Questions & Answers

- *How often should you practise mindfulness meditation?* *Regular, ideally daily, practice is the key and you can go on using this technique every day for the rest of your life. It's something you should plan to practise for years. Remember, self-mastery is a marathon, not a sprint.*

- *How long should your meditation be?* *Meditation teachers have different views. One notable teacher recommends beginners start with 20-30 minutes and work up to an hour after a year or two of practice. I do not claim to be a meditation teacher, I am just a practitioner, but I've found that shorter periods work for me. My advice would be to start with 5 minutes for the first month, go to 10 minutes in the second month and then 15 minutes in the third month. I would stay at 15 minutes from the fourth month onwards, but if you decide to seek the advice of a respected meditation teacher and he or she recommends that you practise for longer, by all means follow their advice. The key is this: don't overdo it, settle on a duration you can keep up! Meditation is like physical training; a little and often is better than lengthy but occasional bouts of exercise.*

Are you thinking, is that it? Is that all I have to do? The answer is yes, mindfulness meditation is simple. But it's not easy. For example, it's not easy to hold your mind on the breathing as it will produce random thoughts and impulses based on memories, previous experiences, long-standing beliefs and how much the collective unconscious affects you. This problem is called "monkey mind" and although it reduces with practice, it remains a challenge for most meditators. The second problem is getting wrapped up in (identified with) your random thoughts, which is hard to avoid because we're so used to believing that we are what we think. How do you deal with these problems? Through repeated practice.

Under point 6 of the meditation exercise it says, "But you don't think about it; meaning you don't describe it in words, get caught inside it, classify it or scold yourself for failing to concentrate on your breathing, you just observe." This is important. Mindfulness meditation is not thinking, but nor is it about emptying your mind. It is about *stilling* your mind by learning to focus your attention and then noticing what happens. If you see this practice as emptying your mind or going into a dreamy trance, you can sink into a state where there is not only no thought, but no awareness, no observation and no will; just a dull sleepy vacuum. This is not mindfulness meditation and if you find it happening, stop the session and return to it only when you feel refreshed. Concentration and mindfulness are not dull and sleep-inducing; the words I would use to describe them are energetic, alert, awake, clear and sharp.

Mindfulness and concentration work as partners in this form of meditation as you can see in figure 14. They are both important, but mindfulness is the objective whereas concentration is only the means to it. Beginners often assume that concentration is the more important and regard moments of mindfulness – noticing when their mind has wandered off the subject of focus – as moments of failure. But that's not the way to see this exercise. Noticing when your attention has wandered is as important as concentrating, which is why you should be pleased when you notice you've been caught up in your mind's activity. Indeed, you could argue that mindfulness is the more important because sensing when you are not acting from your centre, when you are in auto-pilot mode, is a key to self-mastery.

Figure 14

Concentration and Mindfulness

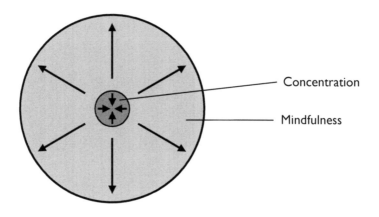

Concentration

Mindfulness

Thus you could say that concentration is 48% of the exercise and mindfulness is the other 52%. Concentration provides the hard focus on the object that stills the mind while mindfulness gives the soft multi-directional focus around it that notices whenever there is a change. Mindfulness decides what to pay attention to, concentration does the work of focusing the attention on it (thus providing a reason to be mindful) and mindfulness notices when attention has wandered off target and nudges the mind to refocus. Can you therefore see that mindfulness is a combination of will and awareness? These are, of course, two of the three facets of Self. Thus, mindfulness is the Self in action.

What are the benefits of mindfulness meditation? Well, studies of its psychological benefits do exist although most are to do with its success in reducing stress and depression. Examples include two studies into the benefits of Mindfulness-Based Cognitive Therapy (MBCT) in 2000 and 2004. The central feature of MBCT is mindfulness meditation to disidentify from negative thoughts and feelings. The studies showed a clear benefit: MBCT halved the rate of recurrence among those who had previously suffered three or more episodes of depression compared with patients who received traditional treatments.[71] However there have also been studies that show the practice of mindfulness improves feelings of well-being. These include feeling a sense of control over one's life, vitality, competence, connectedness to others, fulfilment and life satisfaction.[72]

Here is what mindfulness meditation can offer to leaders seeking self-mastery:

* As you practise, you may experience that your thinking and the space in which it takes place are not the same. This space – which feels like attentive stillness – is the pure awareness linking the Self and its source, the Fountainhead. Now you are experiencing yourself as a Self and at the same time, allowing a greater inflow of the energies of your source.

    You'll find this experience helps you deepen your ability to disidentify and strengthen your sense of centre as a Self. That's because you're no longer just *affirming* your Selfhood as in the disidentification exercise, you are *experiencing* it by accepting and watching the passing thoughts and feelings and realising they're just random currents of the mind. You realise they cannot be all that you are because they come and go, whereas you who are watching them remain. You also realise they are just thoughts – they are not reality, they are not truths, they are just thoughts. You no longer experience them from inside them, that is, while identifying with them. This makes it harder for your passing thoughts, feelings and urges to dominate you. As time goes by and your meditation experience deepens, you will be able to choose to identify with and act on them (or not) in your daily life. Thus, you gain control of your response to inner and outer events, which as you may recall is the first quality of presence, personal power.

* You increase your sense of inner togetherness through strengthening the will – the Self's directing and integrating force – as you repeatedly bring your mind back to your chosen centre of focus. And as your ability to direct your mind grows, so does your personal power and your daily efficiency. You will probably find you use your time better, that you are less easily distracted. This gradually brings you a greater feeling of

competence and control over your life (which psychologists call self-determination). Feelings of self-competence and self-determination are important parts of real self-esteem, the second quality of presence. However, to be clear, together they represent only one of the three facets of self-esteem (the others being self-significance and self-love).

- I found after practising meditation for some years that my creative ability – that is, my capacity to imagine more original solutions or to define a distinctive vision – improved noticeably. My sense is that greater stillness of mind gives us access to what I called the "invisible storehouse of abstract universal knowledge and creative potential" in chapter 5. By reducing some of the useless mental noise, we make space for new ideas, thus building our intuition. And intuition is the fifth quality of presence.

- In learning to see what is happening in your mind as it happens and then letting go of unhelpful passing thoughts, emotions or impulses you're less likely to live in the future or the past (the problem I described in chapter 5). This is because you are practising living in the moment, being in the now, which is the sixth quality of presence.

    So, for example, let's imagine you work in a multinational firm and you are CEO of one of its bigger divisions. And let's say your division's results over the last six months have been well below target and you are getting pressure from head office. Now picture yourself in a meeting with one of your key managers; someone who isn't performing well and whose impact on the division's results is huge. If you are so emotionally attached to your goals that your self-image and happiness are threatened whenever results are below target, you will often find yourself living in the future. That is, your sense of well-being will largely depend on results, achievements and events yet to come – meaning that under pressure you rarely feel good in the now. Living in the future means you will find it hard to stop tension affecting your skill in handling this person. But the practice of mindfulness allows you to notice what's happening in your psyche and let it go, leaving you free to deal firmly and skilfully with the issue in the here-and-now, without getting caught in fears about your personal future. Mindfulness therefore offers a big prize to leaders: to be motivated, to be a catalyst for change, to set high performance standards, to have preferences on outcomes, but not be so attached to results that they define who you are, cause stress and lead you to behave unwisely.

• As you continue your practice, you will probably notice a greater sense of tranquillity during your meditation periods. In the moments of stillness you will see your thoughts as they are without overlaying any meaning or judgement on them. I think you will find this develops into a sense of flexible steadiness and composure when you are working with others and this gradually gives you a sense of freedom. It's the emotional freedom that comes from no longer judging circumstances, yourself and other people on a good-versus-bad scale. This is when you begin to experience a positive state that doesn't have an opposite because it doesn't depend on outer events, including your results, which can take your mood up one day and down another. Instead, it reflects your enjoyment with how you are growing, who you are being and how you are using your life. It's hard to give it a name. Some call it joy, others call it bliss or fulfilment. This is the beginning of the seventh quality of presence.

• Your kindness towards yourself will grow as you get better at noting your passing thoughts, feelings, sensations and urges without criticising or condemning yourself. And as it grows you will probably find yourself extending this kindness to others for as you stop judging yourself you will do it less and less to others. This helps you develop the second part of personal leadership – the belief and feeling that others are as important as you.

Daniel Siegel, a clinical professor of psychiatry and author of The Mindful Brain, argues that what you practise during mindfulness meditation will eventually become natural traits of character and behaviour in your daily life, even when you're not consciously trying to be mindful.[73] How does this happen? Well, neuroscientists are now studying the effects of mindfulness meditation on the brain. We don't know exactly how mindfulness affects the brain's structure – although I've outlined one new theory by Henry Stapp and others in endnote 62. But we do know research strongly suggests that mindfulness meditation changes the brain's neural circuits and can even thicken parts of it. For example, a study by Sara Lazar and others in 2005 showed that seasoned meditators' brains were physically different from those of non-meditators. The zones linked to attention and sensory processing were thicker. The scientists also noticed that the meditators showed less age-related thinning of the cortex (which is key to memory, attention, thought and language).[74]

As you gain experience in daily mindfulness meditation, the aim is to gradually apply it to your daily life. You note any unasked-for thoughts, feelings or urges, view them as though they're just waves in the sea of your mind and bring your attention back to whatever you choose to focus on. And this may or may not be one of those thoughts. The key is that now you are choosing what to identify with; you are no longer a slave of your monkey mind. When you start doing this you will quicken your progress.

It's worth reading more on mindfulness meditation. Two books I have found helpful are Mindfulness in Plain English by Bhante Henepola Gunaratana and The Mindful Brain by Daniel Siegel. The former goes into much more detail on the practice of mindfulness and how to deal with any difficulties that arise. The latter comes in the form of an audio book. It guides you through the practice and the science of mindfulness, especially its effects on the brain.

In summary, mindfulness meditation helps you develop your sense and experience of Self and many of the qualities of presence. However, my experience tells me that long-standing limiting beliefs aren't as visible as passing thoughts, so the practice of mindfulness may not touch them, which is why we need another tool. Thus, I'm including the technique of Self-Enquiry. Depending on your needs, you might also wish to try extra complementary techniques to keep up your momentum and deepen your qualities of presence. These include Mental Rehearsal and Affirmation, Knowing your Values and the Personal Mission-Vision Statement.

Self-Enquiry

Self-enquiry is a version of concentrative meditation that involves honest, penetrating self-observation and questioning. Unlike mindfulness, it does involve thinking, but in concentrated form. Its aim is to help you see and let go of at least some of your most subtle, powerful and previously invisible limiting beliefs – especially those in your higher mental mind – in pursuit of self-mastery. If you can release them, you will express yourself more naturally, powerfully, flexibly and wisely as a leader.

I explained limiting beliefs in chapter 8. To remind you, they are the ideas we think are true (but are in fact false) that control how we interpret and experience life, limit our intellectual, emotional and behavioural choices and cause our defensive behaviours. I gave the earlier example of how a doorbell ringing can produce two different reactions depending on how the person perceives the event. And how they perceive it depends on what they believe. So our beliefs – and notably our limiting beliefs – control our perceptions.

Most limiting beliefs have two parts: they claim something is true and then judge it to be negative. So someone might believe, "I am bad at public speaking and if I have to give a speech it will be a flop, which would be humiliating." Can you see that the first part, "I am bad at public speaking and if I have to give a speech it will be a flop..." is a sequence of so-called truths? And can you see that the second section "... which would be humiliating" is the judgemental part? Note that without the judgement, the belief has no power. Only when you insert the judgement – which adds emotional intensity – does the limiting belief gain control over your feelings and behaviour. It's important you understand the structure of a typical limiting belief because then you know what you're looking for as you carry out the self-enquiry exercise. So the equation is this: LIMITING BELIEF = FALSE TRUTH + JUDGEMENT.

Dealing with limiting beliefs is not straightforward and your progress will probably be faster in the early stages of self-mastery if you work with a qualified professional like a coach or therapist.

The advantage of working with someone else is that they are outside your mental box and can more easily see what you cannot. That way, you'll gain experience in looking for and challenging your limiting beliefs before you break out on your own. Nonetheless, you can almost certainly work on limiting beliefs alone because, without realising it, you have created, used, replaced and discarded many limiting beliefs in your life. Understanding that you did so may give you confidence that you can do it again, although the difference this time is that you'll be doing it consciously. How did you do it in the past? By following the sequence of events in figure 15.

Figure 15

Unconscious Belief Change Cycle

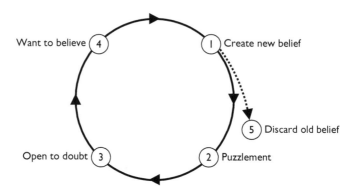

At phase 1, you created a new belief when you experienced something or absorbed an idea from someone influential in your life or instead took on board something from the collective unconscious (for example, through watching television). Sometimes, especially when you were very young, you may have been a passive recipient. But often you would have filtered the event according to any physical sensations you felt, your values, your expectations and your emotional state at the time. As time went by you may have found your belief didn't explain what was happening to you or around you. So at phase 2 you became puzzled. That led to phase 3 where you became open to doubting the belief. From there, you moved to phase 4 where you wanted to believe something more useful; something that would guide you better than the old belief. And eventually you completed the cycle by creating a new belief and discarding the old one (phase 5).

You have done this many times unconsciously. For example, consider your self-image at the age of 15, then at 25, then 35, then 45, then 55 and today if you are older. Ask yourself, what did I believe about myself at these points in my life? I suggest you write down your answers. Did you find that your beliefs changed significantly over time? Most people do. You can try the exercise again by considering what you believed about "success" or "love" at these same points in your life. When clients have done this exercise they've sometimes been astonished to find that within a decade or two they had completely reversed their beliefs. The point is this: you have unconsciously changed your beliefs many times and you can do so again.

So the purpose of self-enquiry is to help you find, let go of and replace your unhelpful but enduring beliefs – the beliefs limiting your effectiveness as a leader – and *you approach it as a Self who knows he has beliefs, but that he is not those beliefs.* The process you will follow, which you can see in figure 16, is similar to the one just described, except that you will be doing it consciously.

Figure 16
Conscious Belief Change Process

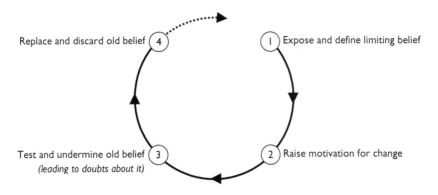

Replace and discard old belief (4)   (1) Expose and define limiting belief

Test and undermine old belief (3)   (2) Raise motivation for change
(leading to doubts about it)

The first stage of self-enquiry is to find, define and expose each key limiting belief by setting it down in writing. I explained in chapter 8 that the False Self's main survival strategy is to stay invisible – which means keeping its limiting beliefs out of sight. You will find that dragging a limiting belief into the clear light of day often weakens it even before you start stage 2 of the process. The second stage is to raise your motivation to let go of and replace the limiting belief. The third stage is to probe and test the belief with questions that undermine it, which is when you start to doubt the belief. The fourth stage is to replace and discard the old belief.

To help you with the first stage, I am offering a tool with eighteen seed thoughts. Each seed thought has its own theme with questions to help you detect your key limiting beliefs. I suggest you take one seed thought a month – but spend longer if you wish – and work on it for 10-15 minutes per day. As a guide, I suggest you spend the first 19-21 days on stage 1 (which is when you will be using the seed thought questions) and the rest of the month on stages 2-4 (when you'll be using some additional questions). Here are the eighteen seed thoughts:

Self-Enquiry Stage 1: Seed Thoughts

Choose no more than one seed thought per month. Reflect on the seed thought questions for 10-15 minutes per day for about three weeks (or longer if you choose) and write down any answers that come to you.

1. **Leadership.** *Note: ask yourself these questions without referring back to the first three chapters. What does the word "leadership" evoke in me – what ideas or feelings immediately spring to mind? And what does being a leader mean to me? What do I believe the leader has to bring to his group, organisation or nation? How do I feel about myself in comparison with those standards? How would I summarise my beliefs around leadership and being a leader? Which of them are limiting beliefs?*

2. **Turning points.** *What have been the main turning points in my life? What special significance do they have for me? What effect did they have on me? How do they live on in my life today? How do they show in my thoughts, feelings and behaviour? What are the beliefs I still hold following these turning points? Which of these are limiting beliefs?*

3. **Key work issues.** *What, in my opinion, are the top three issues facing my*

organisation? How do they affect me personally in my role as a leader? (Note: not just any person facing the same issues in your role, but YOU, how do they affect YOU?) What is it I believe about myself, other people or the world that causes these issues to affect me this way? Which of these beliefs limit my effectiveness?

4. **Difficulties.** *What aspects of my role as a leader do I find most difficult? What are the greatest frustrations I experience in my role? What is it I believe about myself, others and life that lies at the heart of my difficulties and frustrations? Which of these are limiting beliefs?*

5. **Relationships.** *Who are the people with whom I have my key working relationships? Having listed them, consider them one by one and ask, in what ways could my relationship with each of them be improved? What is stopping these improvements? What is it I believe about myself or the other person that is blocking my progress? Are these limiting beliefs?*

6. **Fulfilment.** *What is missing in my life? What would make it more fulfilling? What would that bring me? What is it I believe about life, myself or other people that's stopping me from living a more fulfilling life?*

7. **Resistance.** *Considering what I have read so far in this book, what resistance have I noticed in myself? What subjects, explanations or suggestions have I found myself criticising, rejecting or ignoring? Why am I resisting, criticising, rejecting or ignoring what I'm reading? Is my reaction well-founded or is it the sign of a deeper limiting belief or set of beliefs? If so, what are those beliefs?*

8. **Love.** *Do I feel worthy of another person's love or affection? If the people I work with and those I am close to knew what I know (or rather, believe) about myself, would they love me or like me? So what do I believe about my lovability? And what do I believe about love itself? How do these beliefs affect my leadership?*

9. **Anger.** *How often do I get angry? When I do get angry, is it usually in public or when I'm alone? How do I express my anger? What events, circumstances or behaviour from other people do I tend to get angry about? What are the results of my anger for me and for other people? How does anger affect my leadership? What beliefs are the source of my anger? What do I believe about anger itself? How easy is it for me to forgive myself or other people? If I find it hard to forgive myself or other people, what is it I believe that makes it hard?*

10.*Irritation.* *What part does irritation play in my life? What circumstances trigger irritation in me? What behaviours from other people irritate me? How does my irritation show – what am I aware of inside my psyche as it develops? And how does it show in my behaviour? What effects does my irritation have on other people? In what way is irritation limiting my effectiveness as a leader? In those moments when I'm feeling irritated, what is it I believe about myself, the other person or the event that's causing the irritation?*

11.*Living in the past.* *To what extent do I live in the past and allow old (perhaps painful) private memories and the meaning I have given to them to dominate me in the present? What are the consequences for me of being trapped in the past? How does it affect me as a leader? How does it affect my working relationships? What is it I believe about myself, other people or life in general that is causing this?*

12.*Living in the future.* *To what extent do I live in the future, allowing targets, future possibilities and desires to keep me on a treadmill and not enjoy the moment? To what extent is my happiness – even my self-image – dependent on what happens in the future? What are the consequences for me and my organisation? How does this affect my ability to set the atmosphere as leader? What is it I believe about myself, other people or life in general that is causing this?*

13.*Comparison.* *How important is a sense of comparison and competition with others in my life, especially colleagues? Have I been subtly comparing myself to others, whether in terms of accomplishments, possessions or appearances? Do I subtly put others down, either verbally or in my mind? In carrying out my work or pursuing my career, to what extent have I been doing what I've been doing to win and keep someone else's approval? By what standard do I measure myself? Given these answers, what is it I believe about myself, others or life in general that is driving my attitude?*

14.*Superiority.* *Note: you may wish to review the section on pride earlier in this chapter. To what extent do I view the world through a filter of pride or superiority, perhaps stemming from feelings about my nation, my organisation, my family background, my position in society or at work, my knowledge or perhaps my wealth? In what situations and with which people do I notice feelings of superiority in myself? Am I using the idea of pursuing self-mastery to reinforce my sense of superiority? What is it I believe about life, myself or others that underpins any feelings of superiority?*

15.Inferiority. *How have I reacted to the material in this book? Have I told myself that becoming a more effective leader is beyond me? Do I perhaps feel unable or unworthy to pursue self-mastery? If so, what is it I believe about myself that causes these feelings? Do I fear failure or do I ever feel a need to be perfect? Despite my achievements and career so far, do I sometimes wonder if I will be exposed as not being good enough to be the leader? If the answer to one or more of these questions was yes, what are the controlling beliefs lurking in the background?*

16.Contact with others. *What am I like around people I don't know well? Do I hang back or avoid them or do I make contact with them, include myself or include them in my world? How easily could I adopt a different form of behaviour with people – how easy would it be to include myself (or them) significantly more or less than I usually do? If I notice that it would be hard for me to behave differently, what is it I believe about myself or other people that's causing some rigidity in my behaviour?*

17.Power and responsibility. *How easy is it for me to take close control of a situation and dominate when circumstances demand it? And how easy is it for me to back off and allow others to have control over me when they are better qualified to deal with the situation? Am I able to take responsibility for decisions, projects or initiatives that may go wrong without blaming others? Do I delegate responsibility and give others room to do their jobs their way? Do I notice a habit of avoiding or postponing decisions even when that serves the organisation poorly? Wherever I've noticed that I have difficulty in flexing my behaviour, what is it I believe about myself or others that's causing it?*

18.Openness. *How easy is it for me to be fully honest with my colleagues? What is it I avoid telling them? In working one-to-one with colleagues, what do I find it difficult to say and with whom? What am I like in a group; am I consistently prepared to tell others what I am really thinking and feeling while respecting their right to hold other views? Am I prepared to disagree with others? What feelings does the idea of conflict evoke in me? If my answers suggest that I find it hard to be open in some or perhaps many situations, what is it I fear? And what is it I believe about myself or other people that's holding me back, that's creating the fear?*

Here is what stage 1 of the exercise involves:

- Choose a seed thought (you don't have to do them in the sequence I've shown here) and after reading it over a few times, hold all or part of it in your mind. So, for example, in seed thought #2, you hold the question, "What have been the main turning points in my life?" in your mind and you explore it as deeply as you can. As you reflect, have a note pad with you and write down any thoughts or insights you have there and then – without analysing, criticising or censoring them. It's important to write them down because you will find many of your insights have a curiously short life and if you don't capture them quickly, it's hard to recall them with the clarity they had when they first appeared. Then you move on to the next sentence or question and ponder that. And so on until the end of the seed thought.

- Towards the end of stage 1, review your notes and write down any limiting beliefs you have detected, using the two-part formula explained at the beginning of this section. Try to keep the belief statement as short as you can. Reflect, redraft and redraft again until it feels right to you. If you find that a seed thought leads you to several limiting beliefs, try to distil them down to one or two so you can see the root belief or beliefs. (Note: as I continue explaining this exercise I'll assume, for simplicity, that there's only one limiting belief per seed thought.)

You can expect your False Self to tempt you into believing that after one or two sessions you have exhausted all there is to know on the subject. Do not believe it. Your False Self would prefer you not to expose your limiting beliefs, but if it can't stop you working on this exercise, its next line of defence is to encourage you to think superficially. But it's essential you keep probing the seed thought. There will be times when you uncover nothing new and you'll assume you've learnt everything there is to know and yet the following day you'll see something you hadn't noticed before. Persistence is the key.

Remember that this is an exercise in concentrative meditation. Thus it has two aims. First, to strengthen your will by helping you learn to hold your mind on one subject. You do this not only by keeping your mind on the subject for 10-15 minutes, but by doing so repeatedly for up to three weeks, even when your False Self is telling you there's no more to learn. Second, to help you gain deep, clear insight into each seed thought topic so you can see your (usually hidden) limiting beliefs. Gaining such insight takes time.

Now although persistence is the key, are you thinking that spending 10-15 minutes per day for about three weeks days on each seed thought is too much? If so, ask how yourself, what part of me is thinking that? Could it be a False Self defence?

From day 20-22 onward, you move on to stages 2, 3 and 4. Stage 2 will probably take you only a day, but stay longer on it if you need to. Here are the stage 2 reflection questions:

Self-Enquiry Stage 2:
Motivation for Change

Reflect on the following questions for 10-15 minutes and then write down your answers.

1. *What will it be like for me if nothing changes, if this limiting belief continues to hold me in its grip?*

2. *How has this belief helped me in the past? And how useful is it to me now?*

3. *What would life be like if I let go of this belief?*

4. *How important is it for me to be free of this belief?*

Assuming you want to be free of the limiting belief, you now test and undermine the belief. Again, you have a set of questions to use as a tool and I suggest you spend 3-5 days on stage 3.

Self-Enquiry Stage 3:
Undermining Questions

Reflect on the following questions for 10-15 minutes per day for 3-5 days and write down your answers.

Is it really true...

1. *Can you know for sure that it is true? What is the evidence that it is true?*

2. *What evidence could you point to or what arguments could you offer to suggest that the belief is false?*

3. *How does it always follow that if X happens, Y will be the inevitable result?*

4. *Who says you "must"? (Some limiting beliefs include the word must.)*

5. *Does this belief always hold true? What instances can you think of when it wasn't true?*

6. *Have you ever believed it but overcome it – if so, what was different or what did you do differently?*

7. *Thinking about the [problem situation], what alternative interpretations might also be true?*

8. *Now ask yourself: am I still sure this belief is true? Can I let it go?*

Are the consequences really so dire...

9. *If that happens, how does it mean that... [terrible consequences]?*

10. *What makes that terrible, is there perhaps a more realistic evaluation of the consequences?*

11. *Is this something you absolutely **need** or something you **want**? (Some limiting beliefs assume that what is at stake is something you must have, but in fact it is only something you prefer to have, which is less serious.)*

The judgemental part of the belief is normally harder to undermine, but you will usually find that testing the belief's validity with the first eight questions so weakens it that the judgement no longer makes sense. Sometimes you will so undermine the belief that you can now let it go. Other times you weaken its ability to control you, but it still remains. The key is to ensure that by the end of this third stage you are, at the very least, open to doubting the belief.

In the last days of the month, you move on to the fourth stage to consider and define a replacement belief. Again, you have some reflective questions to use:

Self-Enquiry Stage 4:
Defining a New Belief

Your aim is to write a brief new belief statement. First, reflect on the following questions for 10-15 minutes per day for 3-5 days and write down your answers. Then write down a replacement belief meeting the nine criteria.

Reflective questions

1. *What would and could I rather believe?*

2. *Can I think of a more realistic, helpful belief?*

3. *Or can I restate the old belief to serve me better?*

New belief criteria

1. *It must be something you feel you could believe even though you may not fully believe it yet.*

2. *It must be as short and as specific as possible.*

3. *The new belief must involve change on your part alone. It must not require other people or outer conditions to change. Thus, it must centre on the only thing you can control: you.*

4. *It must have emotional content. Thus, the formula is NEW TRUTH + POSITIVE FEELING.*

5. *It must be something you can verify. In other words, you must be able to see if change is happening.*

6. *The belief must not involve comparisons with others. (If it does, it will weaken your focus on you which, to repeat, is the only thing you can control.)*

7. *It must be stated in the positive. Thus, it must focus on what you are or are becoming, not what you are not or do not want to be. Thus, "I will be less irritable..." is not positively stated whereas "I will be calm..." fits the bill.*

8. *Wherever possible, state it in the present tense – as though it is happening, as though the change is underway. This gives it extra power (see the first example*

below). However, you can use the future tense e.g., "I will…," if you practise mental rehearsal (see next section) as that gives it a present tense feel.

9. *Remember: it must be a belief, not a statement of desire. "I want to be calm" is not a belief.*

Examples:

"I am becoming more expressive as a public speaker and am enjoying the feeling of progress."

"I assert myself powerfully yet respectfully and feel a sense of satisfaction as I do so."

"The more I practise mindfulness, the more I gain control over my irritation and feel a greater sense of peace."

Defining a new belief after spending nearly a month uncovering and undermining an old limiting idea is sometimes enough to help you feel and act differently. But not always. If you are to embed a new belief that's replacing something decades-old you'll probably have to call on the power of sustained attention. This is where you may find it helpful to reread the earlier section headed *Key 7: Understand the psychological laws governing habits and change*. There I explained how we break old habits and create new ones. The main message was this: repeated, conscious, willed attention is crucial. What does this mean in practice? It means using the technique of mental rehearsal and affirmation, which I will present in the next section.

If you do need to work with mental rehearsal and affirmations, I would suggest that you don't move on to another seed thought for another two or three months to avoid losing your focus and trying to do too much too soon. As I mentioned, this is a marathon, not a sprint.

As you become more advanced, you can use self-enquiry not just as a daily technique where you set aside fifteen minutes, but any time you feel mentally or emotionally off-balance. For instance, when you feel a dip in confidence or you are irritated or sense something internal is interfering with your performance as a leader. (This, of course, means you have to be mindful enough to be aware of your inner state. So you can see how these techniques mesh with each other.) The key then is to ask, what is it I believe that lies behind this mental state? As you gain experience, you'll find you can uncover the belief and when that happens it's harder for it to control you from then on. If you find that exposing the limiting belief isn't enough, ask yourself if the belief is true and whether you can realistically believe something else that would help you more.

Whether you are performing self-enquiry as part of a daily routine or as a there-and-then exercise, you will always find a false belief behind your limiting mental state or behaviour. The belief is always an illusion and when you look closely, nothing of it is real. Don't misunderstand me – it can cause real pain and fear, but the cause itself is always an illusion. It will seem real, but only until you put it under the spotlight and examine it closely. You will know this is true when you have tried this exercise several times for yourself.

To repeat something I wrote earlier, dealing with limiting beliefs is not easy to do on your own, but it is certainly possible using the four-stage technique outlined here. However, if you find you are not making progress, you might consider working with a qualified coach or, if your negative memories and beliefs are especially distressing, a psychotherapist.

Finally, let me stress that self-enquiry is not a mechanical process that produces results regardless of how you approach it. It is a creative process and what you get out of it depends on the honesty, concentration, persistence and courage you put into it.

Extra Self-Mastery Techniques

Mental Rehearsal & Affirmation

Mental rehearsal and affirmation is a combination technique to embed new beliefs, create new neural circuits in your brain and develop new habits of thinking, feeling and behaviour before engaging in physical practice. While you can use either mental rehearsal or affirmation on their own, I recommend you combine them for best effect. We'll look first at mental rehearsal before turning our attention to affirmations.

Mental rehearsal uses the imagination. The idea is that you imagine yourself performing a certain act or expressing a chosen quality or responding in a particular way to an outer event. You see and feel yourself experiencing whatever it is you wish to rehearse and doing it well. You can even imagine something going wrong and rehearsing how you will cope with it.

Mental rehearsal is not the same as "positive visualisation." In positive visualisation – a technique you can find in self-help books – you imagine that whatever you are trying to do has a successful result. So for example, an Olympic class sprinter might see herself crossing the winning line with the crowd rising to acclaim her. But mental rehearsal focuses instead on the experience of the performance from within. So staying with the Olympics example, the athlete might see herself standing before the blocks, relaxing her muscles and beginning to block out external noise. Then she may imagine getting in to her starting position, feeling the sensations in her leg muscles as she crouches and the pressure of her hands on the ground. Then she would imagine the sound of a gun, her instant response and the feelings in her muscles as she started to surge upwards… and so on. In other words, you are mentally rehearsing the experience, the performance – not the outcome. Why? Because you cannot fully determine the outcome; you can only fully control your performance. Elite sports men and women use mental rehearsal regularly, but in my experience it is rarely used in organisational life.

We know that mental rehearsal works – several research studies (mainly in the world of sport) have proven it. To summarise their findings, they showed that without physical practice, people who mentally rehearsed performed better than those who didn't. However, they also proved three other points. First, that physical practice was more effective than mental rehearsal alone. Second, that physical practice combined with mental rehearsal was better than physical practice on its own. Third, the benefits of mental rehearsal are greater the more the task calls upon the mind rather than the physical body, which is significant for self-mastery.[75]

Modern technology shows us what takes place in the brain when we mentally rehearse. Alvaro Pascual-Leone, a Professor of Neurology at Harvard Medical School, used neuro-imaging to map what happened when he asked volunteers to practise a five-finger exercise on a piano keyboard. He divided them into two groups: one had to physically practise playing the tune every day for two hours over five days while the other had to simply imagine moving their fingers to play the music for the same period. After five days, scans of the volunteers' brains showed that the area of the motor cortex governing their fingers had reorganised in a similar way for both groups. He also found their playing skill had reached a similar level. In other words, mental rehearsal had achieved the same effect on the brain as physical rehearsal. Thus, the brain changes in response to repeated actions *and* thoughts.[76]

Sports champions and musicians know when their skills and attitudes will be put to the test because their competitions and concerts are scheduled in advance. But that isn't the case for leaders. Leaders don't always know when they are going to face the circumstances or people causing them their greatest challenges. But mental rehearsal gives them the chance to create these moments mentally and practise embedding new beliefs, attitudes and skills in private whenever they want without having to wait for the physical opportunity to test themselves.

So how do you perform mental rehearsal to get the best results? There are four keys: full sensory involvement, vivid detail, image control and repetition.

- Full sensory involvement means you don't just see yourself living and acting out your new belief, you feel it with the other four senses. So as far as possible you also imagine sounds, physical touch, taste and smells. The more you can use all five senses, the more convincing the rehearsal and the more effective you will be in changing your neural circuits.

- Vivid detail means seeing clear detailed images in full colour.

- Image control means two things. First, holding the scene in your mind consistently during the mental rehearsal. Second, controlling it so you experience yourself thinking, feeling and acting exactly as you want, not breaking down or reverting to old habits at critical moments. (Note: on the first point, you will find that mindfulness practice will help you develop the concentration to hold the scene in your mind.)

- Repetition will not come as a surprise. The more you repeat the rehearsal, the more it becomes an ingrained habit.

So the idea is that you take the new positive belief you defined at the end of your self-enquiry work and imagine yourself applying it in circumstances or with the people of your choosing. The first step is to relax and close your eyes. Then imagine the scene. The appearance of the room. Any sounds or smells. The feeling of any table or desk in front of you. The people you are with. The way you are sitting, standing or walking and what you are feeling emotionally. See and feel everything in as much detail as you can. Now you imagine applying the belief in action. From within, see yourself talking, moving and feeling as though the event is real. Experience yourself living from the new belief and expressing whatever qualities and behaviours it brings. Try different ways of sitting, standing or moving and try different ways of expressing yourself verbally until you find what works best for you. Then repeat that perhaps once a day for 5-10 minutes for up to a month. After that you can rehearse on an as-and-when-needed basis.

Mental rehearsal is a skill and like any other it improves with practice. This is important because people vary in their ability to use their mental imagination, so if you aren't good at it you may be inclined to give up after trying it once and finding it hard. What can you do about that? You can practise building your mental rehearsal skill before applying it to your new positive belief by spending five minutes a day until you feel ready to switch to working with your new beliefs. After relaxing, close your eyes and imagine a familiar scene – perhaps a meeting you were in the previous day or a task you were carrying out on your own. Practise recreating a detailed vivid image by imagining what you would see if you were back at the scene. After you have gained some skill in recreating a detailed visual scene, add in sounds. When you can hold mental images and sounds together, try adding in physical sensations – like the pressure of a chair on your back or the feeling of your forearms resting on a table. Once you can imagine physical sensations, try adding a smell; perhaps the aroma of a pot of coffee. In this way, you can practise your imagery skills until you are ready to apply mental rehearsal to your new beliefs.

An affirmation is a spoken positive statement in which you declare the truth of something. You can use the new belief you developed at stage 4 of the self-enquiry exercise as an affirmation. The key is to affirm the new statement aloud repeatedly to yourself in private over a period of time and *mean it*. How often and for how long? There is no scientific answer but Lou Tice, an American coach, believes you may need several hundred repetitions when you're working with new beliefs that represent a significant change from what you have believed for a decade or more.[77] As a guide, you could consider affirming your new belief nine times a day for about a month. I suggest you do the affirmations straight after your mental rehearsal.

The technique of affirmation is controversial. Many sports psychologists think highly of it and recommend it to their clients. But sceptics argue that affirmations are useless. What do scientific studies show? Well, there aren't many of them, but the most recent (in 2009) showed that people with high self-esteem felt better about themselves after repeating a positive self-statement, but people with low self-esteem felt worse. So positive affirmation worked for some, but it backfired for the people who needed it most. Professor Joanne Wood, who led the study, commented in a newspaper interview, "I think that what happens is that when a low-self-esteem person repeats positive thoughts, all they do is contradict what is there already. So if they're saying, 'I'm a lovable person,' they might then think, 'Well I'm not always lovable' or 'I'm not lovable in this way.' Then these contradictory thoughts may overwhelm the positive thoughts."[78]

I think Professor Wood is right. Her view supports my explanation of the mental hierarchy in chapter 8. When we repeat a positive affirmation, we are using the lowest level of mind, conscious mind. I explained that we subconsciously refer potential decisions (and statements of truth, including affirmations) to the beliefs and workings of the higher, unconscious levels of mind. If the affirmation clashes with limiting beliefs in your higher mental mind, for example about your self-identity and character flaws, it will carry no weight. Indeed, it may even remind you of what you truly believe, lowering your self-esteem. So in my view, it is pointless trying to overlay a new belief on to an unprepared mind; it's like sowing seeds on rocky ground. It isn't going to work. Thus, I wouldn't recommend using a positive affirmation unless you had already exposed and undermined your associated limiting beliefs – which is why it's so important to perform self-enquiry before using the technique of affirmation.

Of the two techniques, I consider mental rehearsal the more powerful. But I've found that affirmation does make a difference if you have prepared the ground by making yourself open to doubting old beliefs. And the technique of affirmation does offer you an alternative way of embedding a new belief if you feel mental rehearsal is not for you.

I should add before we move on that you can strengthen the power of mental rehearsal and affirmation by learning new behavioural skills or practising role-plays. But of course to do that you will need to work with other people.

Knowing Your Values

Your values are the ideas, the special class of beliefs, that motivate you most. They are your judgement of what matters most in your life. As the years go by you develop a set of values with some more important to you than others. At the top of your hierarchy of values are your core values. They sit closest to your sense of self-identity, your sense of who you are.

Values guide your priorities, feelings and behaviour. They also influence your mental state when you are not expressing your values. If you lose contact with and stop expressing your core values you can eventually experience frustration, inertia, loss of motivation and depression. If on the other hand you are expressing your core values, you are more likely to experience joy and fulfilment and feel a sense of vitality, which of course are aspects of the fourth and seventh qualities of presence.

It's good to know your values for four reasons. First, it can strengthen (or restore) your sense of purpose, helping you overcome inertia and start working on self-mastery. Second, it can provide the motivation to stay on the road to self-mastery and work through any guilt or shame you feel. Third, it can ensure that *you* set your life agenda instead of trying to meet others' expectations or bowing to social pressure – giving you that sense of fulfilment and energy I just mentioned, thus helping you develop your presence. Fourth, it can help you make leadership decisions that you can live with, whatever happens.

Like self-enquiry, it's not always easy to see your values clearly by working alone, but it is possible. Once again, if this is an area you find difficult, you might consider working with a qualified coach because having someone with a different perspective to ask questions and listen gives you more space to think. But assuming you want to work on your own, here is an outline of a technique you can use. It is in two parts: uncovering and then ranking and rating.

You can see the first exercise as another version of concentrative meditation as it demands deep reflection. The idea is that you take some time to consider the set of questions you will see in the box below and note down your answers in short, preferably one-line statements. You may choose to spread the whole exercise over two or three weeks, working for perhaps 10 minutes a day, but take longer than that if you wish.

Values Exercise 1: Uncovering

Peak Moments

- *Recall a moment when life was especially satisfying. A moment, not a period. See it, feel it.*
- *Ask yourself, what was happening? Who was present? Relive it in your mind.*
- *Now ask yourself:*
  - *What was so satisfying about that moment?*
  - *Probe to get a clearer understanding: (A) What was so important about that? (B) What did it bring me? (C) And what did that give me? (D) And what did that do for me?*

- *When you find your answer keeps coming back to the same value you can end your questioning and note what you have learned so far.*
- *Now you recall another peak moment and repeat the procedure.*
- *Then you repeat again until you have done this perhaps 4-5 times and have at least 3-4 value statements. (You may find that different peak moments are founded on the same value.)*

Concealed Values

- *Remember a time when you were angry or deeply frustrated.*
- *Name and describe the feelings around the occasion.*
- *Ask yourself, why was I so angry or frustrated? What value of mine was being trampled on?*

- *Also ask, what for me would be the opposite of the feelings I experienced? For example, feeling "helpless" might give an opposite of "powerful." Then probe for the value suggested by this positive opposite by asking, what would that give me?*

- *Note down the value and repeat the exercise 4-5 times.*

Essentials

- *What would you miss most in your life if you lost it or it was taken from you?*

- *Why? What is so important about that? What does it bring you that matters so much?*

- *Note down the value you have uncovered in a statement and repeat the exercise 4-5 times.*

Admired Figures & Chief Accomplishments

- *Whom do you admire in life (past or present)?*

- *Why? What is it about their life, character or achievements you admire so much? What is important about that to you?*

- *Repeat 2-3 times, each time noting down the value in a short statement.*

- *In your own life, what do you consider to be your most important achievements so far?*

- *Why? What was so important about them in your eyes?*

- *Again, note down your insights in a one-line value statement and repeat 2-3 times.*

Legacy

- *How would you like to be remembered? What would you like people to say about you?*

- *Why? What is so important about that? And what would that bring you?*

- *Note down what you have learned in a short statement and repeat the exercise 4-5 times.*

You will notice some recurring questions. Questions like "What is important about that?" and "What does that bring you?" These questions take you towards your values because they uncover what it is that matters to you.

When you have completed this exercise you could have a dozen or more value statements, ideally no more than fifteen words long such as, "The sense that I'm fulfilling my potential." The next step is to rank them in importance and assess your degree of satisfaction on each value. You can do this in any way you choose, but below is an exercise to help you.

Values Exercise 2:
Ranking & Rating

* *Write the value statements onto post-it notes (one per note).*

* *Count them and mix them up. Then spread them out on a table in front of you.*

* *Decide which values make up the lowest third in terms of importance to you and put them aside (in no special order).*

* *Then find the values that you judge to be in the second tier of importance. Again, put them aside in no particular order.*

* *This leaves you with your with top third of values. Review them and then take a look at the values in groups two and three. Move any that you feel are in the wrong group.*

* *Take the bottom group and put aside each post-it note one by one, with the least important discarded first. This gives you the bottom third of your total rankings. Now look at it, decide if you're happy with the rankings and make any changes. Then do the same with the middle group and finally the top group. Now you have ranked every value.*

* *Review the total list, check you are still comfortable with the rankings and then write them down, top to bottom, in a table with these headings:*

    Rank   Value Description   Current Satisfaction Score

* *Score your degree of satisfaction on each value (that is, the degree to which are honouring and expressing that value) on a score of 0 to 10, with 10 being the maximum.*

Now you have a league table of your personal values. The ones near the top are your core values, the ones that motivate you most.

Okay, so you have a table of personal values. Now what? Well, now you know what motivates you most. You can use this knowledge in three ways. First, you can see which of the highest ranked values have low satisfaction scores. Those are your frustrated values and you could regard them as your top priorities for action. Second, you can note the high values with high satisfaction scores and ensure you continue to look after them. Third, you can use the table to guide you in defining your next steps, which may include writing a personal mission-vision statement.

One important note before we finish; some people assume that your core values will always reflect the real you. But that is not always true. You may find, perhaps to your surprise, that one or more of your highest ranked values reflect your False Self. For example, a client of mine found that one of his highest values was "feeling better than other people." He quickly recognised this as a False Self value and decided he was going to leave it behind. The point is that you need to be discerning as you review the table.

Personal Mission-Vision Statement

A personal mission-vision statement (PMVS) is one you set for yourself to guide you, not necessarily for the rest of your life, but certainly for the coming years.

Your personal mission (or purpose) is what you are there to do; it is your top priority for the coming years – perhaps even your main reason for being. Your personal vision, on the other hand, is the distinctive way you will achieve your mission. It describes what you want to become in the future and the impact you will have on your world – however you define "your world." Thus, you may have a similar sense of mission to others, but your vision will be uniquely yours. If your PMVS is to motivate and guide you it must, of course, reflect your highest ranking values.

Your personal vision has two facets: being and doing. Although Stephen Covey uses slightly different terminology in The Seven Habits of Highly Effective People (he calls it a mission statement), he caught the essence of what I mean when he said, "It focuses on what you want to *be* (character) and to *do* (contributions and achievements)."[79] The italics are mine.

You can use a PMVS to shape all parts of your life – for example, personal and spiritual development, work, general learning, travel, recreation, relationships with friends and family, money and possessions, service to the wider community. But here we're talking about using a PMVS to guide your development as a leader. So the idea is to create a PMVS defining the kind of leader you want to be – that is, the qualities you want to express and what you want to do with the opportunity of leadership. You can think of it as an act of self-leadership.

Why is a PMVS so helpful to a leader aiming for self-mastery? There are three reasons:

- It energises you and, if you act on it, can bring you a sense of purpose and fulfilment, thus opening the door to the fourth and seventh qualities of presence.

- It sets your agenda in working towards self-mastery, focusing your energy on priorities. This ensures you don't try to "boil the ocean," as a colleague once remarked to me when we were in danger of trying to achieve too many things at the same time.

- It gives you first-hand experience of the leadership value of defining a mission and vision.

What does a PMVS look like? Well, there is no formulaic answer to that because everyone is different, thus each person's PMVS is unique. And that's the way it should be. It could be two short paragraphs. Or it could take the form of a short preamble followed by a set of bullet points. How you present it is up to you – whatever it takes to give purpose, thrust and meaning to your development and work as a leader. The only guidance I would offer is this: don't include specific deadlines. This isn't a performance goal; it's a mission-vision statement. Self-mastery doesn't unfold to a timetable and creating an expectation may only fuel disappointment.

How do you create a PMVS? First, you need to be clear on your values, which is why the previous exercise is a precondition for working on a PMVS. Once you have a league table of values and you can see the main satisfaction gaps, you are ready to start reflecting and writing. As before, I am offering a self-reflection tool to uncover the insights you may need to craft a PMVS that can motivate and guide you.

Personal Mission-Vision Statement Exercise

1. *Looking at the top seven values and seeing where there is a significant satisfaction gap (score of 6 or below), which of these do you want your PMVS to have a positive effect on? For each of these values, write down what you could do to raise your satisfaction level to 8 or more.*

2. *Looking at where you experience high-satisfaction (a score of 8 or more) among the top seven values, which of these values must you preserve at that level in setting your personal direction? Could any of them be False Self values? What might that rule in or out?*

3. *What three character qualities would you most like to develop or strengthen in yourself as a leader? Why? What is important about them? What would they bring you? What would they bring to those you lead? What could you do to develop them?*

4. *Considering your role and development as a leader, what are the three things you would do if you knew in advance that you could not fail? (Note: some people unconsciously rule out certain endeavours they would love to pursue because they assume they will fail. This asks you to forget the idea of failure.)*

5. *Think of the person who knows you better than anyone. If you asked this person to list (a) your greatest strengths and (b) your greatest talents, what would he or she say? Reflecting on these strengths and talents, how could you draw on them more to become a better leader and serve your organisation, community or nation more effectively? What could you do to achieve this?*

6. *Imagine you have only three years to live. What more than anything else would you change in yourself? How would you spend your time as a leader? What leadership accomplishment(s) or contribution(s) would matter most to you? What sense of purpose and urgency emerges from your answers?*

I suggest you take several weeks to reflect on these questions and jot down your answers. They are testing questions so don't expect to have ready answers. Take your time – this could be a life-changing exercise.

When you have enough material and have detected any themes running through your answers, try writing your first draft of a PMVS. Don't expect to finish it in one sitting. Expect instead to have to do several redrafts before it feels right to you. How will you know when it's done? When you look at it and you feel a mixture of excitement and freedom, when you can sense what your first practical steps will be and when you feel, "This is me and I *will* do this come what may or else a part of me will die."

Speaking from personal experience, I found a PMVS essential when, at the age of 49, I decided to exit corporate life and go independent as an executive coach. The urge to change direction was there, but it wasn't focused enough for me to dare to make that leap. Only after I'd defined a personal mission and vision did I feel emboldened to take a step I wasn't sure would be successful, but was so important to me I was determined to try. But of course, if you already have a strong sense of personal mission and vision you may not need this exercise.

Most PMV statements wear out eventually because your values shift, circumstances change or you succeed in what you set out to do and it's simply time to refresh the agenda. Thus, if you want to use the PMVS technique over the long term you need to keep the statement up-to-date.

Putting It All Together – A Long-Term Programme

So you have six suggested self-mastery techniques; three core and three extra. How might you knit them together into a personal long-term programme?

I would start with Disidentification and Centring and work on that daily for at least 6-9 months. During that time, you might choose to reflect on your Values and a Personal Mission-Vision Statement if you want to give more focus to your growth.

When you feel ready to move to the next level, you can end Disidentification and Centring and start practising Mindfulness Meditation. You can go on practising Mindfulness Meditation daily for the rest of your life. I suggest that after, say, a year of meditating you consider adding the Self-Enquiry work to your daily schedule. How long you spend on Self-Enquiry will depend on the pace you work at and how many of the 18 seed thoughts unearth stubborn beliefs needing Mental Rehearsal and Affirmation work. However, I doubt it will be less than two years as you may recall I suggested you spend two or three months on Mental Rehearsal and Affirmation before moving on to another seed thought. Speed is not the priority here so I would advise you not to set yourself deadlines around self-mastery. Growth is what matters; as is enjoying the journey. Did I mention that this is a marathon and not a sprint?

The Key Points...

- There are seven keys to treading the path successfully towards self-mastery. They are:

  - Know the usual pattern of personal change.

  - Move towards, not away from.

  - Concentrate on what you can control.

  - Remember the mental hierarchy.

  - Keep an open mind.

  - Have the humility to ask for and accept help.

  - Understand the psychological laws governing habits and change.

- Where you place your conscious awareness is the key to change and growth as a leader. Research shows that repeated conscious, willed attention to an experience, a movement, an image or an idea can remodel your brain circuits – the circuits underpinning habits in your physical mind.

- The techniques in this chapter draw on your three core faculties: will, self-awareness and imagination.

- There are certain obstacles you are likely to face in working on self-mastery:

  - *Inertia.* The condition of non-will. It is the inability to embark on the challenge of self-mastery or, if you make a start, the failure to persist. One way to counteract inertia is to come back into contact with your highest-ranking values.

  - *Fear of feeling guilt or shame.* Guilt stems from something you have done or failed to do. Shame is harder to deal with as it stems from beliefs in your higher mental mind about your self-identity; that is, who and what you think you are. Many leaders have unrecognised pockets of shame in their psyches. The key to getting beyond shame is to accept that behind this unpleasant emotion there is always a false belief, a belief you knowingly or unknowingly allowed to form. But what you created, you can uncreate.

- *Doubt and discouragement.* Doubt stems from fear. Discouragement can grow from early doubts and unrealistic expectations about your rate of progress. The keys to getting beyond doubt and discouragement are stickability, informed faith and understanding the limiting beliefs behind your doubt and discouragement.

- *Pride.* This is the sense that you know all you need to know, that you are better than others, that you know better, that you don't need to improve or that you're never wrong. Pride stems from ignorance and fear although this won't be obvious in the prideful person. The antidote is a hard one for the prideful person to swallow: it involves self reflection and accepting the need to keep an open mind.

- *Believing that pursuing self-mastery is selfish.* This is a misconception. Self-mastery is self-centred, but it is not False Self centred. In freeing yourself of the most limiting aspects of your False Self in the service of others as a leader you are in truth engaging in an act of sustained unselfishness.

- This chapter outlines six techniques to help you work on self-mastery.

- Three are what I have called core techniques:
  - Disidentification and Centring
  - Mindfulness Meditation
  - Self-Enquiry.

- In practising all three core techniques you adopt the stance that you are a Self; that you have beliefs, thoughts, feelings, desires and behavioural habits, but that you are not them, you are more than them.

- The other three techniques are optional extras depending on your needs:
  - Mental Rehearsal & Affirmation
  - Knowing Your Values
  - Personal Mission-Vision Statement.

- Remember, you can download worksheets for five of these techniques from the book's website at www.three-levels-of-leadership.com.

The only one that doesn't have a worksheet is Mental Rehearsal & Affirmation.

- How you use these techniques is up to you. But remember, self-mastery demands a long-term commitment. The reward is beyond price so you have to think in years, not months.

◇◇◇◇◇◇◇◇◇◇

10

◇◇◇◇◇◇◇◇◇◇

Closing Thoughts

If you have read everything up to this point, you've covered a lot of ground. You may recall that I promised at the start to make the book no longer than it needs to be, but keeping it succinct has meant there's been much for you to absorb in every chapter. So you might want to read this book more than once and make notes in the margins because it's likely you'll notice points you didn't see and have insights you didn't have on first reading. But to make your first reading easier, let's go back over the main points:

- If you don't have a clear view of leadership and your role as leader you are probably making your job harder. Why? Because your unspoken definition of leadership may well be lofty, intimidating and fuzzy. This can lead to unrealistic expectations about the impact you should have and leave you permanently feeling you're not good enough. But if you have a practical understanding of leadership and know what the leader is there to do, you'll increase your chances of being effective and enjoying your role.

- Leadership is a process with four dimensions. First, setting a *purpose and direction* that inspires people to combine and work towards willingly. Second, paying attention to *results and the means, pace and quality of progress* towards the aim. Third, *upholding group unity*. Fourth, *raising and keeping individual effectiveness up* throughout.

- When you see leadership as a process (a series of choices around defining and achieving a goal), you realise it's a challenge that's bigger than the leader. Thus, anyone in a group can exert leadership, meaning anyone could play the leading role in one of the four dimensions. So why have a leader? Because *someone has to make sure there is leadership*, that is, someone has to make sure all four dimensions are being addressed. The leader can do it himself or draw on others' help or allow others to lead for a time. But although he can delegate certain tasks, *the leader can never offload his responsibility to make sure there is leadership*.

* Researchers have been trying to find the secrets of effective leadership for at least 150 years. In the early days of leadership theory, the emphasis was on discovering the key *character traits* of great leaders. But different authors found different traits and the list became so long the theory lost credibility. So as the twentieth century unfolded, four other lines of thinking emerged. I grouped them under the headings of *situational suitability*, *behavioural style*, *flexing behaviour* and *leadership functions*. The last two lines of thinking are the most influential today and their supporters believe the key to effective leadership is simply applying the right behaviours.

  But they ignore the leader's psychology. Sometimes a leader's weakness is that he doesn't know what to do, so you tell him what behaviour to adopt, he does it and that solves the problem. But it doesn't always work that way. You see, although you tell him what to do, you may find he still doesn't act because although he knows what he should do, he doesn't know how to do it. So you give him skills training and feedback on how he is doing. This is as far as most leadership books and development programmes go. But we've all met people who have gone on leadership courses and... nothing's happened. They don't behave any differently afterwards. Why? It's not because the courses are no good. It's usually because what they're being asked to do clashes with their *unconscious limiting beliefs*. These beliefs prevent them from adopting new behaviours through fear or pride. Thus, if you are to grow as a leader you must deal with your key limiting beliefs, otherwise your route to becoming a better leader will be blocked. The solution? *Self-mastery*.

* We can integrate the five lines of thinking on effective leadership and the need for self-mastery into one model: *The Three Levels of Leadership*. The levels are Public, Private and Personal Leadership.

The first two are outer behavioural levels. The third is the inner level and of the three it's the most influential. *Public leadership* concerns the actions you take in a group setting and when trying to influence an organisation or a nation as a whole. *Private leadership* refers to your individual handling of group members. *Personal leadership* centres on your psychological, moral and technical development and has powerful effects on your presence, behaviour and skill and thus on how people respond to you. It's the heart of your outer leadership effectiveness.

- There are over 30 distinct public leadership behaviours. You are unlikely to be good at all of them, which is why it makes sense to share leadership with your colleagues. You don't have to memorise them, but you do need to remember the split between *group purpose and task* and *group building and maintenance* behaviours. This is important because some of us can be biased to one side and neglect or underemphasise the other. Chapter 3 contains a self-assessment tool to help you identify your public leadership learning priorities.

- We can split the 14 private leadership behaviours into the same categories of *purpose and task* and *building and maintenance* although the individual is now the focus, not the group. Once again, in chapter 3, you have a self-assessment tool to help you spot the private behaviours you need to work on.

- Personal leadership has three parts. First, *knowing your technical weaknesses and continually updating your knowledge and skills*. Second, *your attitude towards other people* – that is, believing them to be as important as you and acting on that belief. Third, *self-mastery*. Self-mastery is about committing to self-awareness, self-integration and flexible command of your psyche, enabling you to break old unhelpful habits, keep growing and let your unique presence unfold.

- Your *presence* can inspire people, causing them to want you as their leader. Other people will experience your leadership presence when you have a strong sense of mission and are in the flow, being the natural you, paying full attention to them and current issues, unhindered by fear. You will experience your own presence when you are living and working in the now, feeling focused, able to respond flexibly to events, making things happen easily, skilfully and enjoyably.

- Presence doesn't show as one standard set of behaviours. Why? Because each person's presence is unique. Thus, one leader with presence may be charismatic, but another may not. Presence is not the same as charisma and the leader with presence is more able to endure tough conditions. The root of presence is inner wholeness. Pure presence has seven qualities: (1) *personal power;* (2) *high, real self-esteem;* (3) *the drive to be more, to grow;* (4) *a balance of an energetic sense of purpose with a concern for others' needs and respect for their free will;* (5) *intuition;* (6) *being in the now;* (7) *inner peace of mind and a sense of fulfilment.* Remember, a leader doesn't have to display all seven qualities to be effective; he can consider himself a work in progress. Finally, presence is not a trait of the privileged few. Everyone has the potential to let their unique presence unfold by practising self-mastery and growing their sense of connection with other people.

- Developing your leadership presence, knowhow and skill means paying attention to personal leadership – the focus of the second part of this book.

- On the first part of personal leadership – technical knowledge and skills – I suggested you consider educating yourself in three non-sector-specific areas of knowhow. They are (1) *individual psychology* (2) *group psychology* and (3) *time management.* We also looked at the key skills underlying the public and private leadership behaviours. I classified them under the headings of: (1) *group problem-solving and planning;* (2) *group decision-making;* (3) *interpersonal ability;* (4) *managing group process;* (5) *assertiveness* (6) *goal-setting.* I suggested alternative ways of working on them and offered a self-evaluation tool to help you see your learning priorities.

- We looked at the second part of personal leadership: your attitude towards other people. This is where we saw the moral dimension of leadership, where we moved beyond a focus on good leadership to the idea of leadership for good, which includes the way you treat others, how you see your role and the aims you pursue. In action, it's about viewing your colleagues as people with feelings as real as your own, seeing your connection with them and believing them to be as important as you. I explained that your attitude – along with your competence and the destination you are taking your colleagues towards – will influence how much they trust you as a leader. I argued that the right attitude on your part will drive the right behaviour. The right attitude and behaviour has five characteristics: *interdependence, appreciation, caring, service* and *balance* of concern for your mission and your people. I pointed out that not all leaders display these characteristics and explained why. There are two reasons. First, not every leader is working towards a *compelling, shared purpose or vision.* Second, *the leader may lack self-esteem.* We studied what you can do to prevent those issues becoming a problem for you. In so doing, I stressed the significance of self-mastery in raising your self-esteem and your appreciation of others' importance.

- This second element of personal leadership has an essential message for you as a leader: *if you want to reach the heights of leadership, you must serve those you lead.* This means seeing your role as serving other people's highest interests. Who are the "other people?" They include those who work alongside you, customers and anyone else affected by what your organisation or nation do. A servant-leader aims to serve the greatest number possible – his priority isn't personal benefit or achieving gains for a privileged minority. And "highest interests" may include better products and services. Or improved living conditions. Or a safer, healthier, more sustainable environment. Or political and economic freedom. Or perhaps a greater sense of purpose, personal growth, learning, happiness and community spirit.

- There is a hidden side to this leadership-as-service point. You're not a servant-leader if, *in serving some, you are deliberately enslaving, harming or disadvantaging others – perhaps telling yourself that it's for a greater cause.* Of course, leadership as service doesn't rule out tough actions like firing poor performers or making jobs redundant.

But leaders who kid themselves that violence, suppressing truth and limiting freedom is for the sake of their people aren't serving anyone but themselves – or rather, their False Selves. And it means that leaders who want to serve must know when the majority no longer want to be led by them, recognise it is time to step down and give up their power.

- In looking at the third part of personal leadership – self-mastery – I introduced a new model of the human psyche before outlining how you can work on yourself.

- The model explains that you are a *Self* – a centre of pure self-awareness, will and imagination. The Self is a centre of potential, but not of content. All you can say about Self is that it *is*. But you, the Self, need a sense of identity to express yourself, gain experience, grow, create, connect with and lead others. Thus, you create an identity (a self-image) in your psyche. In that psyche you hold thoughts, beliefs, memories, feelings, desires and behavioural habits, but they are not all that you are. You are more than them. But with your faculties of self-awareness, will and imagination you can unconsciously choose to identify with your limiting beliefs. The sum total of these limiting beliefs is what I called the *False Self*. The False Self is what limits your possibilities, confidence and creative expression, thus blocking you from letting your unique presence flow. Understanding the model and practising self-mastery can free you from the grip of your False Self.

- We looked at the seven principles of personal change and discussed the obstacles you are most likely to face on the road to self-mastery. The seven principles are: (1) *know the usual pattern of personal change;* (2) *move towards, not away from;* (3) *concentrate on what you can control;* (4) *remember the mental hierarchy;* (5) *keep an open mind;* (6) *have the humility to ask for and accept help;* (7) *understand the psychological laws governing habits and change.* The obstacles you may face are *inertia,* the *fear of feeling guilt or shame, doubt* and *discouragement, pride* and *believing that pursuing self-mastery is selfish* and I explained each in turn, suggesting ways to rise above them. If you understand these obstacles, you are more likely to overcome them.

- Finally, I offered you practical tools for pursuing self-mastery. We looked at six techniques: three "core" (*Disidentification & Centring, Mindfulness Meditation* and *Self-Enquiry*) and three "extra" (*Mental Rehearsal & Affirmation, Knowing Your Values* and *Personal Mission-Vision Statement*). I pointed out that self-mastery demands a long-term commitment and suggested how you might combine the techniques into a personalised programme.

Being an effective leader is, ultimately, about you being "you" as you create, express and enjoy your own unique way of leading. Letting the unique "you" flow – unhindered by psychological defences and anxieties – is not straightforward, but the key to it lies within you. The truth is, you and you alone must take responsibility for your development.

To many, the challenge of personal leadership may seem formidable. It may even discourage some. It needn't. I say that because in my experience no leader starts in his leadership role as the finished article. In fact, no leader ends his time as the finished article.

And that's okay because you don't need to be the finished article. You don't need to be perfect, you just need to be willing to grow and keep on growing. If you hold a vague mental image of a perfect leader against which you are comparing yourself, remember it's just that – a mental image. A mental image based on your belief that perfection is a static state you can define. And like every mental image founded on a belief, it's no more real than you think it is. You see, if you try to find a definition of the perfect leader that everyone agrees on, your search will be fruitless. People will base their definition on their own beliefs and culture, so it won't be universal or they'll make it so vague it will be useless as a basis for measuring yourself. Thus, when it comes to your psychological development as a leader, the idea of perfection has no practical use. There is no perfection, only constant inner growth and the only comparison you can make is against yourself. Thus, personal leadership is a growth experience; a voyage rather than a destination.

Personal leadership is worth the inconvenience of what seems like extra work at the start for as well as making you a better leader it offers you a priceless reward: a sense of wholeness, enjoyment and fulfilment. How do you reach that prize? Well, there is an old saying that, "A journey of a thousand miles starts by taking the first step." And of course it's true.

And what's also true is that you travel mile after mile by constantly taking the next step. As it is with a journey, so it is with personal leadership.

As we end, consider this: no matter how exalted or humble your leadership role, the world needs you to be the best leader you can be.

You see, in working on personal leadership, you won't just be doing it for yourself. For as you raise yourself, so you will raise others by your example. Now because leaders can have a major impact on other people, imagine what will happen if you and every leader decide to work on personal leadership, especially self-mastery, to serve others better. You will demonstrate what history teaches us: that it only takes a few committed, insightful men and women in the form of thought leaders and executive leaders to enable change across groups, organisations, nations and even the world. But such change starts with individuals.

Individuals like you.

Notes

Chapter 1. Leadership & The Leader

[1] *A leader's unconscious fears* (page 23)

For example, a CEO might see himself as effective, but ruthless. He might be comfortable with his ability to do the job, but privately feel he's an unpleasant person. Thus, he may believe it's dangerous to be too open with others, as it would let them see him as he really is. And if this happened – so goes his inner script – he may run the risk of painful rejection. So unconsciously, he protects himself by working at arms length – even when it would help the team's performance if he was more open and won greater trust and support from his colleagues.

[2] *Leadership definitions* (page 24)

Examples of such leadership definitions include:

- "Leadership defines what the future should look like, aligns people with that vision, and inspires them to make it happen despite the obstacles." (J. Kotter, *Leading Change*, p. 25, Harvard Business School Press, Boston, 1996)

- "The art of mobilising others to want to struggle for shared aspirations." (J. Kouzes & B. Posner, *The Leadership Challenge*, p. 30, Jossey-Bass, San Francisco, 1995)

- "The creation of a vision about a desired future state which seeks to enmesh all members of an organization in its net." (A. Bryman, *Leadership & Organizations*, p.6, Routledge & Kegan Paul, London, 1986)

- "I define leadership as leaders inducing followers to act for certain goals that represent the values and the motivations – the wants and needs, the aspirations and expectations – of both leaders and followers." (J. Macgregor Burns, p. 19, *Leadership*, HarperCollins, New York, 1978)

[3] *Servant leadership* *(page 27)*

Robert Greenleaf, *Servant Leadership*, Paulist Press, New York, 1977.

[4] *Lists of leader's qualities* *(page 28)*

James Kouzes and Barry Posner carried out surveys of thousands of business and government executives in the 1980s and 1990s. They asked, "What personal traits or characteristics do you look for or admire in your superiors?" They got 225 different answers, which they clustered into fifteen categories. Later versions of the survey led to new characteristics and categories. After surveying over 20,000 people on four continents, they now have a list of twenty top characteristics. We have to be careful with lists of leadership traits because as chapter 2 (and note #6) explains, they differ. Note too that these are not the actual traits of leaders; they are the desired traits. Nonetheless, here is Kouzes and Posner's 1995 ranking of desirable characteristics for leaders from their book *The Leadership Challenge* (Jossey Bass, 1995): (1) Honest (2) Forward-looking (3) Inspiring (4) Competent (5) Fair-minded (6) Supportive (7) Broaded-minded (8) Intelligent (9) Straightforward (10) Dependable (11) Courageous (12) Cooperative (13) Imaginative (14) Caring (15) Determined (16) Mature (17) Ambitious (18) Loyal (19) Self-controlled (20) Independent.

[5] *The "need" to be visionary and inspirational* *(page 28)*

Being visionary (forward-looking) and inspirational are two of the four top qualities desired in leaders, according to Kouzes & Posner's surveys (see previous endnote). I am not challenging the fact that people *want* these qualities in their leaders. Nor am I challenging the idea that it's helpful for a leader to have these qualities. But I am challenging the idea that they *must* possess these qualities. This idea stems, in my view, from a mistaken view of leadership and the role of the leader. It also comes, I believe, from a tendency on society's part to put leaders on a pedestal, to want them to solve our problems and, sometimes, to avoid our responsibility for providing part of the solution.

Chapter 2. The Three Levels of Leadership Model

[6] *Leaders' traits* *(page 34)*

See R. M. Stogdill's article, *Personal Factors Associated with Leadership: a Survey of the Literature*, Journal of Psychology, vol. 25, 1948 (also included in Leadership – Selected Readings, edited by C. A. Gibb, Penguin Books, 1969).

John Adair, a respected author on leadership also comments on this point: "Since 1934 quite a lot of leaders, observers of leaders, and trainers of leaders have been prepared to list the qualities which they believe constitute born leadership. The difficulty is that the lists vary considerably, even allowing for the fact that the compilers are often using rough synonyms for the same trait..." He also noted that, "A study by Professor C. Bird of the University of Minnesota in 1940 looked at 20 experimental investigations into leadership and found that only 5% of the traits appear in three or more of the lists." (J. Adair, *Effective Leadership*, pp. 7-8, Pan Books, London 1988)

David Buchanan and Andrzej Huczynski, authors of Organizational Behaviour, comment: "The problem is that research has been unable to identify a common, agreed set of attributes. Successful leaders seem to defy classification and measurement from this perspective." (D. Buchanan & A. Huczynski, *Organizational Behaviour* (third edition), p .601, Prentice Hall, London, 1997)

Nonetheless, despite the problems with this approach, I have included Kouzes & Posner's survey of leaders' traits in this book – see endnote 4 under chapter 1, Leadership & The Leader.

[7] *Situational suitability* *(page 34)*

One example of the Situational Suitability line of thinking is Fred Fiedler's Contingency Model, published in his book, *A Theory of Leadership Effectiveness* (McGraw-Hill, New York, 1967). He suggested there is no ideal leader and argued that "situational contingency" determines a leader's effectiveness. Situational contingency depends on two points: the leader's leadership style and situational favourableness.

Fiedler defined two leadership styles: task-orientated and relationship-orientated. And he argued that situational favourableness depends on three factors. First, how much trust, respect and confidence there is between leader and subordinates. Second, how tightly the task is defined and how much creative freedom the subordinates have. Third, how much the subordinates accept the leader's power. When there is high mutual trust, respect and confidence; a clear, controllable task; and high acceptance of a leader's power; he considered the situation to be "favourable." He found both task and relationship-orientated leaders can be effective if the situation suits them. Task-orientated leaders do well in more extreme scenarios – whether favourable or unfavourable. Relationship-orientated leaders thrive in the "in-between," more moderate situations.

In essence, he was saying you should match the leader to the situation – and if it changes, change the leader. As you can see, this is a model for selecting leaders rather than developing them.

[8] *Behavioural style* (page 34)

R. Blake & J. Mouton, *The Managerial Grid: The Key to Leadership Excellence*, Gulf Publishing Co., 1964.

[9] *Flexing behaviour* (page 34)

Paul Hersey & Ken Blanchard's Situational Leadership® model was first explained in their book, *Management of Organisational Behavior: Utilising Human Resources*, 5th edition, Prentice Hall, 1988. The model is outlined in endnote 15, under chapter 3.

There was an earlier "flexing behaviour" model from Robert Tannenbaum & Warren Schmidt. They put forward their Leadership Behaviour Continuum in a Harvard Business Review article called *How to Choose a Leadership Pattern* in 1958. This showed the range of choices a leader has around decision-making – from deciding on his own to letting the group decide – and the three pressures he faces in choosing among the options. I outline this model in chapter 6.

[10] *Leadership functions I* (page 34)

John Adair is the most well-known champion of the Task-Individual-Group approach to functional leadership in the UK. Under the label "Action Centred Leadership," he describes it in *Effective Leadership* (Pan

Books, London, 1988). He based his three circles model on group dynamics theory. This model is practical and helpful, but it misses the purpose and inspiration dimension of leadership.

[11] *Leadership functions II* *(page 34)*

Kouzes & Posner's model in their book, *The Leadership Challenge* (Jossey-Bass, 1995) is another example of the functional approach to leadership, but it is more prescriptive than the Task-Individual-Group idea. It comprises 5 practices and 10 behaviours (listed below) that add up to what Kouzes & Posner call exemplary leadership.

- **Challenge the process**
  - Behaviour 1: Search out opportunities to change, grow, innovate and improve.
  - Behaviour 2: Experiment, take risks and learn from the mistakes.

- **Inspire a shared vision**
  - Behaviour 3: Envision an uplifting and ennobling future.
  - Behaviour 4: Enlist others in a vision that appeals to their values, interests, hopes and dreams.

- **Enable others to act**
  - Behaviour 5: Foster collaboration by promoting co-operative goals and building trust.
  - Behaviour 6: Assign key tasks, give power away, develop competence and offer visible support.

- **Model the way**
  - Behaviour 7: Set the example by behaving in ways that fit the shared values.
  - Behaviour 8: Achieve small wins to promote steady progress and build commitment.

- **Encourage the heart**
  - Behaviour 9: Recognise individual contributions.
  - Behaviour 10: Celebrate team accomplishments.

A practical difficulty with this model comes, in my view, when the leader wanting to develop himself tries to apply these practices. You see, just knowing the right behaviours doesn't mean the leader will perform them. Even after leadership skills training, many leaders don't change their behaviour. Often they remain stuck in their old ways of relating to others and will spend their time the way they always did. And if the leader does apply the practices, it doesn't mean people will follow, as the model ignores the question of presence (discussed in chapter 5).

As good as their work is, the missing key, I believe, is the leader's psychology. In my experience, leaders often won't act the way Kouzes and Posner recommend – even after training – because of inner psychological blocks and divisions.

Thus, in my view, leaders need to work on self-mastery. This way, they can let go of their fears, express their presence and use the skills they have learned in a way that suits their personality and feels – and comes across as – genuine. Part 2 of the book goes into this in detail in discussing personal leadership.

[12] *In Search of Excellence* *(page 38)*

T. Peters & R. Waterman, *In Search of Excellence – Lessons from America's Best-Run Companies*, p. 121, Harper & Row, New York, 1982.

Chapter 3. Public, Private & Personal Leadership

[13] *List of public leadership behaviours* *(page 40)*

This table draws on research by Benne & Sheats, published as an article, *Functional Roles of Group Members,* in the *Journal of Social Issues,* 1948. They were the first to note that successful groups exhibit a blend of task and maintenance behaviours. However, I have extended their findings by combining them with John Adair's thinking on leadership behaviours (see *Effective Teambuilding,* John Adair, p. 122, Pan Books, London 1986) and research of my own.

[14] *Tolerating occasional failures* *(page 41)*

This point comes from research by Carl Larson and Frank LaFasto (*TeamWork – What Must Go Right/ What Can Go Wrong,* Sage Publications, 1989). They found that team members have seven requirements of their leaders. One is to create an "action atmosphere" by, amongst other points, tolerating occasional failures.

[15] *Situational leadership (page 46)*

According to Hersey & Blanchard's Situational Leadership® model (see endnote 9 for book details), people can be classified according to two criteria – competence and commitment – into four groups. They are: (1) *High Competence/High Commitment* (2) *High Competence/Variable Commitment* (3) *Some Competence/Low Commitment* (4) *Low Competence/High Commitment*. They argue that the leader should match his or her behaviour to each individual's classification. Thus:

- Group 1 individuals – who are capable, confident and motivated to do well – need a *Delegating* style, where the leader passes over day-to-day responsibility for decision-making.

- Group 2 people – who are competent but lack some commitment or confidence – should receive a *Supporting* style, in which the leader doesn't give much direction, but concentrates on boosting their motivation through praise and follow-up.

- Group 3 people – who have some experience but lack confidence or motivation – will benefit from what the authors call a *Coaching* approach, in which they receive direction, supervision and motivational support.

- Finally, the group 4 people – who have a low level of competence, but are enthusiastic – will receive a *Directing* approach from the leader, with the emphasis on close control through instruction and supervision.

Note: the classification of followers can vary by situation. So, for example, a manager might be good at day-to-day running of her department (group 1), but be nervous about dealing with sensitive "people issues" (group 3). In which case, the leader might switch from a Delegating style to a Coaching approach to help his subordinate on this issue.

The situational leadership model shares a similar problem to the Kouzes & Posner framework. In ignoring the leader's inner psychological world, it assumes he or she can and will flex their behaviour to suit the follower. In my experience, this is often not the case due to limiting beliefs and their tendency to generate rigid, defensive behaviours.

[16] *Neural circuits and habits* (page 50)

Norman Doidge's book, *The Brain That Changes Itself*, gives more detail on how neural circuits underpin old habits (Chapter 3, pp. 45-92, Penguin Books, London, 2007).

[17] *William Schutz's research into interpersonal behaviour* (page 51)

William Schutz first published his research and ideas – known as the Fundamental Interpersonal Relations Orientation (FIRO) theory – in 1958 and updated it over the following 35 years. His key books are: *FIRO: A Three-Dimensional Theory of Interpersonal Behavior* (Rinehart, New York, 1958) and *The Human Element: Productivity, Self-Esteem and the Bottom Line* (Jossey-Bass, San Francisco, 1994).

Chapter 5. Presence & Personal Leadership

[18] *Winston Churchill* (page 74)

Churchill's "black dog" affliction has been well known for decades as was his habit of dismissing others and their opinions. There is an interesting Internet article on Winston Churchill and manic depression at Bipolar-Lives.com (www.bipolar-lives.com/winston-churchill-and-manic-depression.html). The article refers to a letter from Churchill to his wife about his "black dog," mentioning it by name. Bipolar Lives quotes one of Churchill's close friends, Lord Beaverbrook, as saying that he (Churchill) was always either "at the top of the wheel of confidence or at the bottom of an intense depression."

Anthony Storr, the British psychiatrist, also wrote on the subject in his book *Churchill's Black Dog and Other Phenomena of the Human Mind* (HarperCollins, 1997).

An article on Churchill on the PBS website at www.pbs.org/churchill/theman/blackdog.html says this: "As Prime Minister, Churchill's mood and manner were often considered sour by his subordinates. His own Private Secretary, Jack Colville, wrote, 'He is very inconsiderate with his staff'. Later, Churchill's wife Clementine warned him that he might become disliked by colleagues because of his sarcastic manner." The

Bipolar-Lives article also mentions Churchill's sarcasm, his "disdain for other people and their opinions" and his "unwavering belief in himself as a great man."

[19] *Abraham Lincoln* (page 74)

Lincoln's problem with depression has been well documented. An article in *The Atlantic* magazine by Joshua Wolf Shenk in October 2005 describes Lincoln's struggle with depression from his mid-20s onward. Shenk has also written a book on the subject titled *Lincoln's Melancholy: How Depression Challenged a President and Fueled His Greatness* (Houghton Mifflin Harcourt, 2005).

[20] *Peak experiences* (page 74)

Peak experiences are sudden feelings of intense happiness, satisfaction and well-being. Abraham Maslow researched and wrote about peak experiences in *Toward a Psychology of Being* (John Wiley & Sons, 1968) and *The Farther Reaches of Human Nature* (The Viking Press, 1971). He explained his research methods at the start of chapter six in *Toward a Psychology of Being* and in the same book, in chapter seven (pp. 116-124), he listed the many attributes of peak experiences he had discovered. They were:

(1) Feeling whole, at peace with oneself.

(2) Being able to connect with and appreciate others, even feeling a sense of oneness.

(3) Being able to use one's powers to the fullest, feeling fully "in the zone," on top form.

(4) A sense of effortlessness in using one's powers – a sense of flow and ease.

(5) A sense of being wholly responsible for one's actions and perceptions, of being able to act with free will and determine the course of one's life.

(6) Freedom from fears, inhibitions, doubts or inner blocks.

(7) Feeling spontaneous and expressive and being more inclined to be candid with others.

(8) Greater creativity and originality, being prepared to improvise.

(9) Being oneself, expressing one's uniqueness.

(10) Being present to the here-and-now, not being caught in the past or the future.

(11) Respecting and appreciating oneself while, at the same time, equally respecting and appreciating the other person; being able to love another without needing them, clinging to them or limiting them in any way.

(12) Experiencing joy in who you are being and what you are doing, not acting out of any sense of lack.

(13) A tendency to communicate in poetic or even mystical language.

(14) A sense of completion and renewal.

(15) Playfulness, happiness, amusement and a sense of abundance.

(16) Gratitude.

It's not difficult to see the overlap with the seven qualities of presence outlined in chapter 5.

Chapter 6. Working on Element 1 – Technical Knowledge & Skills

[21] *Understand and anticipate the strategic pressures on your industry (page 78)*

Try reading Michael Porter's *Competitive Strategy: Techniques for Analysing Industries and Competitors* (The Free Press, New York, 1980). I found it heavy going, but it was worth reading. If you are pinched for time, my advice is to concentrate on chapters 1, 2, 3 and 7.

[22] *Looking at the business model (page 78)*

The best book I've read on the subject is Gary Hamel's *Leading The Revolution* (Harvard Business School Press, Boston, 2000).

[23] *Teeing up and leading organisational change (page 78)*

Try reading John Kotter's, *Leading Change* (Harvard Business School

Press, Boston, 1996). He outlines an eight-stage change process.

[24] *Abraham Maslow book* *(page 79)*

The book I mention in the text is *Toward a Psychology of Being* (John Wiley & Sons Inc., New York, 1968).

[25] *Jarlath Benson book* *(page 79)*

The book is *Working More Creatively with Groups* (Routledge, London, 2001). It's an easy read packed with practical advice and no waffle.

[26] *Time management – Stephen Covey book* *(page 81)*

The book is *The Seven Habits of Highly Successful People* (pp. 150-156, Simon & Schuster, New York, 1989).

[27] *Tolerating occasional failures* *(page 83)*

This point comes from research by Carl Larson and Frank LaFasto (*TeamWork – What Must Go Right/What Can Go Wrong*, Sage Publications, 1989). They found that team members have seven requirements of their leaders. One is to create an "action atmosphere" by, amongst other points, tolerating occasional failures.

[28] *Tannenbaum & Schmidt's Leadership Behaviour Continuum* *(page 87)*

They published the continuum model in a Harvard Business Review article called *How to Choose a Leadership Pattern* in 1958, reprinted in May-June 1973. I have changed their diagram to fit this text better, but the idea is theirs.

[29] *Group decision-making techniques* *(page 88)*

I'm aware of six ways of reaching a group decision: (1) majority vote (2) minority vote, via a sub-committee (3) consensus, meaning full agreement (4) consensus plus – what William Schutz calls the "concordance" approach in his book *The Human Element* (see pages 197-232, published by Jossey-Bass, San Francisco, 1994) (5) negotiating towards a middle position (6) following an expert's recommendation.

[30] *Projections on to the other person* *(page 89)*

Projection is one of the most common False Self defence mechanisms. Projection is seeing in others what you deny in yourself. In this way, you don't have to face or address your unattractive habits because you tell yourself the problem is with the other person. So for example, you may hear someone claiming, "He never listens" and then hear a colleague of his remark privately to another, "It's strange he should say that, because that's his problem too." The truth is, we often notice in others what we dislike about ourselves but dare not acknowledge. That is projection.

[31] *Emotional intelligence* *(page 90)*

D. Goleman, *Working With Emotional Intelligence*, Bantam Books, 1995. Goleman is probably the most well-known author on the subject of emotional intelligence. He followed the first book with *Working With Emotional Intelligence*, also published by Bantam Books, in 1998.

[32] *Encounter/sensitivity/right relations groups* *(page 90)*

Interpersonal sensitivity training takes place in a group setting. The idea is to give members of the group insight into how they relate to others, how others relate to them and how they can be themselves honestly and effectively while respecting the other people.

Sensitivity training began after the Second World War in the United States and went under various names: training groups, T-groups, encounter groups. Business organisations tried it for a while in the 1960s and 70s but, judging by what older colleagues have told me, it gradually gained a bad name. Why? Because the intense atmosphere and honest (but often distorted) conversation could damage some members' self-esteem if the group wasn't controlled by a skilled facilitator.

I can only describe the sensitivity training I received at the London Institute of Psychosynthesis. They called it "right relations" training. Right relations referred to an inner attitude and outer way of living based on self-awareness, a sense of responsibility for our actions, clarity of intent, assertiveness; respect for the other person and cooperation.

The training would take the following form. We would be in a group of about 12 students, guided by a psychotherapist-trainer. We worked for two days at a time, from nine o'clock to five o'clock, three times a year. We would sit in chairs in a circle with no table and there would be no agenda. We simply sat and talked or, if we wanted, remained silent. You might think that would be dull. I can tell you it was never dull. The challenge was to be true to yourself while respecting the other person and that's not easy.

Working in a group is different to working one-to-one because it feels more psychologically risky. Our fantasies and fears are more likely to influence our behaviour when we're in a group. There's a greater chance that instead of seeing the other person cleanly, as they are, we will project onto them beliefs and stories from our past. And of course with several people present, you can't predict what will happen. Sometimes what you learn about yourself and others is uncomfortable.

Throughout, the psychotherapist-trainer ensures the well-being of everyone present while, at the same time, ensuring everyone gets full value from the training. His or her role is crucial.

I found the training valuable for self-insight and enabling me to connect more honestly, lovingly and powerfully with others. However, you need a degree of emotional resilience to benefit from this training and the facilitator must have years of experience in handling these groups. He or she should also, in my view, have been working on self-mastery for many years.

[33] *Read a book on interpersonal skills* (page 90)

I have no recommendations, but there are more than 5,000 books to choose from when you search under "interpersonal skills" and then "management" on Amazon.

Chapter 7. Working on Element 2 – Attitude Towards Others

[34] *Conditions governing people's trust in a leader* (page 107)

These three conditions are drawn from my reinterpretation of Kouzes & Posner's surveys into the characteristics people want to see in their leaders (J. Kouzes & B. Posner, *The Leadership Challenge*, pp. 19-29, Jossey-Bass, San Francisco, 1995). They report that four characteristics regularly rise to the top: being honest, being forward-looking, being inspiring and being competent. They argue too that these four determine a leader's credibility.

I have combined "forward-looking" and "inspiring" into one condition: direction. I have done so as I believe it isn't essential for every leader to be inspiring. It's very helpful, but not essential. However no leader can avoid the need to make sure his organisation is working towards a purpose they find motivating and, ideally, inspirational. Thus, the purpose must be inspiring, but the leader doesn't have to be – provided he or she is genuine and competent... which takes us on to the next point.

I've also given a different label to what Kouzes & Posner call "honesty." I am not arguing with their findings; just suggesting that in reading their explanation of what they mean by "being honest," the label could be better. They use honesty to mean something multi-faceted. They write that the honest leader is one we can trust to be "ethical, truthful and principled" and they stress "consistency between word and deed" and actions that are aligned with values. For me, a better label for what they mean would be integrity or genuineness. I have chosen to use "genuineness" as the word "integrity" is – and this is a personal view – overused in business to the point where I sense its true meaning has been forgotten.

[35] *Promising executives who run into trouble in leadership positions* (page 108)

M. McCall & M. Lombardo, *Off the Track: Why and How Successful Executives Get Derailed* (Technical Report No. 21, Center for Creative Leadership, Greensboro, 1983).

[36] *Speech by Lt. General Melvin Zais about caring* (page 112)

T. Peters & N. Austin, *A Passion for Excellence*, pp. 290-291, William Collins, 1985.

[37] *Robert Greenleaf quote* (page 113)

R. Greenleaf, *Servant Leadership*, Paulist Press, 1977. The quote is from chapter 1, *The Servant as Leader*, on page 27.

[38] *Vince Lombardi quotes* (page 114)

I found the first Lombardi quote on the Internet. The second comes from *A Passion for Excellence* (T. Peters & N. Austin, p. 290, Random House, 1985). Peters and Austin report that Vince Lombardi made the remark about loving his players in a talk he gave to an American Management Association group not long before he died.

[39] *William Schutz research into interpersonal behaviour* *(page 115)*

William Schutz developed the FIRO (Fundamental Interpersonal Relations Orientation) theory during 30 years of research. He found there are only three fundamental dimensions to our interpersonal behaviour. The first concerns the *amount of contact* we want with other people. The second is to do with the *depth of contact* we want with them. And the third is about the *level of control* we want in our relationships with others. He called these dimensions Inclusion, Openness and Control. He found that people's interpersonal behaviour stemmed from their self-image and their feelings about their self-image, which we call self-esteem. These feelings drive our beliefs and feelings about others and, in turn, determine our interpersonal behaviour.

His two key books are *FIRO: A Three-Dimensional Theory of Interpersonal Behaviour* (Holt, Rinehart & Winston, 1960) and *The Human Element* (Jossey-Bass, San Francisco, 1994).

[40] *Psychology of negative self-esteem* *(page 116)*

The book I mention in the text is *Understanding Shame* by Carl Goldberg, (Jason Aronson Inc., Northvale, 1991).

If you want to read about the childhood origins of low self-esteem and their impact on the brain's development, you could read *Why Love Matters: How Affection Shapes a Baby's Brain* by Sue Gerhardt (Brunner-Routledge, Hove, 2004).

[41] *Peter Drucker quote* *(page 121)*

Peter Drucker, *Managing For Results* (pp. 211 and 219-220, Pan Books, London, 1964).

[42] *The danger of complacency* *(page 124)*

The book I mention here is *Leading Change* by John Kotter (Harvard Business School Press, Boston, 1996).

[43] *The discomfort of change* *(page 124)*

Intuitively, we all know change can be uncomfortable. What few know is that neuroscience is starting to explain why it's so hard. An article called *The Neuroscience of Leadership* outlined what happens. In essence, there are two key influences at work.

First, when we have to consider a new idea or behaviour, we engage the conscious part of our mind, which activates the prefrontal cortex. Now the prefrontal cortex demands more energy than the parts of the brain handling more familiar ideas and behaviours and can only handle a limited amount of data at a time. So changing a long-standing habit demands more effort in the form of mental concentration and that alone feels tiring and uncomfortable to many.

However, the second factor magnifies the discomfort. When we experience what neuroscientists call an "error" – a difference between what we expect to happen and what does happen – the circuits in the orbital frontal cortex send out intense signals. These trigger activity in the amygdala, the part of the brain linked to the experience of fear. This causes us to feel something is wrong. Not only that, it reduces the brain's capacity for reasoning temporarily.

So in summary, handling new challenges and the need for change is hard work for the brain. But not only that, it causes the brain to activate its fear circuits, magnifying the discomfort of change and making to harder to see a way through.

(Source: D. Rock & J. Schwartz, *The Neuroscience of Leadership*, Strategy & Business, issue 43, Summer 2006. Strategy & Business is a magazine published by the management consulting firm, Booz & Company.)

[44] *"They must be concerned about the risks of continuing as they are. They must see the need for a fresh direction and want change before they are ready to consider a new vision"* *(page 124)*

The importance of having your colleagues feel dissatisfied with the status quo and wanting urgent change before developing a vision isn't just my opinion.

Research by John Kotter, a professor at Harvard Business School and author of *Leading Change*, revealed that, "By far the biggest mistake people make when trying to change organisations is to plunge ahead without establishing a high enough sense of urgency in fellow managers and employees." He goes on to comment, "If complacency were low in most organisations today, this problem would have limited importance. But just the opposite is true. Too much success, a lack of visible crises, low performance standards, insufficient feedback from external constituencies, and more all add up to: 'Yes, we have our problems, but they aren't that terrible and I'm doing my job just fine'..." This quote comes from *Leading Change* (pp. 4-5, The Harvard Business School Press, Boston, 1996).

Professor Kotter proposes an eight-stage process for achieving change in an organisation, with the first step being to establish a sense of urgency. He makes the same point I have made in the text: that if people are satisfied with the current situation or trajectory and don't feel an urgent need to change, they are unlikely to welcome a new vision that demands different behaviour from them.

[45] *Paul Dirac quote* *(page 127)*

I have not found the original source for this quote, but Amit Goswami, the theoretical physicist, mentions it in his book, *Creative Evolution* on page 23 (Quest Books, Wheaton, 2008).

[46] *Failure rate of acquisitions* *(page 129)*

There have been many studies into the success of acquisitions. Overall, the finding is that somewhere between 50-80% of acquisitions are failures.

For example, here is a quote from an article entitled *"The Failure of Merger-Acquisitions, Myth or Reality?"* by Emmanuel Metais, a professor at EDHEC Business School in France. It sums up the data succinctly. "In 1987, Harvard professor Michael Porter observed that between 50 and 60% of acquisitions were failures. There have been several other studies since then and the results have continued to support his conclusions. In 1995, for example, Mercer Management Consulting noted that between 1984 and 1994, 60% of the firms in the "Business Week 500" that had made a major acquisition were less profitable than their industry. In 2004, McKinsey calculated that only 23% of acquisitions have a positive return on investment. Academic research in strategy and business economics has taken these conclusions further, suggesting that acquisitions destroy value for the acquiring firm's shareholders, although they create value for the shareholders of the target firm, something that was confirmed by a recent study carried out by the Boston Consulting Group (2007)."

[47] *"...this can make a company look and feel the same to customers, turning what could have been distinctive products and services into commodities. Few firms do well in that scenario."* *(page 129)*

My comments here are influenced by an article titled *"Michael Porter Asks and Answers: Why Do Good Managers Set Bad Strategies?"* Michael Porter is one of the world's leading thinkers, teachers and writers on strategy. He gave a talk on this subject as part of Wharton Business School's SEI Center Distinguished Lecture Series in 2006, which the Wharton article summarises. You can find it on the Internet.

Porter makes the point that firms get into trouble if they try to compete head-to-head with others. He argues that "No one wins that kind of struggle." Instead, he believes, "Managers need to develop a clear strategy around their company's unique place in the market." He goes on to say that, "Bad strategy often stems from the way managers think about competition. Many companies set out to be the best in their industry, and then the best in every aspect of business, from marketing to supply chain to product development. The problem with that way of thinking is that there is no best company in any industry. What is the best car? It depends on who is using it. It depends on what it's being used for. It depends on the budget."

He adds that, "Managers who think there is one best company and one best set of processes set themselves up for destructive competition. The worst error is to compete with your competition on the same things. That only leads to escalation, which leads to lower prices or higher costs unless the competitor is inept. Companies should strive to be unique. Managers should be asking, how can you deliver a unique value to meet an important set of needs for an important set of customers?"

[48] *FIRO Elements series* *(page 133)*

This is a set of tools developed by William Schutz in the early 1980s after years of research. They are not to be confused with FIRO-B – an earlier version that the FIRO Elements series replaced.

Chapter 8. Working on Element 3 – Self-Mastery: A Leader's Map of the Psyche

[49] *Freud, Jung, Assagioli, Ellis, Schutz & Maslow* (page 139)

- *Sigmund Freud* was the founder of the psychoanalytical approach to psychotherapy. He played a breakthrough role in bringing to public attention the idea that the unconscious mind has a powerful influence over our thoughts, feelings and behaviour. He went on to create his Id-Ego-Superego model of the psyche in the 1920s and introduced the idea of psychological defences. Some of his ideas have fallen out of favour since, but he was one of the founding fathers of psychology.

- *Carl Jung,* a student of Freud's, broke away to develop his own theories, which he called Analytical Psychology. He was, with Freud, one of the big names in psychology in the twentieth century and was notable for introducing the idea of the collective unconscious and his own model of the psyche. Like Assagioli, he believed a human being's goal in life is to realise they are a Self and to express their Selfhood.

- *Roberto Assagioli* was an Italian psychiatrist and founder of the Psychosynthesis school of psychology. He believed the psychoanalytical approach was incomplete; that psychology had to explain genius, mystical states and prodigies, as well as problems like neurosis, psychosis, depression, anxiety and shame. Thus, he introduced a model of the psyche as an alternative to Freud's Id-Ego-Superego theory in an article in The Hibbert Journal in 1934.

- *Albert Ellis* was an American psychotherapist who introduced the Rational Emotive Behaviour approach to therapy in the 1950s. In doing so, he became a founder of the Cognitive Behavioural school of psychology, which the National Institute for Clinical Excellence in the UK regards as an especially effective form of talking therapy. His ideas and techniques are now crossing over into coaching.

- *Will Schutz* was an American psychologist and researcher into groups and interpersonal behaviour. He first published his FIRO (Fundamental Interpersonal Relations Orientation) theory in 1958 and continued to refine his thinking well into the 1990s.

- *Abraham Maslow* is famous for his theory of human motivation, which was a breakthrough at the time (the 1950s). The prevailing view then was the Freudian belief that the Ego is in the middle of a tug-of-war between the Id and Superego and its purpose is to perform a balancing role as the person faces the realities of daily life. There was little emphasis on personal growth at the time. Maslow argued for a more hopeful view. He believed we are all striving to become more; an idea he summarised in his "hierarchy of needs" model. In taking this view, he was one of the prime movers in a new approach to psychology called the Humanistic school. Other influential figures like Carl Rogers and Frederick Perls joined with him in taking this view of a human being's drive to express its potential. Maslow, like Jung and Assagioli, also pondered on a human being's potential beyond the purely personal. So he, Jung and Assagioli were unofficial founders of what's now called the transpersonal approach to psychology.

[50] *About the model – key authors and schools of thought* (page 139)

To give you an overview, these were the key authors, influences and schools of thought:

- The psychoanalytical school of Freud, Kohut, Winnicott, Bowlby, Horney and Masterson.

- The more growth-orientated psychological and psychospiritual approaches of Maslow, Perls, Rogers, Jung, Frankl, Gallwey and Assagioli. Assagioli's teachings have been especially significant, having had some training in his approach to psychology, Psychosynthesis.

- The cognitive-behavioural school of psychology of Ellis and Beck.

- The positive psychology of Seligman and others.

- The neuro-linguistic programming (NLP) techniques and presuppositions developed by Bandler, Grinder and Dilts.

- The work of researchers in group psychology, such as Bion and Schutz.

- The influence of eastern and mystical thought. For example, the practice of mindfulness meditation (which is gaining favour in the West as a valuable psychological tool), Zen Buddhism, Raja Yoga and the writings of Patanjali, Wilber, Tolle, Welwood, Michaels and Suzuki.

- Libet's research into free will and conscious awareness and the resulting controversy and follow-up studies.

- Dr van Lommel's report on near-death experiences in the medical journal, The Lancet.

- Recent advances in neuroscience – notably Schwartz's discoveries around self-directed neuroplasticity of the brain – and epigenetics. (Epigenetics is the study of the previously hidden factors that turn genes on and off, such as stress and the environment.)

The specific books and articles I have found helpful are listed in the bibliography.

[51] *Love and Power* (page 140)

Anthony Stevens, in his book, *Jung: A Very Short Introduction*, remarks of Carl Jung, the renowned psychologist on page 46, "Again and again, he refers to the masculine and the feminine as two great archetypal principles, coexisting as equal and complementary parts of a balanced cosmic system, as expressed in the interplay of yin and yang in Taoist philosophy." (See the chapter 8 bibliography for the details on Stevens' book.) I believe Jung was referring to what I have called Power and Love in this book.

[52] *Relation of power and love to Maslow's theory* (page 141)

I am not suggesting Maslow talked about these forces in his writings. But I do contend that Power and Love are the primary forces behind the three purely psychological needs in his hierarchy: belonging, esteem and self-actualisation.

[53] *Maslow's model of motivation* (page 142)

The first four (lower) needs, according to Maslow, are "deficit needs." They are like holes a human being must plug – or partially plug, at least – before he seeks higher needs. But the highest need – self-actualisation – is a "being need." With this, there is no sense of lack, more a sense of the joy of life, of being alive. This is living to our true potential, instead of simply coping with our daily worries. Self-actualisation is about expressing our values, talents and unique strengths to the full; to be everything we are and more… and feel a sense of joy and wholeness as we do so. At its highest level – what Maslow called "transcendent self-actualisation" – the person feels such a connection with others (indeed, experiences a sense of oneness with the world) that he or she works to raise all. This is where self-actualisation, wholeness and presence start to merge.

[54] *Signature character strengths* (page 144)

Martin Seligman is the leading researcher in positive psychology; the study of well-being and happiness. He coined the term "signature character strengths." His research revealed that using our signature character strengths in action – in the service of something greater than us – is what brings durable "authentic happiness." Seligman defines 24 character strengths. According to his theory, the top five are your signature strengths; the ones most deeply characteristic of you. You can read more in his book, *Authentic Happiness* (see bibliography for chapter 8).

[55] *Crisis of purpose and meaning* (page 145)

Some call it a mid-life crisis, although this is a misnomer, as it doesn't always arise in mid-life. Others call it an "existential crisis." It involves deep doubts and questions about (a) the purpose of life in general and (b) the purpose and significance of your own life. It can show as a loss of motivation; depression; or a sense of pointlessness, like being a hamster on a wheel going nowhere. But not everyone experiences a crisis of purpose and meaning. The False Self can suppress the Self's drive for a sense of purpose by making the need for fulfilment seem abnormal. Writers on life purpose include Viktor Frankl, the founder of Logotherapy and John Whitmore (see the bibliography for chapter 8).

[56] "The wellspring of conscience" *(page 145)*

This is not the same as the "shoulds" and "should nots" we take in from society and our parents as we grow up. I am not denying the presence of a superego-type formation in the psyche in which a person internalises the norms and expectations of parents, family and society. However, in this model, the superego beliefs are in what I call the False Self structure. This plays a different, less positive, role to that of the Fountainhead.

[57] "The will is not all-powerful" *(page 147)*

The will is not all-powerful. Other forces can hijack, distort, block or distract the will. They include the imagination, limiting beliefs – working through either a negative self-image, fear or strong emotional attachments – and the untamed goings-on of the mind. We'll look at each in turn.

The imagination can block the will. In a struggle between the will and the imagination, imagination wins. For you can't will yourself to do something you cannot first imagine. Nor can you perform something you can't imagine yourself being able to do, even if you can imagine others doing it. What stops you being able to imagine something? Two obstacles. First, ignorance (for example, a lack of knowhow). Second, limiting beliefs – especially around your right, worthiness or ability to be or do whatever it is you would like to imagine.

Limiting beliefs can also block the will through fear or strong emotional attachments.

- A powerful fear can block the will because it can stop you even considering certain actions. For example, you may fear that following a course of action could embarrass or humiliate you, cause others to reject you or lead you to feel a failure. Such a fear flows from strong limiting beliefs about yourself, others, the world or your abilities.

- Powerful emotional attachments can hijack and distort the will. When we see our aim as a strong preference, we can invoke enough desire to take action. That's when the will is in control; when the will is master and desire is servant. But we can become so attached to a goal that our happiness – and even our self-image – is at risk if we don't reach it. The aim is then no longer a strong preference. It becomes a "must." We believe we must have it or achieve it before we can feel at ease. Examples include finding the perfect partner, becoming rich, getting a certain job or completing a takeover. But the sense of lack, the sense that we're incomplete without the object of our desire, stems from a limiting belief about ourselves. And this limiting belief uses desire – the desire to do or have something that makes us feel better about ourselves – to hijack the will. Thus, that belief – via desire – becomes the controlling force. How is this relevant to leaders? Well, there can be two results. First, if desire hijacks the will, we can go after foolish or even harmful aims, which can lead an entire organisation or even a nation down a path it later regrets. Second, we'll experience stress if we don't – or it seems we won't – get what we want. Not only does this make a leader's job less enjoyable, it induces tension, can harm his decisions, encourage him to look for scapegoats and reduce his ability to inspire others.

The untamed mind's random activity – what Buddhism calls "monkey mind" – can also distract the will. Anyone who has meditated knows this problem. Try focusing your mind on something – an object on the table in front of you, your watch or a mental image – and see how long you can hold it in your attention without thinking about something else. You'll usually find your mind strays on to another subject without you realising it and only afterward do you notice you are no longer focused on your target. This is "monkey mind." It proves what all seasoned meditators know: the untamed mind is a boiling lake of fantasies, worries, ideas, thoughts, feelings and desires that come and go at random. It's got a momentum of its own. So until you strengthen your will with concentration exercises and learn to use it skilfully, your mind's "monkey" tendencies can deflect the will.

Although the will isn't all-powerful, it has the crucial directing role in the psyche. Its place is to skilfully align, focus and direct our intuition, thinking, feelings, desires, body sensations and even our imagination towards ends we consider important.

The trouble is, emergence of a False Self (a scaffolding of limiting beliefs) can thwart this design. When a person is under the control of their False Self, it reduces their capacity for free will because the mind's limiting beliefs are running the show, throwing up the blocks and distractions I've just outlined. So the False Self is at the root of most of a leader's difficulties in applying his will. I say "most" because obstacles also flow from the collective unconscious, but this isn't the place to discuss them.

[58] *The act of will* (page 147)

The act of will is not just a matter of deciding or choosing, as some people think. There is more to it than that. Roberto Assagioli outlined the six stages of the act of will in his book, *The Act of Will* (see chapter 8 bibliography). His six stages were:

1. Purpose (or aim or goal)/evaluation/motivation/intent
2. Deliberation
3. Choice and decision
4. Strengthening faith/conviction/certainty
5. Planning
6. Directing the execution

Before explaining them, I'd like to make two points:

- Not every act of will follows these stages consciously – or needs to follow them – because your aims or problems may not demand such thoroughness, perhaps because what you're aiming to do is so simple or familiar. What he outlined was a model of complete, purposeful action because some important acts of will demand careful thought and step-by-step execution.

- The six stages aren't equally important in every act of will. One act of will may demand close attention to one stage and hardly any to the others. Another may stress different stages. So for example, a student leaving university may have to spend much time pondering her career goals and deliberating on the alternatives. After that, the decision may come easily and assuming her choice fits her talents and values well, she may have no doubts over her ability to reach her goal – meaning the faith, conviction and certainty stage would need no attention. Perhaps she will spend some time on working up a plan, but not use much energy on directing herself as she's so motivated. A top professional tennis player, on the other hand, may have a clear goal to win Wimbledon and spend no time on deliberation and making a choice, nor have difficulty in working out a plan or sticking to it. But he may doubt his ability to reach this prize, in which case working on faith/conviction/certainty would be the key for him.

With that said, here's my summary of Assagioli's six-stage model of the act of will:

1. *Purpose/aim/goal – based on evaluation, motivation and intent.* The act of will always involves a purpose, a vision or a goal you want to reach. But although this is the beginning, it's not yet will in action as it remains in the realm of imagination. Thus will and imagination are closely bound. If you are to act on the purpose, you must evaluate it – meaning you will assess how important it is to you. And for you to act, the evaluation must arouse motives strong enough to create a powerful intent to achieve the goal. What arouses the motives? Your values. Your values are beliefs about what is important to you, what you care about most and, therefore, what naturally motivate you. Thus, your values are the mould on which sit your most naturally motivating goals. This first stage is more complex than it looks as it can come about in more ways than one, which Assagioli explained when he wrote:

> "In the ... [first] stage, four elements have been grouped because they are interrelated in such a way that they should not be treated as different stages. In fact, a purpose is the will to reach a goal, an objective; but a goal is not such if it is not regarded as valuable. Similarly, a motive is not a motive if it does not "move," if it does not impel toward a goal. And the direction of the motive is given by intention.
>
> Moreover, these aspects do not always succeed each other in a fixed order. Sometimes a motive or an intention appears first to the consciousness, for example, a prompting toward some ideal not yet clear or defined. Or one becomes aware of a moral, social, aesthetic, or religious value, which only later becomes connected to an aim, a specific goal to be achieved. At other times the vision comes first, the intuitive flash, the illumination that reveals a goal or a task to which a value is then attributed; and this arouses the motives which urge toward actualisation and the intention to achieve it. Thus there can be

a variety of dynamic relationships among purpose, evaluation, motive and intention."

(The Act Of Will by Roberto Assagioli, Psychosynthesis & Education Trust, 1974, pp.140-141.)

2. *Deliberation.* You may find yourself with alternative aims, all of which you find motivating. So before making a choice, you must decide which you prefer. This is deliberation. It will probably centre on which aim is most important to you right now (that is, fits your values best). It may also consider which goals are most realistic for you, whether this is the best moment to act, the rewards for achieving the aim and the penalties for missing it – for you and others. This is when your beliefs about yourself, the world and other people will act as a filter as you deliberate. Thus, your limiting beliefs can and usually do affect your deliberations, ruling certain directions in or out. For example, if you believe yourself to be a victim of life, doomed to endure disappointment after disappointment, you're less likely to consider bold, risky goals. Of course, it's also important to consider the problem that led you to seek a purpose in the first case and ask, which of the aims best deals with the issue? Finally, the deliberation stage is where you may ask others for their perspective and advice.

Sometimes the deliberation phase will demand you be ruthlessly honest with yourself to see your true motives; motives that may be more selfish than you'd care to admit – motives you wouldn't act on once exposed. The trouble is, your limiting beliefs may have led you to create psychological defences that make it harder to see your true motives. Thus, it can sometimes be hard to stop yourself going after an unwise or harmful goal. Deliberation can therefore be a complex stage in the act of will, demanding great insight.

3. *Choice and decision.* This is where, having deliberated, you choose one goal and let go of the others. This can be hard for those who dislike taking responsibility because of fear of failure or fear of making a mistake. It is the stage some mistakenly think is the act of will.

4. Strengthening faith/conviction/certainty. This is the beginning of the action phase. It's where you must come to believe without doubt that you'll succeed, giving you the energy to drive through to completion. You must have complete faith, complete conviction that despite obstacles, you will achieve your purpose – or at least, enough faith and enough conviction. This stage is therefore about aligning your will and imagination. It's crucial, because as I mentioned earlier, in any battle between the will and imagination, the imagination wins.

Faith largely depends on how we see ourselves – or rather, our beliefs about ourselves. People will vary in their degree of faith about the result depending, of course, on whether their self-beliefs allow them to believe they should even consider such a goal. Conviction is different – it's more intellectual; it stems from believing you will find the means to achieve the goal, that your faith is justified. Faith and conviction together bring the degree of certainty that you're right to push ahead, allowing determined action. This is why it can be essential to strengthen your faith and conviction through affirmation techniques, including mental rehearsal. But it's not only about strengthening work. It's also about seeing and dissolving negative beliefs standing in the way of the goal.

In my experience, this stage of the act of will is one many leaders ignore or don't understand. Top sportsmen and women, however, are more likely to recognise its importance, especially if they work with a sports psychologist.

5. Planning. Next, you need a plan. First, you'll need to consider your starting point and pressures from any other goals you're working towards. With an especially complex or demanding goal you may have to consider alternative means of execution, their different phases and timings, and the money and support you'll need from other people. Here, the will can draw on the imagination to envisage different ways of achieving the plan before you assess the pros and cons and decide which make most sense. It's also important to consider in advance what may go wrong and how you'd respond if it did. Finally, this is where you look at yourself and ask, "What habits do I have that may sabotage what I'm trying to achieve here… and what will I do about them?"

6. *Directing the execution.* This is not the same as carrying out the plan, it's directing it. So will directs execution by skilfully combining the powers of the psyche, including its partner in the act of will, the imagination. Thus, it orchestrates your intuition, thinking and imagining plus the way you use your feelings and body sensations to communicate, connect with and influence others. Direction includes (a) nudging the intellect to check the plan is on track; (b) ensuring problem-solving happens when it needs to; (c) adapting to new circumstances; and (d) seeing if surprise events demand a change of plan. You could liken the will to the conductor of an orchestra. It's not playing any of the instruments, but it's having an effect on what music the orchestra plays and how it sounds.

[59] *How this model fits with Libet's experiments and the resulting controversy (page 147)*

This model is consistent with Benjamin Libet's findings in his "free will" experiments in the 1980s; research that's been controversial in psychology, philosophy and neuroscience since then. You can read summaries of Libet's work in *Conscious Intention and Brain Activity*, an article by Benjamin Libet and Patrick Haggard in the Journal of Consciousness Studies (see bibliography). You can also read about it and the debate following Libet's work on Peter Hankins' weblog, *Conscious Entities*, at www.consciousentities.com. There you will find an article titled *Libet's Short Delay* (dated June 2005), a follow up article, *Unconscious Decisions* (April 2008) and then a second follow-up, *Libet was wrong…?* (September 2009). Jeffrey Schwartz also gives an account of Libet's work in *The Mind & The Brain* – this too is listed in the bibliography.

Libet found that when he asked subjects to flex their wrist whenever they chose, their brains showed a build-up of unconscious electrical activity (dubbed the "readiness potential") in the region governing motor activity about $5/10^{ths}$ of a second before they acted. And yet when they declared their conscious decision to act, this came only $2/10^{ths}$ of a second before the action. In other words, there was unconscious brain activity before they became aware of their decision to flex their wrist. Later, slightly different experiments by other researchers broadly confirmed this finding, with a 2008 study showing unconscious mental activity up to ten seconds before the person became aware of a decision to act.

Many scientists have taken Libet's results to mean we don't have free will. They believe the electrical activity is the brain deciding to act. In their view, the brain is calling the shots unconsciously and we become aware of the already-made decision shortly afterward. Thus, they argue, the will – and therefore our experience of free will – is an illusion. This line of thinking doesn't fit with the model offered in this book, which puts will alongside self-awareness and imagination at the heart of the Self, but it's the dominant view in neuroscience at present.

Now although it's the dominant view, it's not the unanimous view. Some philosophers and scientists have challenged this conclusion. They point out that although the build up of electrical activity is a fact – the assumption that it reflects an unconscious decision driving specific behaviour is just that; an assumption. They argue it could mean something else. Now this is where you need to know that Libet's research showed the brain's unconscious electrical activity didn't always lead to flexing the wrist. Peter Hankins reports that Libet asked some subjects to form an intent to act and then change their mind at the last moment. Libet found the readiness potential appeared and then faded. So this weakened the argument that the build up of readiness potential reflects the firm, unconscious decision to act. It could instead be a preparation to act or a "getting ready" that the subject could still reverse.

This led to new, more recent experiments:

- Christoph Herrmann and others (you will find their 2008 paper in the bibliography) asked people to watch a computer screen and, depending on what it told them to do, to press one of two buttons. They found the electrical brain activity, just like Libet. But intriguingly, it was already present before the computer told the subjects what to do – and therefore before they could decide which button to press. They inferred that the readiness potential does not determine action. They suggested instead that it reflects anticipation of coming activity, but no more than that. This fits what some were already suggesting.

- Judy Trevena and Jeff Miller published another piece of research this year (2010) – see the bibliography. They asked some subjects to strike a key on a computer keyboard whenever they heard a randomly-timed tone. They asked others to do so only half the time, as they wanted to test what happened when the person decided *not* to act. If those believing the "brain is calling the shots" were right, they expected the readiness potential to be greater after the tone whenever a person chose to tap the key. They found the build-up of readiness potential appeared whether the subject pressed a key or not – and they saw there was no change in its strength. In their view, it signalled neither a decision to act nor a preparation to act.

So there's much speculation, but the only thing anyone knows for sure is that during these experiments there was unconscious brain activity before the subjects become aware of their decision to act or not act. The problem comes when we infer what this means. Whatever it means, this much is clear: any new model of the psyche must fit with what Libet found. The model in this book does.

Despite coming up with results that others have used to argue free will doesn't exist, Libet himself didn't accept he'd killed off the idea of free will. Noting that the readiness potential doesn't guarantee an action, Libet suggested the will is present through veto power; that is, stopping the readiness potential from becoming an action. In other words, he'd come to suspect that while we don't have "free will," we do have "free won't" (as one commentator called it).

However, the model outlined in this book says that reducing free will to the vetoing role of "free won't" isn't the whole story. I suggest that – as well as free won't – psychologists, philosophers and neuroscientists consider five thoughts, which may shed some light on the controversy around Libet's work:

1. *Not every willed action needs processing in the conscious part of the physical mind.* The will is not a busybody, constantly interfering in all details of the psyche's work. Take the example of a tennis player. As he waits to receive from the server, he doesn't consciously command his muscles to perform this or that detailed action – there's no

time for that. Instead, his strategic command to the body is to return the ball any way it can. So he gives the order and delegates the means of execution to the unconscious – previously learned – routines of playing tennis shots under pressure. The point here is that the will (the Self) can make a high-level decision and leave the unconscious mental routines to handle the details – including tactical decision-making. This means an unconscious build-up of readiness potential without a prior, conscious decision to act in that specific way, at that specific moment, is what we'd expect.

I suggest this is similar to what happened in the Libet experiment. The receiver would be consciously aware of (a) where the ball was heading and then (b) what his response would be a split second after he had unconsciously decided what to do. And yet before receiving the ball he had consciously decided to get it back any way he could – he just hadn't specified how to do it. It was the same in Libet's experiment; the exact timing of flexing the wrist wasn't important. So once the will had issued a command to flex the wrist randomly, it could delegate the tactical execution to a later unconscious process, which would show up as a build-up of readiness potential. This of, course, could still be vetoed by a further act of will.

2. *The act of will is not just a decision.* It's a series of steps that includes a decision at the halfway stage, as I explained in endnote 58. So it's not surprising to find electrical activity in the brain preceding conscious awareness of a decision to act. This would reflect Assagioli's first two stages and I develop this point further in thought #3.

3. *Third, there is more than one level of mind, with physical mind being the lowest in the hierarchy.* This model says that when a person faces a decision, his psyche unconsciously refers it to the higher levels of mind. (This is in line with the deliberation stage of Assagioli's act of will model.) There, depending on the decision, a limiting belief – or several limiting beliefs – may allow or rule out certain choices. These beliefs will include the person's values (what's most important to them at that moment, their motivating beliefs) and what they believe about themselves (their self-image).

Thus, the beliefs will screen the decision choices with unconscious questions like: "Does this fit my sense of who I am? Is this even possible? Do I have the skill and power to achieve this? Is it morally right to do this? What will happen to me if it goes wrong? What will I feel about myself if it goes well?" (These are the questions Assagioli was getting at in outlining the "deliberation" phase, the second in his six-stage model.) After screening, the decision returns to the conscious part of physical mind and action follows.

This means there's a second reason to expect neural activity before a decision to act comes into conscious awareness. The unconscious neural goings-on picked up on recording instruments may be more than a build-up of "readiness potential." It may also be unconscious checking at higher levels of mind. Whether this happens every time the person is about to perform the task, or only the first time, is something I'm unsure on. This may explain the results of an experiment by Soon and others, reported in Nature Neuroscience, May 2008 (see references). Using more up-to-date equipment than Libet, they noticed the readiness potential wasn't confined to motor control regions, but began in areas of the brain associated with higher-level planning.

4. *Fourth, the will doesn't make every decision.* As I remarked in endnote 57, the untamed mind is like a boiling lake. Our fantasies, desires, urges, worries, memories and feelings can and do bubble up from the unconscious depths to the conscious surface at random, distracting and deflecting the will. Anyone who has tried meditation for even five minutes has experienced this. The unconscious mind has a momentum of it own. Thus, the stronger desires and urges – often stemming from habits we have created or physical drives – can trigger behaviour without a conscious act of will. In fact, they can do so without a strategic command of the kind I described in point #1 (when talking about the receiver in tennis). This doesn't mean the will isn't real. It just means it's not the only decision-making agent in the psyche. However, the leader working on self-mastery will find his unconscious mind deflects him less often as he trains his will (a subject I discuss in chapter 9).

5. *Fifth, the speculation starts from inadequate models of the will and the psyche.* In this model, the four levels of mind and the physical body (brain) are the Self's means of expression in the world. And what is the Self? It is will, self-awareness and imagination expressing itself through mind and brain. Thus Self, mind and brain are integrated, but they are also distinct. The trouble is, when people talk about free will and consciousness they often conflate (a) brain with mind; (b) brain and mind with consciousness and will; and (c) consciousness itself with conscious awareness. This means they can misunderstand what they are measuring and draw unsound conclusions.

To be clear, this model is saying that self-awareness and will are not the products of mind or brain. The registering of a decision in the brain is not awareness itself. Rather, this model says it's the *result* of our power of awareness. And the unconscious goings-on in the brain after a strategic decision, but before conscious awareness of a tactical decision, is not will itself; it's the *result* of our will. It also says the brain is not the source of our higher mental abilities, but as part of physical mind, it is the cause of certain thoughts and impulses.

However, if you're unaware of all this or reject it as a possibility and see the "I" (Self) and mind as the products of neurons firing in the brain, you'll look at Libet's findings and draw two conclusions. First, the brain, not the will, is the decision maker. Second, free will is an illusion.

[60] *"In fact, it would be better to say the Self is pure self-awareness, will and imagination and that you, the Self, are a centre of potential, not of content"* *(page 148)*

Arthur Deikman, Clinical Professor of Psychiatry at the University of California, San Francisco, wrote an article in the Journal of Consciousness Studies in 1996, titled *I = Awareness* that touches on this same point. You will see it in the bibliography for this chapter.

He makes the central point that, *"Introspection reveals that the core of subjectivity – the "I" – is identical to awareness. This "I" should be differentiated from the various aspects of the physical person and its mental contents which form the 'self'."*

I use different language in this book, but in essence, I agree with Professor Deikman. I have distinguished between what I call the Fountainhead – which is pure awareness – and the Self, which is the same, but is also the seat of one's will and imagination. But I make the point strongly that Self is content-free; that the contents of the psyche, both conscious and unconscious – one's self-image, habits, memories and so on – are not the Self. Despite our different labels, this is a clear area of agreement.

[61] *Cognitive behavioural therapy (page 152)*

Cognitive behavioural (CB) therapists recognise a mental hierarchy and use it to help their clients, but they don't distinguish between higher and lower mind – thus they have only three levels. Neither do they talk about physical mind – they refer to behaviour as the level below emotion. They don't mention the Self either. However, the new mindfulness-based approach to CB therapy does imply an observer of one's psychological contents and impulses, but doesn't name it.

[62] *The mind-brain connection (page 154)*

We can find clues to how the link between mind and brain works in the fields of quantum physics, neuroscience and epigenetics. Quantum physics is the study of the fundamental building blocks of the material world: sub-atomic particles. Neuroscience is the study of the nervous system, including the brain. Epigenetics is the study of the previously hidden factors that turn genes on and off, such as stress and the environment.

The mainstream scientific view is that mind – and indeed consciousness – is simply the brain in action; that both are products of the brain. So you are clear, the model in this book disagrees. It says the mind is more than the brain. It also says consciousness is more than mind. As you will learn in this endnote, recent scientific findings are now challenging the mainstream view.

Let's start with what neuroscience can tell us because for over a decade it has been throwing up hard evidence that mental force affects brain structure.

Scientists used to believe that once a human being had grown to adulthood their brain could no longer change. We now know this is false. Late in the 20th century, neuroscientists found that it's possible to rewire the adult brain, repair damaged regions, grow new neurons (brain cells) and reorganise where the brain handles its tasks. They called this "neuroplasticity."

At first, it seemed only repeated physical actions and experiences could cause neuroplasticity. Neuroscientists knew that a brain devotes more space to tasks its owner performs often and minimises how much it gives to rarely used functions. They'd found, for example, that pianists' brains give more space to the zone controlling the fingers than the average person. In line with this, they proved that a stroke victim could rewire his brain and recover lost control of his limbs through repeated physical practice. However, Jeffrey Schwartz, a research professor of psychiatry, found that we can also change our brain through focused mental attention alone, that is, through will-driven thinking. He showed this with patients suffering from Obsessive Compulsive Disorder. By teaching them certain mental techniques, he demonstrated with the help of PET scanners that they could rewire their brains and free themselves from their troubling condition. He called this "self-directed neuroplasticity." You can read about it in *The Mind & The Brain* (see bibliography for details).

Neuroscientists have noticed a similar effect when studying people who practise mindfulness meditation. A study by Sara Lazar and others (see bibliography) showed that seasoned meditators' brains were physically different to those of non-meditators. For example, the zones associated with attention and sensory processing were thicker. The scientists also noticed the meditators showed less age-related thinning of the cortex (which is key to memory, attention, thought and language).

Alvaro Pascual-Leone and others carried out yet another study of the mind's ability to affect the physical makeup of the brain (you will find their article in the bibliography). He and his colleagues asked a group of volunteers to practise a five-finger exercise on a piano keyboard. They had to practise every day for two hours over five days. After five days, the scientists mapped the area of the motor cortex controlling the fingers and found it had grown compared with its size before the exercise began. This is what you would expect to see. But here's where it gets especially interesting. The scientists asked another group of volunteers to *think* about practising the five-finger piano exercise – no physical work, just imagining how they'd move their fingers to play the music. Five days later, they found the part of the motor cortex governing the fingers had expanded just as much as it had in those who played the piano. In short, mental rehearsal had had the same effect on the brain as physical rehearsal at the piano.

Neuroscience is therefore teaching us that mind affects brain in measurable ways. But is the "mind" doing it or is the brain changing itself? Do these findings prove mind is more than just the brain? Some would say yes, but sceptics would say no. So it's worth looking at studies of near-death experiences (NDEs) because they are examples of people being aware of inner and outer events while being clinically dead – that is, when their brain isn't working. But if "the mind is just the brain in action" theory is right, consciousness and memory shouldn't be possible during NDEs.

One of the most impressive reports on NDEs appeared in 2001, in *The Lancet*, one of the world's most respected medical journals. It was by Dr Pim van Lommel and three colleagues and you'll find it in the bibliography. They followed 344 patients, all successfully resuscitated after cardiac arrest in ten Dutch hospitals.

Now a cardiac arrest is not the same as a heart attack. It's much more serious. A cardiac arrest means the blood stops circulating normally, which starves the brain of oxygen, causing loss of consciousness. Breathing normally stops too and measurable brain activity usually ends within 10 seconds of losing consciousness according to Dr van Lommel. When breathing and blood circulation stops, the patient is "clinically dead." There's always the possibility that doctors can revive the patient, which is why they use the term "clinical death" to distinguish it from permanent death. However, if doctors don't start resuscitation within five or ten minutes, oxygen starvation will seriously damage the brain and the patient normally dies. That's how close to death a "clinically dead" person is. All 344 patients in van Lommel's study had been clinically dead.

Here we had patients whose brains weren't working – not measurably anyway – and were within minutes of permanent death. Yet 18% of them reported NDEs. The NDEs varied. Some patients felt powerful positive feelings. Some had an out-of-body experience. Others found themselves moving through a tunnel or meeting with people who had already died. All could recall their experiences when their inactive brain should have prevented consciousness and memory.

The out-of-body experiences are the ones we will focus on here as it's especially hard to deny them. Dr van Lommel describes in detail how, a week after revival, a previously clinically dead patient could tell a nurse where she had placed his dentures. She reported putting them in the drawer underneath the "crash car" while – and this is the key point – he was in deep coma and being resuscitated. The patient reported seeing himself lying in bed, could describe the room in which the resuscitation took place and who'd been there – although at the time he'd been physically unconscious.

The point is obvious. NDEs – and especially out-of-body experiences – shouldn't happen according to conventional scientific theory. The brain is out of action, so the patient should not remember anything about the episode and, indeed, shouldn't be conscious during it. Yet there were patients who could remember, who were conscious and could describe events accurately.

Dr van Lommel notes that stimulating the brain electrically and using certain drugs can trigger near-death-like experiences, which has led others to challenge the idea that mind and consciousness is more than brain. But he argues against this by pointing out the big differences between genuine NDEs and the induced versions, leaving it clear that artificially created NDEs are not the real thing. However, the point here is not whether anyone can induce NDEs or look-alike versions. The point is that van Lommel has given us powerful evidence of conscious mental functioning while the brain was inactive.

Dr van Lommel's report isn't the only one on NDEs. There are thousands of other cases – but his has been perhaps the best-controlled study so far. So we have hard data telling us that consciousness and memory/mind don't depend on the brain – that consciousness and mind are more than the brain. Now the earlier question was, "Is the mind causing the self-directed neuroplasticity or is the brain changing itself?" We have grounds for believing it's the mind.

The next question is, how does mind connect with the brain? And how does mental force affect the structure and wiring of the brain in cases of neuroplasticity? The answer is, we don't yet know for sure. However, Henry Stapp, Jeffrey Schwartz and Mario Beauregard have proposed a theory based on quantum physics to explain how the mind-brain link might work. Their paper, *Quantum Physics in Neuroscience and Psychology: A Neurophysical Model of Mind-Brain Interaction,* is in the bibliography. Here is a brief summary of their ideas:

- The brain is constantly sending out signals through a network of tiny nerve channels. These connect with each other across gaps so small (only one millionth of a millimetre) that rules of quantum physics apply.

- The sub-atomic world isn't like our everyday existence. In our daily life, we know that if an object starts from a known position and travels at a certain speed in a certain direction, we can accurately predict when it will arrive at a specific destination. But this isn't true when we look at the sub-atomic world of electrons, protons and neutrons. Here, we can't predict anything with certainty. The best we can say as sub-atomic particles blink in and out of existence is that at any moment there's a cloud of alternative outcomes. Now this seems weird, but scientists have proven this many times and the mathematics of quantum physics make repeatedly accurate predictions. So there's no debate about the findings – these potential outcomes co-exist in parallel. For example, we know light exists as both waves and particles at the same time. Only when a scientist asks a specific question and sets up an experiment to get the answer does one firm result ("it's a wave" or "it's a particle") emerge from the alternatives. There's no mechanical predictability in the sub-atomic world.

- Why does this matter? It matters because in normal life we don't experience alternative outcomes. We experience only one at a time. For example, we don't see the moon in several positions in the sky; we see it in just one location. So how do we reconcile the "alternative parallel outcomes" with the "one outcome" we're familiar with? This is when physicists start arguing with each other. They can't agree on one explanation. Instead, they've come up with several theories. The original and probably the leading theory is called the Copenhagen Interpretation and it's the one Stapp and his colleagues used. Arguably, the next most popular explanation is the Many Worlds theory.

- The Copenhagen Interpretation brings together the many parallel outcomes with the single result we experience in normal life via the following explanation:
  - When the scientist conducts his experiment, the question he asks and his method of answering it forces one result to emerge. At the moment of producing that one result, all other possibilities collapse and no longer exist.
  - Thus – and here's the controversial point – this explanation says the scientist and the experiment's result aren't separate. It says the scientist affects the result through the choices he makes in setting up the experiment (such as the question he asks and the equipment he uses).
  - Some have taken this to mean there's a connection between consciousness and matter; that the observer's consciousness causes the collapse. This is an uncomfortable line of thinking for many physicists, some of whom see a conclusion like this as pseudo-science – which is why the arguments started. The competing Many Worlds theory says instead that the cloud of alternatives doesn't collapse down to one. It says they all come to fruition in separate parallel worlds. We experience the one "we" have chosen, but other versions of "us" experience different results that "we" are unaware of. So in this theory, the universe is constantly splitting. Thus, champions of the Many Worlds theory say there's no need to consider a consciousness-matter link.
  - Steering clear of this controversy, the bottom line is that the Copenhagen Interpretation says there's no one outcome until the observer or experimenter intervenes.

- Now Stapp and his colleagues believe the brain is constantly throwing up alternative parallel choices and decisions – for example, on how to respond to someone's question – in line with quantum physics theory. Their model assumes these arise from previous history, previous experiences and habits. They believe that when we don't use mental effort to make a willed decision, the brain works in a more mechanical way and relies on previously learned habits and neural pathways to make unconscious choices.

- But they also believe that when we consciously direct our attention to one alternative or one outcome and keep our focus on it, we cause what's known as the Quantum Zeno Effect. This is when the other possibilities fade away and the structural brain changes (neuroplasticity) can begin to happen.

- To explain the Quantum Zeno Effect (QZE) you need to know that atoms and sub-atomic particles are in a constant state of change – whether that's decay or transition to another state. But if we repeatedly and often watch an atom, we can hold it in its current state (i.e. stop the transition) for an extended time, depending on how rapidly we watch it. In other words, the act of observation interferes with atomic and sub-atomic behaviour. This may sound strange, but it's a proven fact. Stapp and his colleagues believe that focusing on one outcome among the many alternatives has the same effect as multiple, rapid observations – that is, it causes the QZE. According to their model, the amount of mental effort we apply is equivalent to how often the scientific observations take place. This "holding" effect, they argue, overrides the mechanical forces in the brain and produces a different result.

- So their theory is that when we don't apply any effort, history or previous responses will direct the outcome unconsciously. But when we bring conscious directed mental effort to bear, we create the Quantum Zeno Effect. This holds one possibility – or indeed a new possibility – in focus, collapsing the other possibilities, creating certain brain connections and causing physical action. If we keep repeating the conscious mental effort to the same end, the QZE will cause changes to the brain structure, regardless of whether physical practice accompanies the mental effort.

The new science of epigenetics is also giving us clues to how the mind-brain-body link works. The latest research is beginning to explain how our beliefs can affect cellular activity and influence our genes. It's changing the widespread idea that our genes control us, replacing it with a view that our perceptions of our environment – filtered by beliefs – influence our genes' behaviour and their effects on the body. Bruce Lipton is one of the key authors on this subject and his book, *The Biology of Belief*, is in the bibliography. Here is a summary of his key points:

- Our bodies are made of trillions of cells (a trillion is a thousand billion). You have different types of cells for your brain, for your skin, for muscles, for bones and so on.

- Scientists used to think the nucleus of a cell was its "brain," its command centre. We now know this isn't true. The main role of the nucleus is to take charge of the cell's reproduction and repair. You see, cells are largely made of proteins and they wear out and eventually break down. The nucleus is responsible for replacing them and it holds the recipes for making new proteins (the recipes are called DNA and they contain a set of genes) – much like the way a library stores books. But the nucleus needs something else to tell it which proteins to make and therefore which recipes to pull from its library. By itself, it doesn't know which proteins the cell needs at any moment. Nor does it tell the cell what to do when something happens in the body that needs a response from its proteins – for example, when there's a wound to the skin.

- What tells the nucleus which proteins need to be replaced and when? And what tells the cell how to respond to changes in its environment, like a wound? What is the real "brain" of the cell? It is the membrane, the cell's outer semi-permeable "skin."

- Environmental information can arrive at the cell in the form of molecular signals or energy signals. We know, for example, that electromagnetic fields affect cells. Signals can originate from a blow to the face, sunshine, hot air, a hormone, a smell – or even a thought.

- So the membrane senses the environment through an incoming signal and converts it into a second chemical signal that selects a particular protein in the cell and tells it what to do, thus directing the cell's response. What the cell does will of course depend on its role – it could, for example, be a cell for moving muscles or aiding digestion.

- Now if the membrane is familiar with the signal, it will know which protein the cell needs to use and the process is straightforward. But what if the environmental signal is new or the protein the cell needs is missing because it wore out? This is when DNA and the individual sections of DNA, the genes – the keepers of the protein-making recipes – come into the picture. However, the genes don't activate themselves – they can't turn themselves on and off or adapt themselves to meet a new signal. What does it take to activate or adapt an existing gene? The answer is an environmental signal, interpreted by the membrane. The environmental signal causes a gene to express itself or to adapt. Or, more accurately, a *perception* of the environment – interpreted by the membrane – leading to a chemical signal in the cell causing a gene to replace a protein or adapt itself.

- As Lipton points out, this means we unconsciously direct our cellular behaviour, turn our genes on and off and adapt them according to the environment we *think* we live in. You see, our environment and our perception of it are not one and the same. When my team (Chelsea) score a goal, I'm pleased. But a supporter of the opposing team would feel differently. And yet we have witnessed the same physical event. So what controls our perceptions? Our beliefs and values (which are just a special class of beliefs). Which means our beliefs decide how we experience our environment.

- In short, Lipton argues that our beliefs drive our perceptions, which determine the signals coming into our cells and control our protein and DNA responses.

- Lipton reinforces this point by telling the extraordinary story of Dr Albert Mason, a case recorded in the *British Medical Journal* (see bibliography).

  – In 1952, Dr Mason tried to treat a 15-year-old boy's extreme case of warts using hypnosis. Most of the boy's skin was hard and leathery but Dr. Mason decided to concentrate in his first session on one arm. A week later, it was looking healthy.

  – When he contacted the referring surgeon, he learned he had misunderstood the boy's condition. He had not been suffering from warts, but from a genetic disease called Congenital Ichthyosis and what Mason and the boy had done together was considered impossible by the medical profession.

- Impossible or not – and encouraged by their spectacular start – they continued their work together and most of the boy's skin returned to normal.

- Now the story is impressive, but it's not over. You see, Dr Mason tried the same hypnosis therapy on other ichthyosis patients, but he couldn't repeat his success.

- Here comes the key point: he reported that his failure (like his initial success) was down to his own beliefs about the treatment. When he treated the new patients, he wasn't as confident as before because he knew he wasn't treating a difficult case of warts. He knew he was dealing with a so-called incurable disease and although he pretended to be upbeat, it didn't work.

- It's clear that Dr Mason was convinced his original treatment would work and it's surely fair to assume his patient picked up on his conviction. But as time went by, his belief waned and the hypnosis didn't have the same effect. This supports the view that our beliefs have physical effects on the cells in our bodies. When we think about it, this shouldn't be a surprise. After all, what is the placebo effect? Why do patients recover from diseases when doctors give them pills with no chemical effect? It's because they believe the pills will work.

To summarise, we don't yet know exactly how mind works through the brain and, frankly, many scientists don't think it does because they believe mind and will are illusions; just products of the brain. However, the data on near-death experiences is making it harder to deny the view that mind – and indeed consciousness – is more than brain. Meanwhile neuroscience, quantum physics and epigenetics are pointing to solutions to the mind-brain problem for those prepared to consider that mind and will are real. What we do know is that mind does affect brain through willed attention – the well-documented cases of self-directed neuroplasticity demonstrate this. So the model in this book has enough scientific data to support it. It's now up to leaders to test it for themselves.

[63] *Is the hierarchical mental flow only one-way?* *(page 154)*

I wrote in the main text, "…the conscious part of physical mind, being the lowest in the hierarchy, can only work with choices allowed by the higher levels. In fact, every level sets the boundaries for what the level below can work with. The choices you consider in physical mind are controlled by emotional mind, which is limited by boundaries set in lower mental mind, which is subservient to the limits set in higher mental mind."

The model outlined here says that thoughts and feelings are not the same as consciousness and that the brain is not the source of consciousness – it facilitates consciousness, but doesn't create it. It takes the view that the physical mind (brain) exists mainly to serve the Self and its three higher levels of mind in (1) enabling physical contact, experience and action and (2) keeping the physical body functioning. Now I'm not saying the brain never exerts a bottom-up effect. But I am saying the unconscious processes in the three higher levels of mind can and often do override the conscious and unconscious workings of physical mind.

For example, I believe we have certain unconscious programs sitting in physical mind. An example is the flight or fight response – the body's reaction to a threat. It triggers an instant protective response without the delay involved in conscious thought. However, we don't all feel the same degree of physical threat when facing identical conditions. Why? Well, consider the difference between a trained martial artist confidently walking down a dark street alone in a scruffy part of town and someone untrained who, feeling scared because he'd been mugged only weeks earlier, sprints along the same road. The physical conditions are identical, but they see different levels of threat as they have different beliefs about themselves and the world. This shows that higher-level beliefs can override the physical mind programs, causing one person to walk and the other to run.

Nonetheless, to be clear, this model accepts that the brain's electrochemical activity can affect our thoughts, mental images, feelings and actions. More specifically, it accepts that the brain can influence thoughts and feelings arising from unconscious physical mind programs like the flight or fight response or modify impulses from the collective unconscious. It also recognises that brain activity can cause some (but not all) dreams.

Dr. van Lommel mentions in his Lancet article (see bibliography) that experiments have shown it's possible to stimulate the brain artificially and cause certain feelings, thoughts and images. The problem is, some scientists assume this means the brain produces *all* thoughts and emotions. From this, they assume that mind and brain are one and the same – indeed that brain produces mind, that your mind is just the brain in action. This model says otherwise. It says they are not the same, but – and this is crucial – neither are they separate. They are distinct and yet connected in one system, with three levels of mind sitting above physical mind/brain in a hierarchy. Thus, you'd expect to be able to stimulate the brain and affect a person's conscious thoughts and feelings because they are facets of one integrated system.

But stimulating the brain doesn't prove that it creates *all* of our conscious thoughts, only that it can cause or affect *some* of them. It only appears to be the sole cause if you have ruled out the idea of mental processes beyond the brain at the start.

[64] ***Will Schutz research*** *(page 157)*

See *FIRO: A Three-Dimensional Theory of Interpersonal Behavior* (Rinehart, New York, 1958) and also *The Human Element: Productivity, Self-Esteem and the Bottom Line* (Jossey-Bass, San Francisco1994).

[65] ***False Self*** *(page 157)*

Some people refer to the False Self as the Ego. I prefer the term "False Self" because "Ego" means different things to different people and varying interpretations can confuse the message. For example, psychologists from the psychoanalytical tradition see Ego as the mediating force between the opposing forces of Id and Superego. But the non-professional refers to Ego when talking about pride and vanity – as in, "He's got a big ego." On the other hand, mystics like Eckhart Tolle and Kim Michaels see the Ego as an internal force preventing the true Self from expressing itself as a spiritual being in the material world.

Others – like Donald Winnicott and James Masterson, both of them psychiatrists – also used the term "False Self" in their writings. Their idea of a False Self is different to what I describe here, but there is overlap in that they see it as a survival formation. They see the False Self as more obviously engaged in self-destructive behaviours, more obviously struggling to live in its social and work environment, more obviously displaying unhelpful emotions, like shame, aggression and despair. I agree those are expressions of the False Self. But I see the False Self as more chameleon-like – that is, able to adapt and update its belief structure even as the Self develops what most would regard as a healthy sense of identity. So in this way, it creates ever more subtle games to survive. Games that remain invisible to most, as they seem so normal, so common. Thus, you can see a False Self at work within what we would otherwise describe as healthy, successful or even spiritual people.

Overall, I agree with Tolle and Michaels, but as explained, I choose not to use their term, Ego.

Chapter 9. Working on Element 3 – Self-Mastery: Principles, Obstacles & Techniques

[66] *The 10 psychological laws* (page 177)

You will find these on pages 51-65 of *The Act of Will* by Roberto Assagioli (The Psychosynthesis & Education Trust, London, 1974). The eight I refer to here are numbers 1-7 and 9 in Assagioli's book.

I mention in the main text that I have updated these eight laws. I have made two minor changes. First, I have included beliefs (a word Assagioli didn't use in writing about the ten laws) alongside ideas and images. Second, I have added to law #4 that emotions not only awaken ideas and images, but also any memories and desires associated with them.

[67] *"Law 4 states that our feelings can awaken and intensify thoughts and desires associated with them. This law can lead us to create expectations that cause us to see only what we want or expect to see, thus filtering and often distorting reality, making it impossible to discern truth. Thus, for example, a scientist who is rigidly attached to a certain theory may find himself looking*

only for data that supports it while ignoring facts that contradict it." *(page 178)*

In this way, the fourth psychological law links with Chris Argyris' *Ladder of Inference* model, which you will find explained in the appendix.

[68] *Obsessive Compulsive Disorder (OCD)* *(page 182)*

Jeffrey Schwartz explained his methods and research in his book, *The Mind & The Brain* (HarperCollins, 2002) which you will find listed in the chapter 8 bibliography.

[69] *Roberto Assagioli and disidentification* *(page 193)*

Assagioli first described the technique on pages 116-124 of his book, *Psychosynthesis* (Mandala, London, 1965). His views on contra-indications are interesting and helpful, but I have decided not to include them in book on leadership because my main audience (leaders) is different from the one he was writing for (psychotherapists) and so I feel the complications presented by borderline cases and psychotics are less relevant.

[70] *Mindfulness meditation* *(page 200)*

Mindfulness meditation comes from the Theraveda school of Buddhism. It is said to be a technique taught by Gautama Buddha to his students. Its original name is vipassana meditation. Vipassana is usually translated as "insight," meaning a clear awareness and understanding of what is happening as it is happening.

[71] *Mindfulness-Based Cognitive Therapy (MBCT) studies* *(page 204)*

I am referring to two studies. One by Teasdale, Segal and Williams in 2000 (*Prevention of relapse/recurrence in major depression by Mindfulness-Based Cognitive Therapy*, Journal of Consulting and Clinical Psychology. And another by Ma and Teasdale in 2004 (*Mindfulness-Based Cognitive Therapy for depression: Replication and exploration of differential relapse prevention effects*, Journal of Consulting and Clinical Psychology. Both sources are listed in the bibliography.

MBCT practitioners believe the key to its success in addressing depression (which is endorsed by the National Institute of Clinical Excellence in the UK) lies in changing the patient's relationship to his or her thoughts and feelings. Rebecca Crane, author of Mindfulness-Based Cognitive Therapy remarks that as the developers of MBCT studied Cognitive Behavioural Therapy (CBT) to see what it was that helped depression sufferers most, they concluded that:

> "... Through a process of engagement with CBT, the client comes to perceive that challenging thoughts and emotions are passing events in the mind that do not necessarily reflect reality and are not central components of the self. This altered or de-centred relationship or stance towards thoughts or emotions is significant. It is this that creates the person's ability to step out of the entanglement of ruminative thinking and the consequences of low mood cycles... Therefore, although not a direct target of CBT, this de-centred relationship to thoughts arises implicitly during the learning process. By contrast, developing the skill to de-centre from one's experience is an explicit and deliberate intention of the MBCT learning process... The focus is on a systematic training to be more aware, moment by moment, of physical sensations, thoughts and emotions as events in the field of awareness... We learn that we can see them as aspects of experience that move through our awareness rather than seeing them as reality."
>
> *Rebecca Crane, p. 12, Mindfulness-Based Cognitive Therapy, Routledge, London, 2009.*

Thus, although MBCT practitioners don't use the word "disidentification," it is the same as a "de-centred relationship to thoughts and emotions."

[72] *Mindfulness and well-being* (page 205)

Again, I am referring to two studies. The first is by Brown and Ryan, *The Benefits of Being Present: Mindfulness and Its Role in Psychological Well-being*, published in the Journal of Personality and Social Psychology 2003, Vol. 84, No. 4, pp. 822-848. The second is *Effects of Mindfulness-Based Stress Reduction Intervention on Psychological Well-Being and Quality of Life: Is Increased Mindfulness Indeed the Mechanism?* This was by Nyklicek and Kuijpers and published in 2008 in the Annals of Behavioral Medicine. You will find both sources listed in the bibliography.

[73] *Daniel Siegel* (page 207)

Dr. Daniel Siegel is a psychiatrist, a clinical professor of psychiatry at the UCLA School of Medicine and co-director of the UCLA Mindful Awareness Research Center in Los Angeles. He wrote *The Mindful Brain* –

The Neuroscience of Well-Being, published as a four-part audio book by Mind Your Brain Inc., 2008. He discusses the scientific side of mindfulness and specifically the effects on the brain in the third part of his book.

[74] *Study by Sara Lazar and others into the effects of mindfulness meditation on the brain* *(page 208)*

They reported their findings in an article titled *Meditation Experience is Associated with Increased Cortical Thickness* in Neuroreport (Lazar, Sara et al, vol.16, no.17, November 2005). While this study does suggest that mindfulness meditation was the cause of the meditators' brain structure, it doesn't provide final proof. Why? Because you could argue that people with such brains are more likely to persist with meditation – in other words, the brain causes the practice, not the other way round. We'll only know for sure when scientists follow two matched groups through time and compare the effects of meditation on the brains of the meditators against what happens to the non-meditators' brains.

[75] *Research into the effectiveness of mental rehearsal* *(page 222)*

The best overview of the subject I found was *Does Mental Practice Enhance Performance?* by J. E. Driskell in the Journal of Applied Psychology, 1994. You will find details in the bibliography.

Other papers you can read: *The Effects of Mental Practice on Motor Skill Learning and Performance: a Meta-Analysis* by D. L. Feltz and D. M. Landers (Journal of Sports Psychology, 1983). *Mental Practice – Does it Work in the Field?* by A. R. Isaac (The Sports Psychologist, 1992). *The Effects of Mental Practice on Motor Skill Performance: Critical Evaluation and Meta-Analysis* by K. E. Hinshaw (Imagination, Cognition and Personality, 1991-92). *Imagining Instructions: Mental Practice in Highly Cognitive Domains* by P. Ginns (Australian Journal of Education, August 2005).

[76] *Research by Alvaro Pascual-Leone* *(page 223)*

See his article, *The Brain That Plays Music and Is Changed by It* published in the Annals of the New York Academy of Sciences. You will find it listed in the bibliography.

[77] *Lou Tice on affirmation* *(page 225)*

Lou Tice is the author of *Personal Coaching for Results* (Thomas Nelson, Nashville, 1997). His view on the number of affirmations you need to create personal change comes on page 137.

[78] *Research into the effectiveness of positive affirmations* *(page 225)*

This refers to a research article titled *Positive Self Statements: Power for Some, Peril for Others* written by Professor Joanne Wood and two colleagues. It appeared in Psychological Science in 2009 and is listed in the biography. The newspaper quote comes from The Times, Saturday 4 July 2009.

[79] *Steven Covey quote* *(page 231)*

Taken from page 106, *The Seven Habits of Highly Effective People* (Simon & Schuster, 1989).

Appendix

The Ladder of Inference

Ladder of Inference Model

Chris Argyris unveiled the Ladder of Inference model in his book, *Overcoming Organisational Defences.* It looks like this:

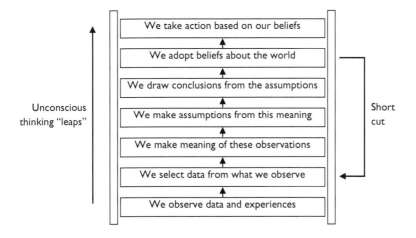

Here's how it works, starting from the bottom and working up:

- At the bottom of the ladder, there are the *directly observable data and experiences* that we have each day.

- However, there are so many of them coming at us during a day that *we choose to pay attention to only some of them.*

- Then we figure out what these experiences and data *mean to us*. The meaning we attach will be influenced by our cultural influences, personal history and psychological characteristics. In other words, we act as a filter as we attach the meaning. Thus, our pure awareness becomes a filtered perception.

- From there we make *assumptions* based on the meaning we gave to the experience and then draw *conclusions* from them.

- These conclusions lead us to generalise about others and the world and we store these in our minds as *beliefs*. These beliefs represent what is true for us.

- We then decide and *act* on these beliefs.

Our actions should give us new experiences and data to check and revise our understanding (that is, the meaning, assumptions and conclusions we draw) and, ultimately, our beliefs. This would enable us to take wiser, more skilful action in future.

However, we don't always work that way. That's because our beliefs are not just the *result* of our experiences; they can be the *cause* of them. Beliefs can – and do – influence which data and experiences we choose to notice and I show this in the diagram as the "short cut." We tend to select the data that reinforces and confirms our beliefs. This means we aren't seeing reality as it is, but through a distorted lens.

Then we compound the problem by making an *unconscious thinking leap*, which is where we make assumptions and generalise without testing our thinking. So a belief can have a limiting effect on our capacity to learn and mature and, of course, our ability to achieve the outcomes we want. That isn't the only problem though – from such beginnings, misunderstanding and conflicts arise as each of us tries to work to our own "truth," which may not match others' worldview.

What It Teaches Us

The ladder of inference model teaches us three things:

- First, we follow distinct thinking patterns as we watch, experience and assess the events in our lives, *without being aware of them*.

- Second, we often *only notice what we are looking for* rather than see everything in front of us because we like to reinforce our existing beliefs (the "short-cut" in diagram).

- Third, we often short-circuit the ladder of inference by *making thinking leaps without knowing it.* This is shown as the arrow on the left of the diagram. In so doing, we trap ourselves in a limited understanding of reality and become subject to unconscious "limiting beliefs." Limiting beliefs can stifle personal growth and creativity, lead to mistakes and reduce the chances of successful teamwork. They are a significant barrier to behaviour change.

An Example

Here is an example of the Ladder of Inference in action, working upwards from the bottom rung to the top:

- Imagine an 18-year-old man. He's in a crowded, noisy room and, four metres away, he sees a pretty girl he's never met before. Their eyes meet. He smiles at her.

- She doesn't smile back.

- He decides this means she doesn't like the look of him.

- He assumes this means she would never want to go out with him.

- He concludes he's probably not good-looking enough to attract a girl like her.

- He starts to believe he'll never have a girlfriend.

- He resolves never to ask a girl out because he doesn't want to risk rejection.

Notice the meaning he took from this episode, the assumptions he drew, the conclusion he reached and the belief this either created or reinforced, leading to a decision or action.

Now it's possible she didn't smile for more than one reason. Perhaps he's right. Or perhaps, despite what he thought, she didn't notice him. Or perhaps she thought he was attractive, but was in a steady relationship with someone else… and so on. You might think this is a ridiculous example; that it would never happen, but unless we know ourselves well we are prey to such emotional thinking patterns. That's why we can start to filter out data that doesn't match our beliefs (which is one way the False Self manages to survive) and why we can make unconscious thinking leaps.

In life, we'd hope that, in time, this young man would have a different experience – for example, a favourable response – that would challenge and eventually undermine his initial belief. In this way, we update and dispose of beliefs that don't serve us well. But sometimes they become so ingrained that the only "data" we notice are those that fit and support our beliefs. That's when the normal "beliefs update" cycle is blocked.

Using The Model

How does the ladder of inference model help leaders? In my view, it helps in two ways. First, it explains how limiting beliefs develop and trap our mental processes. Second, it can help us to be more aware of our thinking – when we are on our own, in teams and in larger groups. We can therefore learn to coach ourselves and others to reduce the effects of limiting beliefs. And if we do that, we can improve our team's cohesion and creative thinking. That's why I mention it in table 9 (chapter 6) when listing the Problem Solving & Planning Skills.

How can we do this? We can't go through life without attaching meaning, drawing conclusions and creating beliefs. But that doesn't mean we have to consider every step of the ladder of inference each time we think – that would be tedious! Nonetheless, through greater awareness of how we think and timely reflection we can ask ourselves questions like:

- What are the unconscious assumptions I'm making here?

- Are there facts and possibilities I could search out that I haven't looked for so far?

When we are in a group, we can raise the quality of our joint thinking by becoming familiar with the ladder of inference and getting into the habit of asking:

- What are the facts behind that statement?

- Can you talk me through your reasoning?

- What unspoken assumptions are we making here?

So this model helps us understand our thinking processes to reduce the power of unreliable limiting beliefs and unconscious assumptions. It's also helpful in a leadership role as it prompts questions to help align people's thinking and raise their collective effectiveness.

Bibliography

Chapter 8, *Self-Mastery: A Leader's Map of the Psyche*

Assagioli, Roberto. *Psychosynthesis: A Manual of Principles and Techniques.* Mandala, London, 1965.

Assagioli, Roberto. *The Act of Will.* The Psychosynthesis & Education Trust, 1974.

Bailey, Alice. *The Light of the Soul: The Yoga Sutras of Patanjali.* Lucis Publishing, New York, 1927.

Begley, Sharon. *Train Your Mind. Change Your Brain.* Ballantine Books, New York, 2007.

Campbell, Joseph (Editor). *The Essential Jung.* Viking Press, New York, 1971.

Clarkson, Petruska. *Gestalt Counselling in Action.* Sage Publications, London, 1989.

Deikman, Arthur J. *I = Awareness.* Article in the Journal of Consciousness Studies, Vol. 3, No. 4, 1996, pp. 350-356.

Dilts, Robert. *Changing Belief Systems with NLP.* Meta Publications, Capitola, 1990.

Doidge, Norman. *The Brain that Changes Itself.* Penguin Books, 2007.

Frankl, Viktor E. *Man's Search for Meaning.* Rider, London, 1959.

Frankl, Viktor E. *The Doctor and the Soul.* Souvenir Press, London, 1969.

Gallwey, W. Timothy. *The Inner Game of Work.* Orion Business, 2000.

Gerhardt, Sue. *Why Love Matters: How Affection Shapes a Baby's Brain.* Routledge, London, 2004.

Hankins, Peter. *Libet's Short Delay.* Article available at his website at www.consciousentities.com.

Hankins, Peter. *Unconscious Decisions.* A follow up article to Libet's Short Delay at www.consciousentities.com.

Hankins, Peter. *Libet was wrong?* A second follow up article, also at www.consciousentities.com.

Herrmann, Christoph et al. *Analysis of a Choice-Reaction Task Yields a New Interpretation of Libet's Experiments.* Article in the International Journal of Psychophysiology (February 2008, pp. 151-157).

Lazar, Sara et al. *Meditation Experience is Associated with Increased Cortical Thickness.* Article in Neuroreport (vol.16, no.17, November 2005).

Libet, Benjamin & Haggard, Patrick *Conscious Intention and Brain Activity.* Article in the Journal of Consciousness Studies (no.11, 2002, pp. 47-63).

Lipton, Bruce H. *The Biology of Belief.* Mountain of Love/Elite Books, 2005.

Lommel, Pim van et al. *Near-Death Experience in Survivors of Cardiac Arrest: A Prospective Study in the Netherlands.* Article in The Lancet, Vol. 358, 15 December 2001, pp. 2039-2045.

Lommel, Pim van. *About The Continuity of our Consciousness.* Chapter in Brain Death and Disorders of Consciousness, edited by C. Machado & D.A. Shewmon, Springer, 2004.

Lommel, Pim van. *Consciousness Beyond Life – The Science of the Near-Death Experience.* HarperCollins, New York, 2010.

Maslow, Abraham H. *Toward a Psychology of Being.* John Wiley & Sons, New York, 1968.

Maslow, Abraham H. *The Farther Reaches of Human Nature.* Penguin Books, New York, 1976.

Mason, A. *A Case of Congenital Ichthyosiform Erythrodermia of Brocq Treated by Hypnosis.* Article in the British Medical Journal, 23 August 1952, pp.422-423.

Masterson, James F. *The Search for the Real Self.* The Free Press, New York, 1988.

Michaels, Kim. *Master Keys to the Abundant Life.* More To Life Publishing, 2005.

Mitchell, Stephen A. & Black, Margaret. *Freud and Beyond: A History of Modern Psychoanalytic Thought.* Basic Books, New York, 1995.

O'Connor, Joseph & Seymour, John. *Introducing Neuro-Linguistic Programming.* Thorsons, London, 1995.

Palmer, Stephen (Editor). *Counselling and Psychotherapy: The Essential Guide.* Sage Publications, London, 2000.

Paris, Bernard J. *Karen Horney's Vision of the Self.* Essay in the American Journal of Psychoanalysis, June 1999.

Pascual-Leone, Alvaro et al. *Modulation of Muscle Responses Evoked by Transcranial Magnetic Stimulation During the Acquisition of New Fine Motor Skills.* Article in Journal of Neurophysiology (No.74, September 1995, pp. 1037-45).

Pauen, Michael. *Self-Determination: Free Will and Determinism.* Paper presented at the Fifth International Congress of the Society for Analytical Philosophy, at the University of Bielefeld, September 2003.

Pauen, Michael. *Does Free Will Arise Freely?* Article in Scientific American Mind (January 2004).

Schutz, William. *FIRO: A Three Dimensional Theory of Interpersonal Behaviour.* Science & Behavior Books, Palo Alto, 1966.

Schutz, William. *The Human Element.* Jossey-Bass, San Francisco, 1994.

Schwartz, Jeffrey M. & Begley, Sharon. *The Mind & The Brain.* HarperCollins, New York, 2002.

Schwartz, Jeffrey M. & Rock, David. *The Neuroscience of Leadership.* Article in Strategy & Business, issue 43, Summer 2006.

Stapp, Henry P. *Attention, Intention & Will in Quantum Physics.* Article in the Journal of Consciousness Studies, Vol. 6, Nos 8-9, August-September 1999, pp. 143-64.

Stapp, Henry P. & Schwartz, Jeffrey M. & Beauregard, M. *Quantum Physics in Neuroscience and Psychology: A Neurophysical Model of Mind-Brain Interaction.* Article in Philosophical Transactions of the Royal Society, 2004.

Seligman, Martin. *Authentic Happiness.* Free Press, New York, 2002.

Siegel, Allen M. *Heinz Kohut and the Psychology of the Self.* Brunner-Routledge, London, 1996.

Soon, Chun Siong et al. *Unconscious Determinants of Free Decisions in the Human Brain.* Article in Nature Neuroscience, May 2008, pp. 543-545.

Stevens, Anthony. *Jung: A Very Short Introduction.* Oxford University Press, Oxford, 1994.

Storr, Anthony. *Freud: A Very Short Introduction.* Oxford University Press, Oxford, 2001.

Suzuki, Daisetz T. *Zen and Japanese Culture.* Princeton University Press, Princeton, 1970.

Tolle, Eckhart. *The Power of Now.* Hodder & Stoughton, London, 1999.

Tolle, Eckhart. *A New Earth.* Penguin Books, London, 2005.

Trevena, Judy & Miller, Jeff. *Brain Preparation Before a Voluntary Action:*

Evidence Against Unconscious Movement Initiation. Article in Consciousness and Cognition (Volume 19, Issue 1, March 2010, pp. 447-456).

Trower, Peter et al. *Cognitive-Behavioural Counselling in Action.* Sage Publications, London, 1988.

Welwood, John. *Toward a Psychology of Awakening.* Shambhala Publications, 2000.

Whitmore, John. *Coaching for Performance.* Third edition, Nicholas Brealey Publishing, London, 2002.

Wilber, Ken. *Outline of an Integral Psychology.* Article available at Wilber's website at www.kenwilber.com.

All Other Chapters

Adair, John. *Effective Leadership.* Pan Books, London, 1988.

Adair John. *Effective Teambuilding.* Pan Books, London 1986.

Argyris, Chris. *Overcoming Organisational Defences.* Allyn & Bacon, 1990.

Baer, Ruth A. *Mindfulness Training as a Clinical intervention: A Conceptual and Empirical Review.* Article in Clinical Psychology: Science & Practice, 2003, 10, pp. 125-143.

Baer, Ruth A. et al. *Using Self-Report Assessment Methods to Explore Facets of Mindfulness.* Article in Assessment, March 2006, 13, pp. 27-45.

Benne, Kenneth & Sheats, Paul. *Functional Roles of Group Members.* Article in the Journal of Social Issues, 1948.

Benson, Jarlath. *Working More Creatively with Groups.* Routledge, London, 2001.

Blake R. & Mouton J. *The Managerial Grid: The Key to Leadership Excellence.* Gulf Publishing Co., 1964.

Brown, K.W. and Ryan, R.M. *The Benefits of Being Present: Mindfulness and Its Role in Psychological Well-being.* Article in the Journal of Personality and Social Psychology 2003, Vol. 84, No. 4, pp. 822-848.

Bryman, A. *Leadership & Organizations.* Routledge & Kegan Paul, London, 1986.

Buchanan, D. & Huczynski, A. *Organizational Behaviour* (third edition). Prentice Hall, London, 1997.

Covey, Stephen. *The Seven Habits of Highly Successful People.* Simon & Schuster, New York, 1989.

Crane, Rebecca. *Mindfulness-Based Cognitive Therapy.* Routledge, London, 2009.

Doidge, Norman. *The Brain That Changes Itself.* Penguin Books, London, 2007.

Driskell, J. E. et al. *Does Mental Practice Enhance Performance?* Article in the Journal of Applied Psychology, 1994, Vol. 79, No. 4, pp. 481-492.

Drucker, Peter. *Managing For Results.* Pan Books, London, 1964.

Fiedler, F. *A Theory of Leadership Effectiveness.* McGraw-Hill, New York, 1967.

Gardner, John W. *On Leadership.* The Free Press, New York, 1990.

Gerhardt, Sue. *Why Love Matters: How Affection Shapes a Baby's Brain.* Brunner-Routledge, Hove, 2004.

Goldberg, Carl. *Understanding Shame.* Jason Aronson Inc., Northvale, 1991.

Goleman, Daniel. *Working With Emotional Intelligence.* Bantam Books, 1998.

Greenleaf, Robert. *Servant Leadership.* Paulist Press, New York, 1977.

Gunaratana, Bhante Henepola. *Mindfulness in Plain English.* Wisdom Publications, Boston, 2002.

Hamel, Gary. *Leading The Revolution.* Harvard Business School Press, Boston, 2000.

Hersey, Paul & Blanchard, Ken. *Management of Organisational Behavior: Utilising Human Resources* (5th edition). Prentice Hall, 1988.

Kotter, John. *Leading Change.* Harvard Business School Press, Boston, 1996.

Kouzes, James & Posner, Barry. *The Leadership Challenge.* Jossey-Bass, San Francisco, 1995.

Larson, Carl & LaFasto, Frank. *TeamWork – What Must Go Right/ What Can Go Wrong,* Sage Publications, 1989.

Ma, S.H. and Teasdale, J.D. *Mindfulness-Based Cognitive Therapy for depression: Replication and exploration of differential relapse prevention effects.* Article in the Journal of Consulting and Clinical Psychology, 2004, 72(1): pp. 31-40.

MacGregor Burns, James. *Leadership.* HarperCollins, New York, 1978.

Maslow, Abraham. *Toward a Psychology of Being.* John Wiley & Sons, 1968.

Maslow Abraham. *The Farther Reaches of Human Nature.* The Viking Press, 1971.

McCall, M. & Lombardo, M. *Off the Track: Why and How Successful Executives Get Derailed.* Technical Report no. 21, Center for Creative Leadership, Greensboro, 1983.

Nyklicek, I. and Kuijpers, K.F. *Effects of Mindfulness-Based Stress Reduction Intervention on Psychological Well-Being and Quality of Life: Is Increased Mindfulness Indeed the Mechanism?* Article in the Annals of Behavioral Medicine 2008, vol.35, no.3, pp.331-340.

Orlick, Terry. *In Pursuit of Excellence* (third edition). Human Kinetics, Champaign, 2000.

Pascual-Leone, Alvaro. *The Brain That Plays Music and Is Changed by It.* Article in the Annals of the New York Academy of Sciences, Volume 930, June 2001, The Biological Foundations Of Music, pp. 315–329.

Peters, Thomas & Waterman, Robert. *In Search of Excellence – Lessons from America's Best-Run Companies.* Harper & Row, New York, 1982.

Peters, Tom & Austin, Nancy. *A Passion for Excellence.* William Collins, 1985.

Porter, Michael. *Competitive Strategy: Techniques for Analysing Industries and Competitors.* The Free Press, New York, 1980.

Rock, David & Schwartz, Jeffrey. *The Neuroscience of Leadership.* Article in Strategy & Business, issue 43, Summer 2006.

Schutz, William. *FIRO: A Three-Dimensional Theory of Interpersonal Behavior.* Rinehart, New York, 1958.

Schutz, William. *The Human Element: Productivity, Self-Esteem and the Bottom Line.* Jossey-Bass, San Francisco, 1994.

Shenk, Joshua. *Lincoln's Melancholy: How Depression Challenged a President and Fueled His Greatness.* Houghton Mifflin Harcourt, 2005.

Siegel, Daniel J. *The Mindful Brain – The Neurology of Well-Being* (audio book). Mind Your Brain Inc., 2008.

Stogdill, R.M. *Personal Factors Associated with Leadership: a Survey of the Literature.* Article in the Journal of Psychology, vol. 25, 1948 (also included in *Leadership – Selected Readings,* edited by C. A. Gibb, Penguin Books, 1969).

Storr, Anthony. *Churchill's Black Dog and Other Phenomena of the Human Mind.* HarperCollins, 1997.

Tannenbaum, Robert & Schmidt, Warren. *How to Choose a Leadership Pattern.* Article in the Harvard Business Review, May-June 1973.

Teasdale, J.D., Segal, Z. and Williams, J.M. *Prevention of relapse/recurrence in major depression by Mindfulness-Based Cognitive Therapy.* Article in the Journal of Consulting and Clinical Psychology, 2000, 68(4): pp. 615-623.

Wood, Joanne V. et al. *Positive Self-Statements: Power for Some, Peril for Others.* Article in Psychological Science, Vol. 20, No. 7, May 2009.

About The Author

James Scouller is an accredited coach and partner of The Scouller Partnership, an executive coaching practice in the UK. He was a chief executive of international firms for 11 years before becoming a professional coach in 2004, so he understands the pressures leaders face. He holds two postgraduate coaching qualifications and trained in applied psychology at the Institute of Psychosynthesis, London.

He lives in Bedfordshire, about 40 miles north of London.

Readers with comments or questions about the book can contact the author through the Contact page on the book's website. You can find this at *www.three-levels-of-leadership.com*.

Index